Flyi

Flying with the Spooks

*Memoir of a Navy Linguist
in the Vietnam War*

HERBERT SHIPPEY

McFarland & Company, Inc., Publishers
Jefferson, North Carolina

The manuscript of this memoir was submitted for prepublication review to the NSA at Fort George Meade, Maryland, and was determined to be unclassified and approved for public release. The material and views presented in the memoir are those of the author and in no way reflect official approval or endorsement by the NSA or the U.S. Navy.

LIBRARY OF CONGRESS CATALOGUING-IN-PUBLICATION DATA

Names: Shippey, Herbert, 1944– author.
Title: Flying with the spooks : memoir of a Navy linguist in the Vietnam war / Herbert Shippey.
Other titles: Memoir of a Navy linguist in the Vietnam war
Description: Jefferson, North Carolina : McFarland & Company, Inc., Publishers, 2022 | Includes index.
Identifiers: LCCN 2021062284 | ISBN 9781476686721 (paperback : acid free paper) ∞
ISBN 9781476645476 (ebook)
Subjects: LCSH: Shippey, Herbert, 1944– | Vietnam War, 1961–1975—Personal narratives, American. | United States. Navy. Fleet Support Detachment—Biography. | Vietnam War, 1961–1975—Aerial operations, American. | Vietnam War, 1961–1975—Military intelligence—United States. | Linguists—Vietnam—Biography. | BISAC: HISTORY / Military / Vietnam War
Classification: LCC DS559.5 .S55 2022 | DDC 959.704/3092 [B]—dc23/eng/20220107
LC record available at https://lccn.loc.gov/2021062284

BRITISH LIBRARY CATALOGUING DATA ARE AVAILABLE

ISBN (print) 978-1-4766-8672-1
ISBN (ebook) 978-1-4766-4547-6

Front cover: Painting of the EC-121 Warning Star (top) and P-3 Orion by an anonymous Japanese artist in Atsugi, Japan (photograph in author's collection)

Printed in the United States of America

McFarland & Company, Inc., Publishers
Box 611, Jefferson, North Carolina 28640
www.mcfarlandpub.com

To the men who served in
NAVCOMMSTA PHIL Fleet Support Detachment Da Nang
(DET BRAVO)
during the Vietnam War.

Also, to the officers and enlisted men of
Fleet Air Reconnaissance Squadron ONE (VQ-1),
who piloted and maintained the aircraft
in which the Big Look Spooks flew.

"If I take the wings of the morning
and dwell in the uttermost parts of the sea,
even there your hand shall lead me,
and your right hand shall hold me."
                                    Psalm 139: 9–10 (ESV)

To sing of Wars, of Captains, and of Kings,
Of Cities founded, Common-wealths begun,
For my mean Pen are too superior things;
Or how they all, or each their dates have run,
Let Poets and Historians set these forth.
My obscure lines shall not so dim their worth.
                    "The Prologue" by Anne Bradstreet

Table of Contents

Acknowledgments

I am hardly the first to write about Det Bravo. Wayne Care, who served as a CTI with the detachment, wrote *Vietnam Spook Show* (1989), a fictional account about Det Bravo, which he called Det Tango. The novel narrates the adventures and misadventures of Craig Nostrum, the central character, a CTI with reconnaissance flight duty out of Da Nang. Norman Klar wrote an article for the February 2003 issue of *Vietnam* magazine that gives a brief account of Det Bravo's reconnaissance activities. The article, titled "The Naval Security Detachments in Vietnam Played a Significant Role in the Gulf of Tonkin Incident," also provides information about other Naval Security Group activities during the Vietnam War. An article by William Leppert titled "Crypto Duty at Rocket City" appeared in the spring 2009 issue of *Cryptolog*, a publication of the Navy Cryptologic Veterans Association. The article describes a rocket attack on July 15, 1967, that heavily damaged the VQ-1 and Spooks barracks at Da Nang. Fortunately, there were no fatalities, although there were a number of injuries. This article was republished with the title "CT Duty at 'Rocket City'" in *Knowing the Enemy: Naval Intelligence in Southeast Asia* (2015) by Richard A. Mobley and Edward J. Marolda, a book that also includes some information about VQ-1 reconnaissance operations in the war zone. Robert Morrison, one of my roommates in Da Nang, completed a history of the detachment in 2017.* The history also includes some reminiscences by det members, as well as Leppert's article. Morrison sent copies of the history to the *Big Look Spooks*, *Navy CT History*, and *VQ Association* websites, as well as to *Station Hypo*, another site about Navy cryptology. In August 2020 *World Watchers* by Angelo Romano was published. The volume is number 305 in the series *US Navy Squadron Histories* and has the subtitle *A Pictorial History of Electronic Countermeasures Squadron ONE (ECMRON-1) Fleet Air*

---

*Robert Morrison. *United States Naval Communications Station, Philippines (NAVCOM-MSTA PHIL): Fleet Support Detachment, Da Nang, Republic of Vietnam (Det Bravo) Command History*. 2017. https://www.navycthistory.com/pdf/HistoryofDetBravoDaNang.pdf.

Reconnaissance Squadron ONE (VQ-1). The book contains an abundance of excellent photographs of VQ-1 planes, along with copious statistics about the aircraft, and provides a history of the squadron from its inception to the present. Information about missions flown by Det Bravo during the Vietnam War is included, along with some quotations from Morrison's history.

During the last few years several members of the detachment have contributed numerous reminiscences and photographs to the *Big Look Spooks* website, set up and maintained by Steve White. The site includes a roster of those who served in the detachment, maintained by Morrison, with the dates of service database updated by Bill Dillon. Also, there have been many posts about life in the detachment in the Facebook group *Friends Who Like Big Look Spooks Danang,* administered by Duane Mann and Don Tremain, as well as an earlier Facebook group, *Big Look Spooks of Danang*, created by Tim Yerdon. I am also grateful for information from members of the Facebook group *Fleet Air Reconnaissance Squadron One (VQ-1) and ECMRON ONE ECM-1.* These resources, especially Morrison's history and the *Big Look Spooks* website, have provided me with inspiration and some information that I have included in a few places in the memoir.

I am especially grateful to Bob Morrison and Steve White, who read an earlier draft of the memoir, marking corrections and making recommendations for improving it. For the photographs included in the memoir, I am indebted to the *Big Look Spooks* website and CDs provided by John Phipps. Acknowledgment of the photographers is included in the captions with the photos.

I began writing some brief sections of this memoir many years ago and during the last several years worked, as my teaching schedule permitted, to complete the manuscript. Consequently, I must thank my wife and sons for their patience in listening to me talk about the book.

My greatest debt of gratitude goes to the men of the Fleet Support Detachment with whom I served. What we experienced together while flying and undergoing rocket attacks, as well as what they did and said in Da Nang and San Miguel, inspired me to write about those days during the Vietnam War that had an indelible impact on our lives.

Preface

As I look back from the perspective of age, I realize that my time in the Navy was one of the greatest learning periods of my life, and I venture to say that the other men in the Naval Communications Station Philippines Fleet Support Detachment at Da Nang, where I served in Vietnam, would say the same. What we experienced and learned, of course, was quite different for each of us because we were all unique individuals with our own interests and areas of specialization. Apart from what we learned in relation to our mission, my interests pertained to literature, art, history, and culture in general. Wherever I was stationed or traveled while I was in the Navy, I visited as many libraries, museums, churches, temples, parks, and historical sites as I could, and I was always reading on something, even though for a while in Da Nang I experienced so much anxiety and restlessness that I could bear to read only a few pages at the time. All of this, though, was only part of the picture. I also had to study for advancement in rank in the Navy, and that involved learning more about radios and radio technology than I would ever have undertaken on my own in civilian life.

Learning Vietnamese at the Defense Language Institute East Coast (DLIEC) in the Washington, D.C., area was a significant cultural experience that added to my knowledge of languages and helped prepare me for my duties in Da Nang. Through this study I also developed a greater interest in the culture and history of the Far East than I had formerly possessed. Today, I have forgotten much of my Vietnamese, recalling only certain words, and phrases, but I value what I learned and still use those phrases in talking to myself. A few years ago, in speaking with a Vietnamese student who was taking one of my composition classes, I tried speaking some Vietnamese, and he said, "Dr. Shippey, your Vietnamese is very bad." I had to acknowledge that his English was much better than my Vietnamese.

Traveling added immensely to my knowledge, and I relished every moment. I realized that the Navy fulfills the promise that I used to see on posters at the post office: "Join the Navy and see the world." I did not travel all over the world, but I saw much more of it than I would have been able to visit on my own. At home I often did not have enough money to travel five miles to the local shopping center to buy something. Uncle Sam made the difference. Perhaps most important of all, I met a lot of people while I was in the Navy and learned much through talking with them and just observing them. The friendships I made were especially valuable and helped shape who I am. The men of the detachment in Da Nang, as well as those I knew at Orlando, Fort Myer, San Angelo, San Miguel, San Diego, and Fort Meade, were all part of that learning experience. I must also include the many civilians that I encountered in Washington, D.C., New York, the Philippines, Vietnam, and Thailand.

In writing about what I learned, I do not want to come across as boastful or proud since I am keenly aware of my deficiencies. The men of the detachment in Da Nang were an intelligent and lively group, and what I knew paled in comparison to the knowledge and experiences that many of them had. They had agile minds and often could size up another person or situation better than I could. Some of them also had more book knowledge than I could muster up, in addition to technical expertise, common sense, and pragmatic knowledge. In later years, the CTIs (Communications Technician Interpretive) who stayed in the Navy continued to expand their linguistic skills, and some of them learned languages other than Vietnamese. My own areas of learning by comparison seem very small. I recall one evening at San Miguel in the Philippines when I was part of the night watch at the Receivers building. I went to a room that had a chalkboard and, to while away the time, practiced writing some sentences in French. Then I sat down in one of the chairs. Shortly afterwards, another "I" beat also on watch duty came into the room and, noticing the French sentences on the board, picked up a piece of chalk and corrected the errors. I was embarrassed and said nothing; I did not acknowledge that I had written the sentences.

Over the years my humility before the vast extent of knowledge has only deepened. After a lifetime of learning what I can, I feel like a beggar who comes in off the street to a festival where a full buffet is laid out on the tables, music is playing, beautiful artworks adorn the walls, and sophisticated men and women in glittering garments are laughing and talking with one another in the warm, light-filled room. I have time to snatch only a few canapés from the abundant feast before returning to the cold, dark street.

Instead of being in the forefront in Da Nang and the other places where I was stationed, I tended to draw back to the sidelines, to blend into the shadows. I was certainly no *wunderkind* nor the cynosure of all eyes. I was more like Joseph Addison's Spectator in the early eighteenth-century London coffee-houses, mingling with the crowd, but seldom speaking, preferring to sit in the back of the room listening and observing. Perhaps a more apt comparison would be to T.S. Eliot's Prufrock, who says, "No! I am not Prince Hamlet, nor was meant to be; / Am an attendant lord, one that will do / To swell a progress, start a scene or two…." I am an introvert and somewhat prudish, often missing out on the grand adventures and the keen insights experienced by others. In short, I am a total nerd, but being a nerd can have its compensations.

This memoir is a personal reminiscence written almost fifty years after the occurrence of the events related. Memory tends to be faulty, especially after so long a period of time. I have done my best faithfully to record what I witnessed, did, and thought, all of which may be quite different from what other men of the detachment experienced. I have used the real names of those men I could remember, but I have also used fictitious names for those whose names I could not recall and for occasions when I did not remember who was present. No doubt, there are errors in my recollection and in facts about the details of the Vietnam War, which the Vietnamese today refer to as the American War. As a result, the book may be accurately labeled as creative nonfiction. Maybe I should have written the work many years ago when I was young since it is about the experiences of a much younger self, but there were good reasons for not doing so at that time. To explain why I waited so long, I offer the excuse that age can give perspective to what occurred in youth, thus perhaps allowing me to write about things that I might not have thought of at an earlier time. Moreover, some of what I discuss was classified for approximately forty years.

I hope that the memoir will be of interest to at least some of the men with whom I served, as well as to members of my family, but should it fail to interest them, that is all right. I needed to write the book for my own reasons. In fact, I felt compelled to write it. Since it may not interest the general public, it is appropriate to quote what the sixteenth-century French writer Michel de Montaigne wrote in the preface to his *Essays*: "Thus, reader, myself am the matter of my book: there's no reason thou shouldst employ thy leisure about so frivolous and vain a subject. Therefore farewell."

Introduction

Nearly five decades have passed since I served in Vietnam as a CTI (Communications Technician Interpretive). For several years after I returned home, I relived the vivid experiences of being stationed in Da Nang every few days. Usually late at night while walking around in my living room, I would begin remembering, and suddenly, I was there—sights, sounds, smells, feelings, all as they had been at the time.

Sometimes I recalled sitting at night in the dark canopy of the A-3 jet somewhere 30,000 feet over Laos, listening to air activities out of North Vietnam, one in each earphone. I watched the green spikes on the panoramic scope that displayed the bandwidth for radio signals of MiG-21s trying to intercept Arc Lights (code name for B-52s) over the Ho Chi Minh Trail. I could hear the telltale whisper of a MiG-21 mic, and then the ground controller out of Hanoi Bac Mai booming out, "Forty-eight, the golden calf is in front seventy kilometers." Pilot number 48, the reputed North Vietnamese Red Baron, was being told in a GCI (Ground Controlled Intercept) that his target was straight ahead, and I wondered if we were the target rather than a B-52. I informed the officer in the tail of the plane, and he issued an alert: "Bandit, bandit! One blue bandit, vicinity of Squid. Heads up all aircraft!"

One night our pilot, Mr. Andrews, heard the warning from the tail of his own plane and took a steep dive. I saw the night sky suddenly flip and panicked, thinking we had been hit by a heat-seeking missile. "Did I miss one," I thought, afraid there had been another GCI that I had not noticed. Then I knew what was happening. We dove several thousand feet over the jungle. The dive seemed to last forever. The plane was vibrating, and from my position I could see the amperage and voltage meters across the aisle going haywire. My hand reached for the parachute release. I was strapped into the seat right behind the pilot and heard the navigator ask him, "Do you think the wings will hold when you pull it out of the dive?"

If the pilot gave the bail-out order, it was, as I understood, my duty to get up, stand on the hatch beside my seat, pull up a cap, and then stomp on it. According to what I recall, this would blast the hatch open and send me first out of the jet. In bailing out of an EA-3B, I did not know if I would hit the radar hump on the belly of the aircraft and be instantly killed or perhaps be deflected off it into one of the engines. Supposedly, the yellow lanyard attached to my chute would automatically pull so that it opened barometrically. There was a "green apple" oxygen bottle beneath the cushion of the seat in case we were still at a high altitude. I fumbled, all thumbs, trying to get my oxygen mask on. The thing was floppy rubber and did not fit into the grooves. I abandoned the effort. It occurred to me that my glasses would probably be knocked off when I exited the jet. There I would be, if I survived, caught in a tree, or circling in the mountainous jungle below without glasses, trying to determine if someone approaching was friend or foe.

Then slowly, agonizingly, we began to come out of the dive and leveled off. We were all right; we were safe, at least for the moment. This is just one example of what might go through my mind on those nights when I relived being in Vietnam. My heart pounded, and I talked out loud like an insane man. Then it all subsided, and I was home again, home, and safe.

That was a time that now seems far away, part of another life, but even today I can occasionally be transported back to those days when I flew with the Big Looks Spooks out of Da Nang. But how did it all come about? How did I become an air crewman with hazardous flight duty?

CHAPTER 1

Entering the Navy
and Recruit Training

During the early years of the Vietnam War, I was in graduate school at Emory University in Atlanta. From time to time there were anti-war protests on campus. I remember one occasion when many students stood silently with posters on the steps of the cafeteria in a non-violent demonstration, but I also saw on television demonstrations that included clashes with police. News programs showed hundreds of thousands of young people marching down Pennsylvania Avenue chanting, "Hey, hey, LBJ, how many kids did you kill today?" There was also the protest at the Pentagon, where demonstrators confronted the military police with flower power, stuffing flowers into the barrels of rifles pointed towards them. Coming from a small-city background in southern Georgia, I was not moved to protest against the government, although I doubted the wisdom of the war.

As I was finishing my master's degree at Emory in the 1968–69 academic year, I realized I would probably be drafted. I had planned for many years eventually to join the military for a while because I felt that it was the duty of a young man in good health to do this. My father, after all, had served in the Army during World War II under General Patton, and I had often listened to his war stories and had grown up looking at his war photographs. As the Vietnam War heated up, and the demonstrations increased in number and intensity, I had some doubts. The hippie movement was in full swing, and many songs were on the radio protesting the war and celebrating the hippie counterculture. I remember humming to the words, "If you're going to San Francisco, be sure to wear some flowers in your hair." A number of young men evaded the draft by going to Canada or Europe, or they became conscientious objectors and went to jail. While I was troubled by the war, these protests seemed like extreme reactions to me. I still felt that I should go into the military. But one night while standing at the stove cooking supper, my mother surprised me. She said she would rather I evade the draft and leave the country than go to Vietnam. I understood what she meant. She did not care about the war protests as such; she was just worried lest her only child should go to the war and not return.

Then the matter was decided for me. I was called to the induction center in Atlanta for a physical. I went to that huge building on Ponce de Leon Avenue, went through all the exams, filled out all the papers, and waited in long lines. It turned out I was abominably healthy. Although I had not yet been drafted, it was clear that I was likely to receive a notice. I preferred going into the Navy rather than waiting to be drafted into the Army, so I signed up. Later in Da Nang my friends and I would sometimes sit in the upstairs mess of our barracks at night, and someone would ask, to no one in particular, "So why did you join the Navy?" Someone would reply, "To avoid having to go to Vietnam." Another would say, "So here we are in beautiful Da Nang!" On the wall there was a black light poster showing a soldier with a bayoneted rifle lunging forward. In bold letters at the top were these words: "This Year Vacation in Beautiful Vietnam." Irony and sarcastic humor were the order of the day in our detachment. Some wore love beads, hardly anyone got a haircut, flight boots went unpolished, and many opposed the war. But like me, they decided to join the Navy and ended up in Nam anyway.

I volunteered at the Navy recruiting office in Albany, Georgia, my hometown. I chose the delayed enlistment option so that I could finish up my master's thesis at Emory University. After working for a few more weeks, I finally completed the thesis on the house as a symbol in Robert Frost's poetry. Dr. Peter W. Dowell was my directing professor. I typed the thesis on a manual typewriter and submitted it. Then I went back to the induction center in Atlanta for processing into the Navy. Filling out all of the necessary paperwork and having a physical examination were part of the process. Most of the rest is a blur. Mainly, I remember sitting for a long time waiting my turn—"Hurry up and wait," an expression I came to know well. I recall one of the NCOs arguing with a recruit whether white perch fish should be called "crah-pee" or "crap-pee." The NCO was from North Georgia and held to the former pronunciation, whereas the recruit, holding the other opinion, was from South Georgia. The examining physician had to listen to my heart twice because he thought he heard something the first time, but the second time he said I was ok. We were led into a room where we held up our right hands and took a solemn oath to defend the United States. Afterwards, we were loaded onto a bus and taken to Hartsfield Airport. We boarded a jet plane bound for Orlando, Florida. This was the first time I had ever flown on a jet. While I was a student at Emory, I had on one occasion taken a flight home to Albany on a Southern Airways prop plane, and I had also flown for the first time in a small plane over Macon, Georgia, with my Arab roommate from Georgia Southern College, but that is another story. I was a bit nervous as the plane turned onto the runway and the engines began to roar for takeoff. We sped down the runway and lifted off at a sharp angle. I felt something wet on my foot. Then I realized what had happened. It was the first time to fly for the recruit sitting in front of me.

It was nighttime as we flew south, and looking out the window, I saw the whole Florida east coast lighted up with cities and towns. In the distance lightning flickered around thunderheads. A bus met us at the Orlando airport and took us to the Recruit Training Center. There we lined up outside the bus and were led to our temporary barracks while being processed. It was 1:30 a.m. when I finally crawled into my rack. At 4:30 a.m. the lights clicked on with a loud command of "Attention on deck," and my first full day in the Navy began. While we stood in line on both sides of the barracks in our tee shirts and skivvies, a PO1 proceeded to tell us in no uncertain language how worthless we were and how much work it would take to get us into shape. Every sentence was embellished with colorful figures of speech. I realized that no one can outdo a Navy man in cursing and vividness of language. As an English major, I was impressed.

That first morning we had to line up in the base clinic for medical examinations and shots. The hospital corpsmen kept walking along the line, insisting that we keep quiet and make a tighter line. In the process they used some vivid expressions referring to certain parts of the anatomy. This kind of language, along with much cursing, was common throughout my days in recruit training. It was obviously no place for a sensitive mind, part of the process of making us tougher. During that examination, a corpsman removed my glasses and told me to look into a scope and identify in order the colors I saw. Without my glasses the colored lights looked like fuzzy blobs that merged into one another. The corpsman doing the examination instructed the one writing down the results to say that I was colorblind. I replied, "Wait a minute! I know that I am not colorblind. Let me have my glasses so that I can see properly." They agreed, and when I looked into the scope again, I saw that the colors were small points of light instead of fuzzy blobs and correctly named them in sequence. Afterwards we lined up again to get our shots. We rolled up the sleeves of our tee shirts and walked between corpsmen on either side who administered the shots in both arms simultaneously with injection guns.

From 27 April through 27 June, I was at the Recruit Training Center (RTC) in Orlando. I was assigned to Company III, or Triple Sticks, as we called it, in Regiment 1, Battalion IV. From what I have read, we were among the first companies to go through training at the RTC. The barracks were modern and from the outside looked somewhat like college dorms, but they were definitely not like dorms inside. I recall that our commanding

Interior of the barracks for Company 111, Orlando Recruit Training Center, June 1969. The RTC was commissioned July 1, 1968, and officially closed March 31, 1995 (photograph by William Mulherin).

officer, an NCO named Pickett, took us to the bathroom on the first day and pointed to the long line of gleaming lavatories and urinals. He informed us we could use the first two toilets and two urinals; the rest were there only to look good during inspections. A similar rule applied to the lavatories. "On the day you graduate from recruit training," he said, "you can take a leak anywhere you please."

Chief Pickett was a good company commander. Every sixth word was an obscenity, but he was not trying to be vulgar. It was just his usual manner of speech. On one occasion when we did not do well on a company inspection, he lined us up on both sides of the barracks by our racks. Everyone had a rifle, and he made us hold the pieces above our heads and march in place. With many epithets he yelled that we had better hold those pieces high or he would march us all the way to Georgia and back. If we did not pass the next inspection, he threatened, he would make us hold two pieces above our heads and march us all the way to Great Lakes (the main Navy recruit training center near Chicago). On the second or third morning he called me into his office to talk to me privately. He told me that, since I had the highest education in the company and was also the oldest man at age twenty-four, he wanted me to be the yeoman, or company clerk. I expressed some doubts about whether I could do a good job, but instead of cussing me out, as I expected, he said, "Look, Shippey, this is a game. That's what it is, but we've got to get through it, and I need someone who's more mature to help lead and keep track of these young guys. You're the best qualified man for the job." He leveled with me and spoke in kind words, and after that, regardless of how much he blessed us out, I always respected him.

Reveille at the RTC was at 5:30 a.m., and "lights out" was at 9:00 p.m., if I remember correctly, but as yeoman, I was sometimes up earlier and went to bed later than the rest of the men, working in the company office, preparing duty rosters and doing paperwork to keep track of where every man was at all times. The wake-up call sounded over the loudspeakers this way: "Reveille, reveille, reveille! Heave to and trice up!" I was not quite sure what "trice up" meant but assumed that it was a relic of sailing days when a ship's crew had to take up the hammocks in which they slept. There was a flurry of shaving, dressing, making up racks, and squaring away lockers before the men assembled to march to breakfast. The blankets on the racks were supposed to be stretched so tight that a quarter could bounce on them. I made out chits for men who needed to be away from the company for some reason. Each detail apart from the company had to have written permission, or the men in that group would be in trouble if they encountered an NCO inspector. Mr. Pickett told us what to do if we saw an NCO approaching when we were by ourselves outside of the barracks: "Salute sharply, about face, and haul boogie!"

After assembling each morning, we marched towards the mess hall. In the pre-dawn darkness, I could hear the sound of other companies marching with commands of "Left turn, march!" and "Forward, march," from the RCPOs (Recruit Chief Petty Officers). Wherever we went, we had to march if we were in the company or a detail. Three men constituted a detail, so they could march. If we needed to be out alone on some duty, we had to double time. On extremely hot days, though, a black flag was flown, and that meant we could walk. The company practiced marching on the grinder with rifles just about every day, if I recall correctly, but we also marched to swimming classes, the firing range, tear gas training, and other classes. An RCPO or a platoon leader would occasionally sound out the cadence: "Left, left, left, righter, left." Sometimes a company used a singing cadence. One of the men would lead off: "I've got a gal in New Orleans." The men would repeat the first line, followed by a man leading with the second line: "Prettiest thing you've ever seen," which was also repeated by the whole company. Another singing cadence that caught my attention went like this: "Birdy, birdy, in the sky / Dropped a whitewash in my eye / I'm no wimp, so I won't cry / I'm just glad that cows don't fly." These and other cadences made marching some distance not so monotonous.

Shortly after I became the company yeoman, I had an unpleasant experience with a battalion inspector because I was not yet knowledgeable about all of the responsibilities of my new position. I knew that I was supposed to keep a record of all men who were away. Almost every morning someone had to leave the company for laundry detail, KP duty, or sick bay, and I wrote out chits for them and kept a copy. One guy who had not learned how to swim had to report to the pool every day for lessons. He said, "I'm afraid of that water," and I wondered why in the world he had joined the Navy. I kept chits for each man who was absent, stating where he had gone and when he had left, but did not know that I was also required to keep a list of absences on a form. At the beginning of our first battalion inspection, our RCPO (Recruit Chief Petty Officer), yelled, "Yeoman, post," and I went forward to meet the inspector. This NCO asked for the away list, and I replied that I did not realize I was supposed to have the names on a single list. This was not the answer he wanted. He yelled, "You *what!*" He grabbed the back of my shirt and ripped it while dragging me the length of the company, chewing me out as he went. Then he threw his hands away from me as though I were too filthy to touch. He grabbed my clipboard, which had a compartment beneath it for storing chits, papers, a razor, and various other items. The razor was for last-minute touch-ups that might be needed to get a man who had not shaved close enough ready for inspection. The inspector dumped the contents of the clipboard onto the grinder, and the wind scattered my papers and chits. Then he suddenly changed his demeanor and acted as if nothing bad had happened, saying in a calm voice, "Yeoman, gather up your things and then follow me and take notes as I inspect the men." I followed along behind him, and occasionally, he would turn to me and tell me to take a note about brass belt buckles that had not been polished sufficiently or aligned properly with the fly of the jeans, shoes that had not been correctly spit shined or laced, and men who had not shaved close enough. I mended the ripped work shirt as best I could and from that time on kept an away list.

On one occasion Chief Pickett was away and asked a POI to drill the company that day. This man, whom I will call Mr. Gillis, marched the company back and forth on the grinder all morning, but he gave us a breather in the barracks before lunch. He had us line up in front of our racks on each side of the room and then talked some about how marching is fatiguing and can

On the roof of my barracks, Orlando RTC, June 1969. The clipboard I am holding is an indication of my duties as yeoman for Company 111. I prepared duty
rosters for the company and kept a record of where all the men were located at
any time of the day. I submitted this record to the NCO in charge of reviewing
and evaluating the company during battalion inspections. In the background:
The USS *Blue Jacket*, a small-scale mockup of a Navy destroyer escort used for
training purposes; however, our company never went aboard for training (photograph by William Mulherin).

make a man's legs hurt. He asked, "Does anyone have aching legs?" I knew
better than to reply, but one recruit remarked that he did have some soreness
in one of his legs. Mr. Gillis walked over to him and looked him up and down.
"Which leg is it, sailor?" The man pointed to his right leg, and Mr. Gillis gave
him a swift kick to the left leg. "Now you have *two* sore legs! Does anyone else
have any pain in the legs?" he asked. This time no one said anything.

Our company failed a battalion inspection and was ordered to undergo a repeat inspection the next Saturday morning at a distant spot on the grinder. It had been raining during the night, and the morning was overcast. The company waited in formation for a long time for the arrival of the battalion inspector. Finally, we saw him approaching on a bicycle. It was Mr. Gillis in his white uniform with his hat cocked to one side of his head. The RCPO called us to attention. The bike wobbled toward us, and as Mr. Gillis dismounted, it fell into a mud puddle, splashing his white trousers. It was obvious that he had enjoyed a good time the previous night. He stood before us unsteadily and delivered a long, maudlin speech about how shameful it was that he had to come out on a Saturday morning because we had failed a battalion inspection. At one point, almost sobbing, he asked, "What will you tell your grandchildren about this?" In slurred words he told us how disappointing it was that we had not measured up. All of us stood at attention, pursing our lips to keep from smiling or laughing outright, but we passed that inspection, as well as the rest of them.

Shortly after arrival at the training center, we had "the talk." One of the base chaplains met with us to discuss appropriate sexual behavior in the Navy. He was tactful and circumspect in what he said, but it was soon obvious what he was referring to, namely, homosexuality. I think that at the time a "Don't ask; don't tell" policy was in effect. The chaplain talked with us for several minutes and then mentioned that anyone who wanted to stay behind and talk with him could do so. As we left the meeting room, a few of the recruits went forward to see the chaplain. Not long afterwards, we attended a worship service at the base theater since the modernistic chapel was still under construction. Upon entering, I recognized that some of those who had remained to talk with the chaplain were handing out bulletins for the service at the door and inside. So far as I know, they did not return to their companies, and I can only guess what happened to them after that Sunday service. During the service we sang the "Navy Hymn," and I remember the verse, "Oh hear us when we cry to Thee / For those in peril on the sea," and I realized that in the Navy there were perils other than those on the sea.

During my time in the Navy, I did not go to church much, even though I was a devout Christian. To some extent, I distrusted military chaplains. I wondered how they could serve two masters, God and the military, and in view of this, which loyalty took precedence. Today, I realize that my views of chaplains were unfair since throughout U.S. history chaplains have served faithfully during peace time and times of war. On the battlefield and aboard battle-damaged ships, a chaplain has often given comfort to injured and dying men, praying with them, listening to their final words, and administering last rites. I think, though, that part of my distrust came as a result of "the talk" during recruit training. It did not seem wise to me to confide in a chaplain who was under military authority.

While in Vietnam, I often had duty on Sundays, and there was no convenient way to go to services, even though I heard that they were held at Da Nang. As I traveled about in the Navy, I visited several churches and had respect for them and their congregations whether I agreed entirely with their theology or not. I recall visiting St. Matthew's Cathedral, the Shrine of the Immaculate Conception, and National Cathedral in Washington, D.C. I remember the baroque columns, like twisted licorice sticks, on the cloistered walk at the Franciscan Monastery in Washington, and I marveled that, while a service was in progress at the Shrine of the Immaculate Conception, I could walk along the side aisles without disturbing the proceedings and that on the ground floor many people were enjoying a late Sunday morning breakfast in the dining hall while others were browsing in the gift shop. In New York I visited St. Patrick's Cathedral, Trinity Church near Wall Street, and the Cathedral Church of St. John the Divine in Spanish Harlem. At the latter church I admired the front bronze doors that depict scenes from the Bible. In looking back now, I wish I had gone to more of the services at the base chapels where I was stationed.

Our company marched to the mess hall for each meal. When we arrived on the grinder near the building, we did a right face and came to parade rest, to wait our turn. Most of the time, this posed no problem, but on some days while waiting to enter for the evening meal, we had to stand in the rain and got soaking wet. During the heavy afternoon showers common to Florida in the late spring, our white hats filled with water, and we occasionally had to dip our heads to pour the water out. It was as if we were wearing a water bowl for a dog. Once in the mess hall, we often had only fifteen or twenty minutes to eat by the time we had gone through the serving line. As we ate, recruits with KP duty walked around shouting, "Eat up and get out!" Signs on the columns and walls stated, "Take all you want, but eat all you take." I rarely finished a meal before time was up, and as a result, lost a lot of weight.

One morning while I was sitting in the company office, working on the duty roster, the telephone rang. It was a chief wanting some information about the men from our company assigned to kitchen duty. He gave me some instructions about this, and I replied, "Very well, sir." He then thoroughly chewed me out, shouting into the phone, "You don't 'very well' me!" He had some choice epithets with this admonition. I thought "very well" would be a nice, polite way of acknowledging what he said, not realizing at the time that this was the response of officers to enlisted men giving them information or reports aboard ship. Afterwards, I always said, "Yes, sir," or "Aye, aye, sir!"

Horton was the RCPO for our company. He marched at the head of the company and gave all of the marching orders. Mullins was the Master at Arms, making sure that everything was squared away in the barracks for inspection, and I was the yeoman, tagging along by myself at the end of the company with a clipboard instead of a rifle. The company was divided into two platoons led by Baker and Richards. Mullins had a camera, and I asked him to take some photos for me to commemorate my recruit training. He took one of me on the roof of our barracks, holding the yeoman's clipboard. In the background on the north end of the grinder was the USS *Blue Jacket*, a down-sized mock-up of a destroyer intended for training purposes, although our company was never taken there. Another photo showed several recruits sitting on an outside landing of our barracks spit shining their shoes. Once Mullins caught me unawares. Having just come from the shower, I had on nothing except a towel around my middle as I knelt down beside my rack to arrange my clothes. One photo that he gave me showed Horton, himself, and me standing near the clotheslines on the roof where we tied our white hats to dry. Burgamy, another recruit, sometimes worked with me in the office, helping to prepare duty rosters and answer the phone. When I needed him, I yelled his name, and he came to assist.

I got along reasonably well with all of the men in the company, although some of them did not like the way I made assignments on the duty roster, but I also put myself on the roster. I remember standing watch one night on the roof of the barracks. I believe the watch was for four hours, and this was good preparation for the times in Vietnam when I had to stand a midnight to dawn watch. Horton, Mullins, and Burgamy were my friends, and I enjoyed talking with them in the company office sometimes. In turning through the pages of *The Rudder*, the recruit picture book for the Orlando RTC, I recognize many of the faces of the men in Company 111. Most of their names I had forgotten over the years, but I remembered Horton, Mullins, and Burgamy, as well as Rossi, a gruff-speaking recruit from New York. When I first met him, I thought he was always angry about something, but this was just his usual manner of speech. He helped me have a better understanding of a certain type of New Yorker. In later years I realized that he reminded me of Tony Danza in the way he looked and talked. I recalled Langston, an African American recruit. He was the one who did not pass his swimming test on the first try and kept having to go every morning for swimming lessons. Unfortunately, one inspector sometimes singled him out for rougher treatment than the rest of us received. Maybe he had not shaved closely enough, or his shoes were not laced the right way. The inspector on one occasion grilled him while he was standing at attention with the rest of the company and hit him several times over the head with his clipboard. My heart went out to Langston as he tried both to dodge the blow with his head and still remain at attention. I empathized with him because of the way a battalion inspector had chewed me out and ripped my shirt while dragging me along the grinder. There was Eason, who, like me, wore glasses and always seemed to be in trouble with Mr. Pickett because of some minor infraction. The chief would yell out "Ea-son, you're not in step," with impatience in his voice. He was a good guy, though, trying to do his fumbling best, and I think he might have been the one who, because of his own experiences, took pity on me and gave me a boost over the wall that I was unable to climb when we were taking our JFK physical fitness test. Then there was Pritchett, whom some of the men jokingly called "Mama" because of the concern he expressed about various irregular things they were doing. In remembering these men, I have wondered where they were assigned after our time in Orlando.

Mr. Pickett was reassigned by the Navy to another duty station after about four weeks. I was sorry to see him go because of the way he had leveled with me; his fairness in dealing with us, even though he cussed a lot; and the humorous sea stories that he occasionally shared at the end of the day. Mr. Dews replaced him as our company commander, and he was a good, somewhat taciturn but agreeable NCO. Our training continued smoothly under him, and I was grateful for his quiet but firm approach in leading. We knew that he would deal fairly with us but not brook any violation of Navy training protocol.

Our training included various classes. One was marlinspike seamanship, i.e., tying knots, a skill I never mastered since I did not serve aboard ship. We also had training in voice-activated radiotelephones and in firing and cleaning the M16 rifle. The irony of the latter training class is that we could not actually fire the M16 since there was no firing range at that early time in the center's history, and Orlando had an ordinance against firing weapons in the city limit that applied even to the Navy. As a result, we simply aimed the M16 over the neighboring lake and clicked the trigger. When I arrived in Vietnam, my commanding officer was astounded to learn that I, as well as a few other men, had never fired the M16. He immediately ordered a range party.

One of our classes was tear gas training. Our instructors taught us how to wear the gas mask and how to clear it before putting it on if gas was already in the air around us. Once in the tear gas chamber, we wore the mask while the gas was deployed. Then we took off our masks and blew into them to clear them before putting them back on. After a short time, we were ordered to take the masks off to experience the effects of tear gas. We all exited the building with burning and watering eyes.

Other classes taught us how to rappel from a height, how to fight fires, and how to swim if we had to stay in the water a long time. The instructors demonstrated that almost every part of the work uniform could be used as a flotation device. We could take off our trousers, knot the legs at the end, lift them into the air with the legs up and bring them down suddenly, thereby creating water wings. We could make sure our shirt was tightly buttoned and blow into it to create an air bubble. The white hat, if turned down, would also hold a bit of air. We were advised not to try to swim if we were a long way from shore and had no flotation device. Doing the dead man's float and coming up occasionally for air was the best way to avoid becoming fatigued and drowning. Later in SERE school I would receive more instructions on surviving in the water.

I recall one morning when we were given a bathroom break after drilling for a long time on the grinder. The entire company had to line up in the head in our barracks to use two toilets. I was very nervous because I really needed to urinate, but it often took me a while to get started, especially if anyone else was in the bathroom with me and I felt rushed. On this occasion a considerable part of the company was waiting in line behind me, and I was under pressure to go as quickly as possible. We also had only a short time to return to the grinder. Fortunately, when my time came, I was able to go after a brief pause.

One of Mullins' photographs shows me standing in front of a chalk board with the schedule for June 23, 1969. This gives some idea of the classes during the latter part of recruit training:

Period	Time	Class
1	0645	Shipboard Orientation 22
2	0735	Naval History 9
3	0825	TV Class
4	0915	TV Class
5	1005	Shipboard Orientation
6	1055	Shipboard Orientation
	LUNCH	
7	1315	DC 22 * [Damage Control]
8	1405	DC 23 *
9	1455	Military Drill
10	1545	Military Drill

By the time of the first class each morning, the company had already finished breakfast. Supper was somewhat late in the day. Although no schedule was posted for the evening, the time was not really free. We had duties to perform to get ready for the next day, and as yeoman, I had to make sure that all men were present and accounted for.

During the sports competition day, our company lost at tug of war and did not do so well on some of the other sports events, but we won the camp championship for volleyball, a game I have always enjoyed. I got into the game that day in a way I had never before experienced with any other sport. There was something about the dynamics of working with my teammates to set the ball up for a spike that appealed to my sense of competition. As we volleyed the ball back and forth, we kept yelling, "Come on Triple Sticks! Come on!" As a result of that win, we proudly flew the championship banner on our company guidon whenever we marched.

Not long before graduation, each training group at the RTC had a supervised liberty day to go as a group on an outing. Disney World on the west side of Orlando was still under construction, so we were not able to go there. Instead, we went to Rainbow Springs, several miles west of Ocala, Florida. I do not remember much about this outing, but I think that we were able to ride on glass-bottom boats on the river. It is possible, though, that I am confusing this trip with one I took with my parents to Silver Springs at a later time. We also walked around in the gardens simply enjoying being away from the training center for the day; otherwise, there was not much to do. Rainbow Springs was privately owned at the time, so the owners apparently did not mind having hundreds of Navy recruits descend on their property at one time since this brought in extra profit.

My parents were not able to come for my graduation from recruit training on June 27. That morning our company, along with all of the other companies, marched on the parade ground in our white dress uniforms, wearing leggings. As we passed the reviewing stand, where the base commander and other officers and dignitaries were standing, in addition to families of the recruits in the bleachers, Horton gave the command of "Eyes right!" The men on the outside column towards the stand continued to look straight ahead, while the men in the other columns looked to the right, carrying their rifles. I was at the end of the company by myself and saluted with eyes right, as did the platoon leaders, since we were not carrying pieces. Horton, as RCPO, was carrying a sword and looked eyes right without saluting. A Navy drill team demonstrated their skill with rifles as part of the program. At the end of the ceremony, families came onto the field to hug their recruits, and I returned to the barracks to finish packing for my flight home. I think I also went to the bathroom to exult in using any urinal I chose.

I flew from Orlando to Jacksonville to catch my flight home to Albany. En route from Orlando, I remember looking out the window and seeing the St. John's River below us. Somewhere near Palatka we must have passed within sight of the fish camp on the river owned by my cousin Eunice and her husband, George Stanley. I visited there with my parents while I was in high school. One afternoon my Grandmother Shippey, during a visit to the camp, fell off the dock into the river while fishing. She was a bit exasperated that her sister, my Aunt Zellie, did not come to her rescue. She asked, "Sister, why didn't you help me?" And Aunt Zellie replied, "I might have fallen into the river, too."

According to the travel request form that I signed, the fare for my flight from Orlando to Jacksonville was $17.00, and the fare from there to Albany was $18.00. The form also showed the cost from Albany back to Jacksonville after my leave ended was $13.00, and the flight from there to my next duty station in Washington, D.C. was $31.00, a total cost of $82.95 when the tax was added. Quite a difference from airfares I later paid once I was a civilian!

Within a day or two after I arrived home, we went to Laura Walker State Park near Waycross, Georgia, for the Shippey family reunion. I was self-conscious about going since I still had the buzz haircut of a recruit, but I was also tanned from marching on the grinder, thinner from not eating so much, and stronger from physical training. In short, I probably looked better that weekend than I have ever looked since then. My Uncle DeWitt and his family hosted the reunion, and it was good to see everyone. The food, as usual, was outstanding and became part of the way I recalled family gatherings while I was in Vietnam, something I sometimes did when I was homesick.

When my leave ended, I took a Southern Airways two-prop plane back to Jacksonville. Over the Okefenokee Swamp we experienced some rather heavy turbulence, and when I glanced back at the flight attendant strapped to her seat at the rear of the cabin, she was gripping the armrests firmly and looked nervous. This turbulence, though, was mild in comparison to what I later experienced while flying in aircraft out of Da Nang over the Gulf of Tonkin during typhoons.

As my jet took off from Jacksonville Airport that afternoon, I saw the water of many estuaries reflecting the sky. Somewhere among them was the Trout River, where my parents and I had lived when I was two to four years old not long after my father returned from World War II. My first memories were of this river. I remembered going out on the river in a boat with my father and being amazed at how black the water was from all of the tannin in it. I also recalled one afternoon when I went down to the river alone and tried to wade out to a houseboat anchored a short distance from the bank. One of my mother's brothers, who was supposed to be watching me while she went into town, had fallen asleep at the house. I wanted so much to reach that houseboat, but the water kept getting deeper and deeper, and I finally realized I had to turn back. When I was almost to the shore, I fell and cut my hand on some broken glass. This was one of several times in my life when the shadow of death has come near me. In Vietnam I was to have a few more of those times.

CHAPTER 2

Washington, D.C., and New York

In recruit training I took the test to see where I might best fit. The results showed I was high in linguistic skills, so I filled out paperwork requesting to be sent to language school to study Russian. Back came the assignment: Vietnamese, Saigon dialect. The other guys in my company chuckled at this and said, as if they had come up with a rich joke, "You know where you're going!" They all seemed to think that, after language training, I would be hauled off to Vietnam and forced to bail out somewhere over the jungle. That was the picture in my mind, too.

But I was first sent for over a year to DLIEC (Defense Language Institute East Coast) in Arlington, Virginia. Officially, I was stationed at the Anacostia Naval Station, but I was quartered across the river at Fort Myer, North Post, right beside Arlington National Cemetery. Every day I could look out the window of my room and see hundreds of tombstones. Not an encouraging sight! I went to classes five days a week at an office building in Rosslyn, Virginia, but later the school was shifted to a new office tower in Crystal City, just south of the Pentagon. From one of the classrooms, I could see the jets landing at National Airport (now Reagan National Airport). It was a ten-minute walk from my barracks to President Kennedy's gravesite and the Tomb of the Unknown Soldier. I often walked down to the Custis-Lee Mansion and looked across the Potomac toward central Washington. On a sunny day I could clearly see Memorial Bridge, the Lincoln Memorial, the Washington Monument, and the dome of the Capitol Building. If I looked to the left, I could see the towers of Washington National Cathedral, misty blue on the heights in the distance. While standing in front of the mansion, I sometimes pondered the irony of all the Yankees buried in General Robert E. Lee's yard.

On Sunday, July 20, 1969, shortly after my arrival in Washington, I went to the TV lounge in the barracks and watched the *Apollo* lunar landing. The other men in the room and I sat entranced when Neil Armstrong

Oil painting by me of buildings bordering the parade ground at Fort Myer, Virginia. While quartered at Fort Myer, I visited the art galleries in Washington, D.C., and was impressed by the paintings of the nineteenth-century French Impressionists at the National Gallery of Art and the Phillips Gallery, so I decided to try my hand at painting. I continued to paint occasionally when I was later stationed at Goodfellow Air Force Base in Texas and the Naval Communications Station in the Philippines (photograph by the author).

stepped down from the lander's ladder onto the lunar surface and began his walk. The next day I purchased a copy of the *Apollo* edition of *The Evening Star* newspaper, which featured a blurred TV image of Neil Armstrong and Edwin Aldrin walking on the moon. This image covered the entire front page, except for the headlines and the masthead. The headlines in huge letters read, "Man Walks on Moon 'One Small Step.... One Giant Leap.'" I still have this edition of the Washington *Evening Star*.

Almost every weekend I visited one of the art museums in town. I especially enjoyed the Impressionists paintings at the Phillips Gallery on Massachusetts Avenue. Renoir's *Luncheon of the Boating* Party at the head of the stairs leading to the second floor was particularly striking in its freshness and beauty. Several Saturday mornings I went to the National Gallery to the theater downstairs and watched the *Civilisation* series narrated by Kenneth Clark. After the film I had lunch in the cafeteria and bought prints in the museum gift shop. Then I went upstairs and sometimes saw works by artists mentioned in the film. On Sunday evenings I attended chamber music concerts performed by members of the National Symphony in the East Garden Court of the National Gallery. Then I strolled around one of the galleries briefly, maybe viewing the Vermeer paintings or the water lilies of Claude Monet. Exploring the gardens at Dumbarton Oaks in Georgetown in the springtime was a pleasant experience when the golden forsythia and pink and white Japanese magnolias were blooming. I admired the Byzantine bronze medallions on exhibit in the house. One evening I went to the Arena Stage Theatre for a performance of Jean-Paul Sartre's *No Exit,* a play developing the theme that shifting relationships with other people can be hell, a concept that I to some extent agreed with. I also saw a production of a Noel Coward play at the Kennedy Center and in the intermission enjoyed walking around the exterior of the building and looking out over the Potomac River.

One cold weekend in November 1970 I traveled to Philadelphia to visit the art museums and other places of interest. I especially liked the Marc Chagall paintings at the Philadelphia Museum of Art. I stood at the elevated entrance to this museum, looking down the Benjamin Franklin Parkway towards the tower of city hall before the iconic scene from *Rocky* was shot depicting Sylvester Stallone as Rocky standing at the same spot. I also walked to the Rodin Museum, where, in addition to the *Thinker* on display outside, I viewed numerous small sculptures by Auguste Rodin, the nineteenth-century French sculptor. The small pieces apparently served as studies for such full-sized works as *Balzac* and the larger-than-life figures of *The Gates of Hell.* A trip to Philadelphia was not complete without a visit to Independence Hall, where I saw the Liberty Bell, which was housed at that time in the entrance hall. I also visited the grave of Benjamin Franklin.

In October 1969 I went to New York City for the first time. I traveled by bus but in future trips preferred to take the train since it took me to Pennsylvania Station, which was nearer to the place where I stayed. It was nighttime when the bus reached the New Jersey suburbs of the city, and I kept wondering why I could not yet see the famous New York skyline. In the distance I saw two points of light protruding above the horizon, and as we neared the city, I realized these were the tops of the twin towers of the World Trade Center. I could not determine, though, why I could see only their tops. In the distance I saw flames burning from what appeared to be the catalytic cracking towers of an oil refinery. Flames were glowing on different parts of the horizon. At one point we crossed a marshy place where I saw an oil slick reflected in the black water. This was a hellish nocturnal landscape where it appeared Armageddon had already happened. As we approached the Lincoln Tunnel, we came down off a hill, and there spread out before me was the Hudson River and on the other side the glorious New

York skyline. We emerged from the tunnel with a policeman blowing his whistle and directing traffic, and this was New York just as I had dreamed it would be from the many movies and TV shows I had seen about the city.

I went to the Soldiers', Sailors', Marines', Coast Guard and Airmen's Club on Lexington Avenue to get a bed for the night. If I recall correctly, the charge was $1.50 for each night, a marvelous boon for servicemen visiting New York. My bed was in a room with several other beds. I stowed my things and then went out to explore the city. Upon emerging from the club, I immediately encountered a young African American streetwalker. She was an attractive woman with short platinum blond hair (or wig), and she was wearing huge gold earrings that hung almost to her shoulders. She had on an auburn-colored leather coat tied with a sash and wore high-topped boots. She asked if I would like some company for the evening, and I politely declined. Anyone reading this memoir may think it not likely that a sailor would decline, but I was living according to how I had been raised and what I believed as a follower of Christ. This perhaps makes me come across as a "goody two-shoes," and I am reminded of the narrator in Ursula K. Le Guin's story "The Ones Who Walk Away from Omelas," in his/her effort to convince the reader that the city of Omelas was not quite so good as it might at first appear to be. Certainly, I had many faults, as will later appear in this narrative. For one thing, I was too much the introvert and did not reach out to others in friendship and compassion the way I should have done. I often remained on the sidelines, being content merely to observe. I was too much the bookworm and pedant. I was aware of this, and in an entry in my journal made while I was in Da Nang wrote the following, imagining what some critic of my way of life might say:

> Go out and get drunk. Raise hell along with everyone else! Man, this stuff don't go. Like, it don't make it. Go out and get yourself a woman of the night and forget all this egghead crap. You trying to be a priest, man? You'd think it, the way you're going at it…. Get out and get your hands down in the mud; get dirty. Come on in, son, the mud's fine, or are you too holier-than-thou to associate with us mere mortals? Well, damn you! Go on back and knock on the gate and say, "Lord, let me back in the Garden of Eden 'cause I don't like it out here in the world." Go on back!

So no, I did not accept the young woman's invitation nor the invitations of pimps and other streetwalkers I encountered while in the Navy. That evening I continued on my way to Times Square and marveled at how much it reminded me of the crowded midway of a state fair where everyone was on the make. I was the incorrigible nerd walking the streets of Vanity Fair.

I visited the Metropolitan Museum of Art and was surprised at how difficult it was to see the paintings. In places the crowds were so thick that I could not get close to the paintings. Also, some of the paintings were placed one above another and were so high that it was impossible to view them clearly. I compared the museum unfavorably to the National Gallery in Washington, where all of the paintings were at eye level, and the different galleries were rarely crowded. Sometimes I could stand in a gallery alone, except for a nearby guard, and have the paintings of Monet or El Greco all to myself for several minutes.

I attended the musical *Man of La Mancha*, but since I could not afford an expensive ticket, I sat in the nosebleed section on the last row of the upper balcony. The stage seemed far away, but I greatly enjoyed the show since the story of Don Quixote's quest appealed to my sense of romanticism. Also, "The Impossible Dream" had long been one of my favorite inspirational songs. I reflected that those of us going to Vietnam were, in a sense, also on an irrational, impossible quest filled with dangers and absurdities, and I could identify with Don Quixote, mocked and scorned, striving for the "unreachable star."

On subsequent weekend trips to New York, I visited the Whitney Museum of American Art, the Guggenheim Museum, the Frick Collection, and the Metropolitan Museum of Modern Art. The Guggenheim had an exhibit of Roy Lichtenstein's paintings, which resembled enlarged frames from comic books depicting World War II aircraft firing their guns and beautiful women crying over romance gone wrong. At the Metropolitan Museum of Modern Art, I noticed in particular the works of Picasso. I saw his *Guernica* before it was returned to Spain and was amazed at the simplicity and ingenuity of some of his sculptures, for example, the head of a bull suggested by a bicycle seat with upright handlebars welded to it as horns. In touring the art museums in New York, Philadelphia, and Washington, I enjoyed having access to original great works of art by the masters of the past and the noted artists of the present. This was an eye-opening experience for me since at that time there were no art galleries in southern Georgia. So far as art was concerned, the region still fit H.L. Mencken's description of the South as "the Sahara of the Bozart."

While stationed at Fort Myer, I visited the Georgetown University library and paid to get a library card so that I could have access to scholarly books. At the time I was doing some research on Walt Whitman, and among other books, I remember checking out Roger Asselineau's *The Evolution of Walt Whitman* from the library and then reading it in the barracks lounge. I also went to the Library of Congress to do research on Whitman. I sat in the main reading room of the library and waited for the books I had requested to be brought from the stacks. I was overawed simply to be sitting there in so distinguished a library, and I must have looked like a hick from the backwoods as I gazed up into the dome and admired the architecture of the room. The north post of Fort Myer also had a library, and I often went there to read and check out books. Some of the books I read while stationed at Fort Myer were *Clock Without Hands* by Carson McCullers, *Everything That Rises Must Converge* by Flannery O'Connor, *How I Believe* by Pierre Teilhard de Chardin, *Civilization on Trial* by Arnold Toynbee, *Mr. Sammler's Planet* by Saul Bellow, and *The Autobiography of Mark Van Doren.* Bellow's book had received mixed reviews upon publication, but I enjoyed reading it because of the protagonist's devotion to ideas. I was interested in Van Doren's autobiography since he had been an English professor at Columbia University, as well as a poet and literary critic. I recalled that his son, Charles Van Doren, had appeared on the 1950s quiz show *Twenty-One* and impressed the TV audience with the breadth of his knowledge and congenial personality. My parents and I watched this show and had been amazed by Van Doren's winning streak. It turned out that it was all a deception. The organizers of the show had given him the answers in advance. This incident led some viewers to distrust both game shows and the media in general. His father, Mark Van Doren, along with Mortimer Adler, had helped develop the Great Books curriculum at St. John's College in Annapolis. For several years I had been an admirer of the *Great Books of the Western World* series developed in the early 1950s by Adler and others.

Outside the cafeteria at Fort Myer, I could buy copies of *The Washington Post* from a newspaper box. I frequently bought a copy to read while I ate breakfast before going for the day's classes at DLIEC. I liked to buy the Sunday edition so that I could read the reviews in the books section, but I also enjoyed reading the editorial pages. Sometimes I went to nearby convenience stores, where I could purchase copies of the *Philadelphia Inquirer,* the *Baltimore Sun,* and the *New York Times.* I especially liked the *New York Times Book Review* and spent Sunday afternoons and evenings reading over whatever papers I had bought. Occasionally, when I was in downtown Washington, I bought a copy of the London *Times* from a newsstand on the street. The pages of the paper were thin and flimsy since it had to be sent by air to the United States.

I believe it was sometime in 1970 when digging for the Washington Metro system began. I recall walking across boards covering the digging at Connecticut Avenue near Farragut Square. The boards and the dirt piled along the sidewalk reminded me of frontier towns that I had read about that used boards to cover muddy streets.

One Saturday night I was walking by Farragut Square when I heard moans and anguished cries coming from a car parked at the curb. I looked through the window and saw a young African American woman rolling back and forth on the front seat apparently in some kind of seizure. I was concerned and tried to get her attention by tapping on the window, but she did not respond. She kept squirming and screaming. A middle-aged African American man wearing an all-weather coat and Fedora passed by, and I asked if he could help. He took a brief look into the car and said, "She's on something." Then he continued on his way, not wanting to become involved. I tried to get two or three more passersby to assist, but they just waved me away as they walked by. Eventually, I saw a D.C. police car, and I waved it down. The two officers tried to speak to the woman and tap on the window, but they also could not get her attention. Finally, one of them broke the back window on the driver's side with his night stick and reached around to unlock the door. At this point I felt embarrassed and a bit guilty, realizing that I had perhaps caused this woman to get in trouble with the law; however, I was also concerned about not trying to help in case she might have been having a heart attack or seizure that threatened her life. As I walked away from the scene, I hoped the officers would be able to get her some help for her drug problem. I also realized how naïve I was about life on the streets of Washington.

Sometimes I enjoyed just walking along Wisconsin Avenue in Georgetown, looking at the shops and the people. In those days hippies congregated in the area, and I recall that one afternoon a young woman who looked like a hippie came up to me and asked for money. She said that she needed money for herself and her "old man." Whether the "old man" was her husband, boyfriend, or father she did not say. She looked somewhat impatient as I fished in my pockets for some coins and departed without saying "thank you." I remember the balloon man who walked along this street. He was a middle-aged African American man who held an array of colorful helium-filled balloons in his hand, saying, "Make the kiddies happy. Make the mama and daddy happy. Make everybody happy! Buy a balloon!" He reminded me of the bird woman in the movie *The Sound of Music*.

Another place in Georgetown where I went a few times for dinner was Chez Odette, a small French restaurant not far from the Francis Scott Key Bridge. The tables were covered with white cloths, and the place was so crowded that the waiter had to pull the table out so the diner could sit on the cushioned bench against the wall. I recall ordering the veal scallopini, and it was succulent and delicious. The restaurant had a good assortment of cheeses, and I enjoyed slices of Camembert with my after-dinner *café au lait*. I could not afford to invite anyone to go with me, so I dined at Chez Odette and other pricey restaurants alone. At one of those restaurants, the maître d' took one look at me in my red sweater and narrow tie and seated me at a table near the kitchen. I did not mind, though, because I was near the fireplace, and the *coq au vin* that I ordered was superb. Sometimes I purchased a copy of *Le Figaro litteraire to* read while I waited for my dinner. Looking back now, I smile, realizing that my preoccupation with fine restaurants, French wines, and foreign papers was rather pompous and naïve. Being from rural South Georgia, though, this was the first time I had ever had access to this lifestyle, and it was good to savor it for a while.

During the spring of 1970, Patrick, a friend at DLIEC, and I rented a canoe near the Francis Scott Key Bridge and paddled a good distance up the C & O Canal (Chesapeake & Ohio Canal). The day was warm and pleasant, and a number of people were walking on the towpath along the canal. We portaged the canoe when we came to a lock, and I climbed onto one of the huge wooden levers that open the lock and sat down for a photo. We went as far as some rapids on the Potomac, which flows beside the canal, and then explored the boulders at the edge of the river. Before we reached the rapids, we saw a fire truck parked beside the canal. An African American man, who had apparently been fishing in the river, had become stuck near the middle of the stream when a spillway for the dam upstream opened, and he was not able to return to the bank because of the rising water and swift current. The firemen waded out as far as they safely could and threw a rope to place around his waist. They then helped the man slowly to walk back to safety on the bank. After watching the rescue, Patrick and I began our return trip. Dusk came, and the evening star was reflected in the canal as we paddled back to the rental place to return the canoe. I recalled a passage from Wordsworth's *Prelude*, in which he described how, in ice skating on one of the lakes near his home when he was a youth, he tried to cut across the reflection of a star on the ice. I paddled towards the reflection of the evening star, which moved with us. Later, when I was stationed in the Philippines, I saw the reflection of the star in a rice paddy as our bus passed by. It was comforting that in a world wracked with war and turmoil the stars were constant whether we were in the Western or Eastern hemisphere.

As interesting as it was to be in Washington and enjoy the cultural delights of its historical sites, museums, libraries, parks, and restaurants and to take trips to Philadelphia and New York, I realized that this was just a brief respite, a peaceful prelude to war, and all of those white tombstones visible from my barracks window, each with its own small American flag on Memorial Day, gave me pause for thought. It was obvious that many of the men buried in Arlington National Cemetery had died in Vietnam, and I wondered if the body count was not higher than the official figures published in the newspapers. But there were other reminders of the war while I was in Washington.

Every month during the fall of 1969 there were moratorium marches against the war with hundreds of thousands of people coming into the city each time to protest. I attended a demonstration one October night at the Washington Monument when Coretta Scott King spoke. I stood on the fringe of the crowd because it was impossible to get near the speaker's podium. After the speeches, the demonstrators lit candles and marched past the White House. Many of them left their candles on the wrought iron fence of the nearby Treasury Building. Months after the march, melted wax was still visible on the fence, a poignant reminder of the smoldering resentment of young people against the war and the draft. In November another big demonstration took place, and Navy officers warned the enlisted men not to attend because FBI agents would mingle with the crowd and take photographs. If we were seen, we could be in big trouble. But this was a historic occasion, and I wanted to see some of it, so I waited until late in the day and then went downtown. I walked to National Square near the White House, where I could look down Pennsylvania Avenue towards the Capitol. The end of the march was visible in the distance, and beyond that the street was littered with discarded posters and scraps of paper. The last of thousands of marchers were entering the square, chanting, "Peace now! Peace Now." Their angry voices reverberated off the surrounding buildings. I stood on the sidewalk watching but then realized that a small group of war supporters was on the other side of me carrying posters that said, "Support Our Boys in Vietnam!" When the marchers spotted their placards, the volume of the shouts increased, and I saw that I was in a precarious position if the opposing sides clashed. I cleared out as fast as I could.

It was a bitterly cold November day. I took a city bus down K Street and got off to have supper at a cafeteria. I recall that I ate warm rhubarb pie, while sipping my coffee, and read *The Washington Post*. Outside young demonstrators sat huddled beneath blankets on the street curbs while others walked in search of a ride out of the city. To protect the White House that day, city buses were parked end to end around the Ellipse and the surrounding streets. A reporter asked President Nixon what he thought about the moratorium march, and he responded, "It's a great day for football!"

In May of 1970 the national guard confronted demonstrators at Kent State University and fired on the students killing four of them. I remember the iconic photo of the young woman in shock, screaming while squatting beside the body of a student. Not long afterwards Crosby, Stills, Nash, and Young came out with the song "Ohio" with the lines "This summer I hear the drumming / Four dead in Ohio." The song was everywhere on the radio. In the same month University of Maryland students, protesting the entrance of American troops into Cambodia, confronted the national guard in College Park and for a time occupied the administration building, setting fire to it. That summer I attended a concert with Margaret Shippey Cook, a distant cousin, and her husband at the Goddard Space Flight Center, and in returning to Washington, we rode through the campus of the University of Maryland to see the places where the students had protested.

I met Ms. Cook, originally from South Carolina, shortly after being stationed in Washington. She and I were both interested in doing genealogical research on the Shippey family, and we enjoyed discussing this subject when she invited me to dinner at their home in Anacostia. When I returned from Vietnam and was stationed at Fort Meade, I often took the bus down U.S. Highway 1 past the entrance to the University of Maryland campus. We passed by the low stone wall behind which I recalled seeing the Maryland national guard lined up, facing the protestors, in news broadcasts.

CHAPTER 3

Language Training

While stationed at Fort Myer, I took language classes with the Defense Language Institute East Coast (DLIEC) five days a week. Each morning I waited with the other students outside the cafeteria for the bus ride to classes at Rosslyn Plaza in Arlington and later at Crystal City in Alexandria. Our teacher was a short, thin Vietnamese woman, whom the men sometimes referred to as Minnie Mouse. She spoke English reasonably well and wore an áo dài to class each day. I got on her bad side one afternoon by saying that something we were discussing was nonsense. I do not recall what the subject of the discussion was, and I did not mean to be insulting. The word just came out wrong. She took offense and from then on treated me with cool detachment. She maintained a cheerful, joking manner with the other men in the class, but always assumed a serious, noncommittal look when it came my turn to respond. She was, nevertheless, an excellent teacher, and we made good progress in learning the language. I remember her joking with one of the Navy men in the class. Sometimes he would become tired during the long day, and his head would begin to nod. The teacher would then rap on the desk and say, "Ông Schneider, you take nap. Exactly, I see you!" Schneider would protest that he was not asleep, and she would reply in a joking manner, "Nói láo, láo, láo! (Speaking lies, lies, lies). Exactly, you take nap!" She enjoyed this kind of repartee, and all of us had a good laugh.

We were issued several volumes of Vietnamese workbooks, many of which dealt with military subjects. These books included cartoon drawings portraying various scenarios in which the language might be used. I recall one set of drawings that depicted a downed American pilot who approaches a Vietnamese couple working in a field. He says in Vietnamese, "Sir, Ma'am, I am an American pilot, and my plane has just crashed." They reply, "Xin anh đừng lo sẽ. Chung tôi sẽ bảo vệ anh" ("Please do not worry. We will protect you"). My classmates and I responded by saying, "They will protect him all right." Thereafter, whenever we discussed some problem or difficulty, we often joked with one another, "Don't worry. We will protect you."

Our teacher talked with us about interesting places in Vietnam and also shared some stories about its history. She mentioned that Dalat is a beautiful city. She then asked, "Đà Lạt có đẹp không?" ("Is Dalat beautiful?"). We replied, "Đà Lạt đẹp lắm" ("Dalat is very beautiful"). She also told us about the Cao Dai religion, which, from her description, seemed to hold that all religions are one. She mentioned that the religion venerates various people, including Jesus, Muhammad, Moses, Shakespeare, Lenin, and Victor Hugo, among others. She related stories about the heroic Trung sisters, who almost two thousand years ago led the Vietnamese in resisting Chinese domination.

Other students in the class included the Navy men (Chief Ortiz, Jackson, Rossiter, and Schneider) and the Army men (Banks, a Harvard graduate; Taylor, a Yale graduate; and a guy from New Jersey whose name I cannot remember). Our first day in class at Crystal City, where the classes were relocated and reorganized, we all introduced ourselves. When I announced that I was from Georgia, the New Jersey man said, "Georgia! Yuck! Did you vote for Lester Maddox?" Maddox was well known in the media for trying to maintain segregation at his Atlanta restaurant, the Pickrick, by brandishing an ax handle at any Blacks who tried to enter. When asked by the media how he was, he would reply, "Everything's just Pickrick!" One of his talents was riding a bicycle while sitting backwards on the handlebars. I replied that I had not voted for Maddox.

Banks was a large bald-headed man with a love for satire. Sometimes during the break for lunch, if we were discussing the war, he would look very serious and then smash his fist onto the desk, saying, "Nuke 'em, by God!" This was his way of satirizing hawkish military leaders, especially General LeMay, or Curtis "Bomb 'em" LeMay, as his detractors sometimes called him. Then he would point a finger at one of us with a quizzical look on his face and say, "You! You like to kill people? Good! We can use you." Banks and Taylor often ribbed each other in the stereotypical Harvard versus Yale tradition, but whereas Banks was loud and vociferous, sometimes punctuating his satire with feigned maniacal laughter ("Mwa-ha-ha-ha-ha!"), Taylor was quiet, completely the gentleman, sitting cross-legged at his desk, holding a copy of *The Wall Street Journal*, and responding with dry humor. Chief Ortiz, a mild-mannered middle-aged man, was the genial arbiter of any disputes that might arise. I later met him again in the Philippines when I was stationed there for a time before proceeding to Nam. Rossiter, younger than the rest of us, enjoyed talking about deer hunting in the woods of Pennsylvania and had a straightforward sense of humor. He learned the language faster than any of us. Jackson, from Minneapolis, often joked with our instructor and sat at his desk drawing amusing cartoons with Vietnamese side notes, which he slyly showed to me whenever the teacher's back was turned. After we graduated from language school, Schneider, Rossiter, and Jackson were all assigned to the Naval Security Group at Fort Meade with duty at the NSA. The only one I ever heard from again was Jackson, who wrote me about how boring his duty was and how messed up he thought the Navy was. His closing words were "Don't change."

While taking classes, I was quartered at the New Enlisted Men's Barracks on the North Post of Fort Myer, Virginia. There were four of us to a room. One of the guys was a driver for the Navy's top brass at the Pentagon. Another, Mitchell, from Nebraska, was a clerk at the Navy Bureau of Personnel. The other roommate, Gerald, also at DLIEC and studying Russian, was from Ohio, and he loved to put on his bathing suit, spread a towel on the grass behind the barracks, and sunbathe. As a result, he had a nice tan. He teased me about being from Georgia, and I jokingly referred to him as King Farouk of Egypt, enjoying his sybaritic lifestyle. Whenever he came back to the room, wearing his sunglasses and flip-flops with a towel on his arm, I would say, "Well, if it isn't Farouk himself!" At Thanksgiving Mitchell's girlfriend invited us to her apartment for dinner. I carried a bottle of French burgundy, which I had bought at the Eagle Wine & Liquor shop in Georgetown. Mitchell's girlfriend was intrigued by my accent and asked if I was British. Gerald guffawed, choking on his wine, and then blurted out, "No! He's from *Georgia!*" Later Brandon Stokowski, another friend at DLIEC, met me in San Francisco while we were en route to Vietnam. We sat next to each other on the plane, and he told me that Gerald had been assigned to Adak, Alaska. "Think we should send him a bottle of suntan lotion?" I asked, and we both pondered the irony of Gerald's being stationed in Alaska. Gerald later wrote to me that Adak was the worst place to be stuck since it was over a thousand miles from Anchorage, the nearest city. He had to work thirteen to fourteen hours a day in the galley. My heart went out to him. Fortunately, he later received orders to Misawa, Japan, a duty station that he enjoyed.

Samuel Kronberg was another friend at DLIEC, but he lived off base with his wife. He was a photographer and hoped to have a career taking photographs after he got out of the Navy. Sometimes he invited me to go with him on excursions around the city. One afternoon both of us in our white summer uniforms visited the Tomb of the Unknown Soldier and, as a result, inadvertently became part of the ceremony. The changing of the guard took place while we were there, and the officer of the guard stated that all men in uniform should render the hand salute at the commands of "present arms." People in the crowd looked around to see who was in uniform. Kronberg and I stood out, and we saluted at the appropriate times. I wondered as I held the salutes how Kronberg felt because I knew that he was adamantly opposed to the war. I made a mental note not to wear my uniform around Washington in the future when not on duty.

At Passover Kronberg and his wife invited me to their apartment for supper. They lived near the Scottish Rite Temple in central Washington. His wife served a delicious meal of Cornish game hens stuffed with yellow rice. There was also gefilte fish, my first encounter with this item of Jewish cuisine, and I liked it. I accompanied Kronberg on several of his photography outings. One Saturday we visited the National Zoo to see the panda, and while we were there, Kronberg took photos of the children who crowded around him. On other occasions he took snapshots as we walked around the Tidal Basin. His primary interest was people just being themselves.

That spring Kronberg and his wife invited me to go on a road trip with them to tour Civil War battlefields. First, we stopped at Manassas and walked across the meadow, where during the First Manassas, when the battle was not going well for the Confederates, General Barnard Bee said, "There stands Jackson like a stone wall." I plucked a cloverleaf from the spot and placed it in my guidebook about the battle. That afternoon we crossed the Potomac into Maryland and traveled to Antietam. By that time we were all a bit tired. Kronberg's wife had packed a delicious lunch, which included cheese, so from the back seat I remarked, "We're off to Sharpsburg with a dull wit and a sharp cheese." The South, of course, referred to Antietam as Sharpsburg, the town near which the battle was fought. On the battlefield, we visited Bloody Lane, where so many Union and Confederate troops died, and later crossed the stone bridge over Antietam Creek and climbed to the bluff overlooking the bridge, a site defended by Georgia troops.

Thinking about those battlefields that I visited with Kronberg and his wife that day reminded me of my family's involvement in war. While in graduate school at the University of South Carolina, I spent some time working on the family history at the South Carolina Archives and found original eighteenth-century documents showing that my great-great-great-grandfather Samuel Shippey was part of a mounted unit during the American Revolution. It is likely that he fought against the British at the Battle of the Cowpens since the family farm was only ten to twelve miles from the battlefield. My great-grandfather Joseph Johnston Shippey fought in both the Mexican War and the Civil War. A book that I found at the Georgia Archives revealed that he was with General Winfield Scott's army at the siege of Vera Cruz. According to an elderly cousin who remembered him, he was a sharpshooter in the Civil War and was present at Gettysburg. Near the end of the war, he was taken prisoner by Union troops after the Battle of Petersburg and was imprisoned for a time at Point Lookout, Maryland. On my mother's side of the family, my great-grandfather Isaac Bailey was a Confederate courier during the Civil War, and my mother, when she was a little girl visiting her grandmother, remembered seeing letters that he had written from the battlefield. My father served as a cook and helped load huge Long Tom artillery guns during World War II. He was with General Patton's Third Army in the Battle of the Bulge. When I was growing up, my father sometimes brought out his war photos after supper when we had company and described in some detail what every photograph depicted. I listened with great interest and now have those photos. One of my father's brothers and four of my mother's brothers were in World War II. Another younger brother joined the Marines just as the war was ending. In short, I was part of a family tradition of going off to war. But some of my male cousins who played baseball, ran track, hunted, and fished did not go to war, only the nerdy cousin, who did not often engage in those macho activities. I thought that it was ironic that I should be the one in Vietnam. A young officer in Da Nang, knowing that I planned to be a college professor, once asked me, "Shippey, do you think your students will ever believe what you did in Vietnam?" I replied that I did not know since I myself had difficulty believing that I was there involved in hazardous flight duty. At the time I was regularly flying in A-3s over Laos at night, a track that was exposed to MiG attacks and SAM launches.

Late one summer afternoon Kronberg and I were in the vicinity of the Capitol when a thunderstorm arose. The entrance to the Rotunda was closed for the day, so we took shelter on the east portico amid the huge columns while the lightning flashed and the thunder roared overhead. I had the impression of being under artillery fire and was reminded that I would soon be assigned to Vietnam, where I did, in fact, experience the roar of outgoing ordnance and incoming rockets. I wondered if the storm was perhaps an ominous portent for the nation. Certainly, Washington during those days was under siege by regular demonstrations against the war that involved hundreds of thousands of marchers.

While taking refuge from the storm with Kronberg, I recalled seeing the TV broadcast of President Kennedy's inauguration from the east portico, followed by Robert Frost's unsuccessful attempt to read the poem he had written for the occasion. The sun glare and the smallness of the typing made it impossible for the eighty-seven-year-old Frost to read the poem, so from memory he recited "The Gift Outright," perhaps a more suitable choice anyway.

Kronberg and I talked about many things, including the war. He was from Miami, and I gathered he did not strictly observe Jewish religious customs, although he was willing to discuss them with me. Later, when we deployed to Goodfellow Air Force Base in San Angelo, Texas, for radiotelephone training, he separated from the unit. In a meeting shortly after our arrival on base, an officer asked if there was anyone who objected to going to Vietnam, and Kronberg held up his hand. He was sent to Philadelphia to a mental unit in a hospital supervised by the Navy. He wrote to me, saying that, if someone in uniform objected to the war, then, according to the establishment, he was obviously insane. A psychiatrist and other officials at the hospital tried to persuade him to return to active duty, but he refused. Kronberg openly shared his thoughts with me, and I admired his independent spirit. His letters were always filled with humor, and I never knew what to expect as I opened them. He confided that the favorite TV program in the "insane" ward was *Star Trek*, knowing how much Dooly, another friend of ours, and I enjoyed this program. I never saw him again, but from time to time, even after I was in Vietnam, he would write. He chided me sometimes for being slow in corresponding and jokingly asserted when I did write that the Messiah must be coming because I had finally responded. He received an honorable discharge from the Navy, moved to San Francisco, and later entered the journalism program at Syracuse University in New York. In one of his letters he sent newspaper clippings containing some of his photos of a street musician playing the drums with a woman dancing to the beat. The photos were published in the Sunday supplement of the *San Francisco Chronicle*.

As mentioned earlier, my barracks at Fort Myer was next to Arlington National Cemetery, and I often went for walks within its precincts. The chapel for the cemetery was only a short distance from my barracks and situated just outside one of the gates. Often, I saw a horse-drawn caisson, with a flag-covered casket secured to it, depart from the chapel and enter this back gate, accompanied by an honor guard. I could hear the muffled beat of the drums and the clop, clop, clop of the horses' hooves on the pavement leading into the cemetery. Several times I walked to the Tomb of the Unknown Soldier and watched a soldier from the Old Guard march back and forth in front of the tomb. One afternoon while at the tomb, I saw a little girl, a toddler, break free from her mother's hand and crawl under the chain that separated the crowd from where the guard marched. The guard immediately halted, turned, clicked his heels, and snapped his rifle to port arms. In a loud voice he said, "It is requested that parents keep their children outside the perimeter!" The horrified mother snatched her child back across the chain. The guard said, "Thank you," shouldered his rifle, pivoted, and resumed his march. The incident reminded me that the guard has a solemn duty that allows no show of disrespect at the hallowed site, whether intentional or unintentional. In thinking about all of this many years later, I am reminded that those who have made the ultimate sacrifice for the nation, either in the military or as private citizens, deserve unmitigated respect, whether at the Tomb of the Unknowns, the Vietnam Wall, a memorial on a courthouse square, or an individual grave in a country cemetery.

Occasionally, I went across the Potomac to the Naval station at Anacostia, where I was officially assigned. I was working to advance in my rating and needed to get copies of books on radiotelephone technology, so I visited the warrant officer who was our immediate supervisor. He was a man strictly devoted to business and indulged in no small talk or polite formalities. Each time I went to his office, he sat behind his desk, and as I tried to explain why I had come, he interrupted me, saying, "The point, the point, what's the point? Come quickly to the point!" He repeatedly interrupted with this command so that it was almost impossible to get a word in edgewise to explain why I was there. But somehow, I got the books and was able to study so that I eventually obtained my PO3 rating. Because of my college education, I had entered the Navy as a Seaman, so I had an advantage in beginning to move up in rank. I hoped that I might be able to go to officers' training school but never had the opportunity. I think that the Navy at that time had more officers than it needed.

On one of my visits to Anacostia, it was late in the day, so I decided to eat supper at the station's cafeteria, knowing that the Navy's food was generally better than what the Army served at Fort Myer. I do not recall what was on the menu that evening, but I enjoyed the meal, sitting at a table by myself. After a while I noticed that at a table on the far side of the room was a man who had been with me at DLIEC. He was eating with two other men, and they were dressed in the work uniform—dungarees, blue shirt, and cap. I guessed they must have been on some kind of work detail. I spoke to the man I knew, asking him how he was doing. He responded, "Shut your trap, or I will go over there and shut it for you!" The aggressiveness of his reply surprised me since I was just trying to be friendly. Then I recalled that the brig was at Anacostia and realized that he and his companions were on a work detail connected with their detention. The anger in his response to my greeting gave me a clue as to why he was there, and he obviously did not like being reminded of his previous status. I ate the rest of my meal in silence and caught a DOD bus back to Fort Myer.

CHAPTER 4

Goodfellow Air Force Base, San Angelo, Texas

Upon completing language study at DLIEC, I went home on leave and then traveled to Goodfellow Air Force Base in San Angelo, Texas, for radio-telephone and technical training. I landed at Love Field in Dallas and then took a flight to San Angelo. Along the way this plane with two propeller engines stopped three times, and I realized why the airline had once been derided by its competitor as "Texas Tree Tops." A bus met me and other arrivals and carried us to the base. It was nighttime when I stowed my sea bag in the barracks and took a drink from the water fountain. It had a slight oily flavor, and I realized I was in Texas oil country.

The next day, I and another enlisted man went to see the Navy warrant officer who was in charge of the detachment. He gave us duties to perform. In fact, he was a bit gruff in talking to us. The other man was assigned to carry coffee mugs to the head and wash them, and if I recall correctly, I had the duty of cleaning the toilets. My companion washed the mugs all right. He told me that he swished each of them around in one of the commodes, dried them off, placed them on a tray, and then returned them to the office of the warrant officer with a smile on his face. I realized then that anyone in charge of other people needs to be careful about who prepares his food or washes his dishes. Over the years I have occasionally read on the Internet of similar actions by enlisted men towards their officers.

I do not remember much about the actual training at Goodfellow. A few men who had already served a tour in Da Nang were there to help us. I briefly had similar training when I arrived at San Miguel in the Philippines. One of the trainers who had been in Da Nang was Borawski. He entertained us with stories about lively times in the bars at the Crossroads, a community just outside the gate of the communications station at San Miguel. What I remember most is simply enjoying what San Angelo had to offer. Some of the men who were accustomed to larger cities did not like the city and the region in which it was located. They considered it too isolated and provincial. But San Angelo was about the size of Albany, Georgia, my hometown, and I found plenty to do. When one of the Air Force officers welcomed us soon after our arrival, he acknowledged that a lot of men did not care for that part of Texas, and that was fine with him because it meant that not many people would move there, and it would retain its unique character.

Sometimes when I was standing outside of the barracks, I saw a fighter jet approach the field, descend, and do a touch and go on the runway. Goodfellow was set up to give pilots of these jets from another airfield practice in Ground Control Approaches.

San Angelo was indeed a place quite different from my part of the country. There were relatively few trees, except along the course of rivers and those that had been planted in the town. I often went for walks out into the country near the base, and it was hot, dry, and dusty, even though it was autumn. One of the first things I did was to visit the local library and get a card that allowed me to check out books. A pleasant middle-aged woman was one of the librarians, and I enjoyed talking to her sometimes. Occasionally, on Saturday afternoons I stayed at the library and read for a while. Some of the books that I checked out and read during my stay in San Angelo were *The Heart Is a Lonely Hunter* by Carson McCullers, *Main Travelled Roads* by Hamlin Garland, *All the King's Men* by Robert Penn Warren, and a biography of Francis Bacon by Catherine Drinker Bowen. I also remember going downtown to the movie theater, where I saw the 1968 version of the film *Night of the Living Dead*. A cultural side note: I learned that in Texas you should never refer to a man wearing a Stetson hat and boots as a "goat-roper," unless you were ready to fight. That term had about the same effect as "redneck" in South Georgia.

Occasionally, I watched TV in the upstairs of our barracks. I was interested in the accent of the local speakers. If anything, the announcers for the ads had more of a drawl than the people back home in South Georgia. I recall one advertisement for bedspreads in which the female announcer gave the word "spread" three syllables: "Stop by and see our new 'spare-ads.'" I also occasionally went out to eat. At a restaurant one evening, I ordered a steak and tea to drink. I saw the waitress coming with what appeared to be a small punch bowl. I assumed she was carrying it to guests in the private dining room to the side of where I was sitting, but I was surprised when she placed it on my table and proceeded to pour sweet tea into it. To drink from this Texas-sized goblet, I had to use both hands. Then she brought the steak. It was nearly a foot long and two inches thick. I had never seen such a steak, and it was tender and delicious.

The food at the base cafeteria was good. I do not recall particulars other than the ubiquitous SOS and eggs cooked however the men wanted them. Dining in the cafeteria was somewhat entertaining. If someone dropped and broke a dish, everyone simultaneously groaned, "Ohhhhhh!" At the end of the meal, Air Force guys amused themselves by blowing paper straw covers at the ceiling. If one of the covers stuck to a ceiling tile, they gave a cheer. At times several of these covers were hanging from the ceiling like festive decorations. Some of the men enjoyed flicking cardboard butter patties at the ceiling, and here and there some of them stuck and hung perilously over the tables below.

Sometimes I went for a walk in a brushy area near the entrance to the base. This place was covered with scrub oak trees and tall grass. Spiders had stretched huge webs between the trees, and I recall having one of these webs break across my face as I walked. Then I wiped my face and rubbed my head vigorously to get rid of the huge spider I imagined to be crawling towards the nape of my neck with fangs extended. I was also aware of the danger of rattlesnakes, but I wanted to go for walks because back home I was accustomed to hiking along the dirt roads and in the swamps near my neighborhood. Sometimes at the edge of this wooded area I squatted and looked out over the neighboring cotton field and thought about the fields back home, remembering the times when I was a child and wandered along the rows of cotton and corn planted by my father and my Uncle L.P. I missed home and was uncertain about what the future might hold.

While stationed at Fort Myer, I had begun to do some painting in oil and watercolors. I suppose this hobby was inspired by my regular visits to the art museums in Washington and New York. The parade ground at Fort Myer, surrounded by old red brick buildings, and a nighttime view from my barracks window are two scenes that I painted. In San Angelo I continued to experiment with watercolors. I went one afternoon to a spot across the Concho River from downtown and painted the skyline, using watercolor tubes. The Hotel Cactus was prominent in the painting. I was apparently on a hotel kick and later painted the multi-storied Holiday Inn. While in the Philippines I still had my watercolors and did some painting in the barracks when it rained.

Many of the men at Goodfellow went to Acuña, Mexico, on the weekends. This was the nearest city of any size on the other side of the Rio Grande. As might be expected of military men away from their girlfriends back home, they did not go just for the sights, although they returned with souvenirs and interesting stories. I never went to Acuña, but one weekend I did travel to San Antonio with two friends, one of whom, George Carson, had a car. We toured the Alamo and its garden and then visited the Hemis-Fair Park, site of the 1968 World's Fair. While there, we went to the top of the Tower of the Americas, where we had an excellent view of the city. This was my first experience with glass elevators that moved along the exterior of a tall structure, and the ride made me somewhat nervous, perhaps not a good sign for someone soon to have flight duty in a war zone. After dinner at a restaurant, we strolled along the Paseo del Rio, a beautiful, winding walk on the banks of the San Antonio River. I remember in particular the river barges on some of which people were dining or enjoying drinks by candlelight. I thought how wonderful it must be to dine while moving along the river in such a pleasant setting, but this experience was too pricey for us. The river walk was lined with fashionable hotels and cafes with *al fresco* dining.

The next morning, we returned to San Angelo by way of Johnson City, Texas. We wanted to see the LBJ Ranch, home to former President Lyndon Johnson. We parked the car on the side of the road and walked along the fence, trying to get a glimpse of the ranch house, but all we could see were some trees in the distance that marked the course of the Pedernales River. Standing near the entrance to the ranch, I noticed a cream-colored Cadillac riding around in the pasture among the cattle. The car eventually turned onto the lane leading to the entrance. It stopped at the gate, where I was standing with my camera just a few feet away from the passenger side of the vehicle. I saw that the driver was wearing a Stetson hat, and then I realized that the man in the front passenger seat was President Johnson. He was wearing a short-sleeved plaid shirt. He put his hand to his mouth and yawned, and the car turned onto the highway towards Johnson City. I informed my friends who was in the car because I was not sure that they were close enough to tell. Then we resumed our journey back to San Angelo. I kept marveling at the changing levels of the countryside and the fact that there were no tall trees, just mesquite bushes. When I went home on leave after my duty at San Angelo, I could not take my eyes off the trees.

CHAPTER 5

En Route to Vietnam

After completing training at San Angelo, I went home on leave. Stokowski, Walinski, and I rented a car and rode all night across the Texas midlands to Dallas to catch our flights for home out of Love Field. They dropped me off in downtown Dallas because I wanted to see Dealey Plaza, where President Kennedy had been shot. I also took a taxi to the Dallas Museum of Art and toured it. I remember in particular a Henry Moore reclining sculpture near the entrance and Thomas Hart Benton's painting *Prodigal Son*. At the airport, dressed in my uniform, I was on standby status, but as luck would have it, I got a seat in first class, the only time I have ever flown in that class. While waiting for takeoff, I chatted with the man next to me. When he saw that I did not intend to drink the whiskey that the flight attendant had served in a mini bottle, he leaned over and asked if he might have it. I did not mind and gave it to him.

I cannot recall what I did at home. The various times I was on leave back in Albany all merge together now, and it is hard to sort out one visit from another. But I can recollect the sadness of saying goodbye to my parents at the Albany airport. It was sobering to realize that I was flying to a war on the other side of the world and that I might never see them again. During those final days at home, I kept thinking about all of this, but for some reason I was certain that I would return home. I had no fatalistic sense of doom. I remember lying in bed the night before I left and staring at the space just above the door to my room and thinking that I would see all of this again when I returned and resumed sleeping in my own bed.

In those days, there were no security checks at the airport. Family members could go outside to the gate to have the last hugs and kisses before the passenger walked across the tarmac to the plane. My memory of this departure probably merges with others, but I recall looking out the window of my jet as it streaked down the runway past the terminal for takeoff. I could see my parents still standing at the gate. It was raining, and the raindrops streaming across the window seemed like tears as the plane lifted off the runway and rose sharply into the sky, with me straining to continue looking at the terminal. Then the plane banked to head northward. We passed over Old Pretoria Road, and we crossed over the fields in front of our subdivision where my best friend, Skip, and I used to walk and imagine the rise and fall of empires with the cities we built out of dirt and granite rocks from the railroad that ran through the area to an industrial park. Looking down, I saw the clump of mulberry trees where we had built one of those cities and named it Forest Glen. Then the clouds intervened, and I was on my way to the Atlanta airport for my next flight.

I flew a National Airlines jet to San Francisco, and there were only a few passengers on board. The pilot came over the intercom and offered a bottle of champagne to anyone who could guess when we were abeam the Sangre de Cristo Mountains. I saw the Rockies below me covered with snow and then the Sierra Nevada. The snow looked like rich whipped cream covering a delectable dessert. In the distance I caught sight of an icy blue expanse of water just east of the mountains and realized this was probably Pyramid Lake in western Nevada. I had enjoyed studying maps for years, as I still do, so I was familiar with the geography of America. It was exciting to be crossing the continent for the first time, and I wished I could be down among those mountains traveling in a car. Then the pilot announced that, if we looked out the windows on the right, we could see Yosemite National Park as we began our descent towards San Francisco. All that I could see were dry-looking mountains spotted with clumps of dark-green forest. As we were preparing to land, we approached from the south, and I saw the southern end of the bay. The pilot came on the speaker again to thank us for flying with National Airlines and announced that, since there were so few passengers, everyone would receive a complimentary bottle of Great Western Champagne upon deplaning.

I walked into the terminal to the baggage claim area, and holding my champagne bottle in one hand and my sea bag in the other, I went outside to try to decide how to get downtown. A black limousine waited at the curb with the driver, dressed in cap, boots, and black jodhpurs, standing beside it. On impulse, I hired him to take me downtown and rode into San Francisco in style. Now I laugh at the absurdity of a Seaman taking a luxury car to get to the YMCA, where he intended to spend the night. The car would have been appropriate if I had been staying at the Mark Hopkins. I was young and naïve. I remember, though, what my Uncle DeWitt said on one occasion when I had dinner with him and his family. He was a Methodist preacher and had known what it was to live an abstemious life during his younger years of ministry. That night my Aunt Grace, who had superb taste, served shrimp cocktails on crushed ice as an appetizer. This was a dish I had never had before, so I was not quite sure how to approach it. I noticed my cousin Marvin snickering with his hand to his mouth. Seeing me hesitate, my uncle quietly remarked that it was good occasionally to enjoy the finer things served in style. He was aware that the Shippey men, recalling the Great Depression, tended to live as cheaply as possible, never laying out money for luxuries, except perhaps for a good bird dog, a bass boat, or a nice car or truck. So, although I felt a bit foolish spending far more money than necessary on my chauffeured limousine, I later justified my expenditure by remembering Uncle DeWitt's advice.

That day in San Francisco, I walked to Union Square and was amazed that there were elderly men sitting on benches discussing the philosophy of Plato and Aristotle while nearby a shirtless young black man did break dancing to the beat of bongo drums. There were street musicians with their cups on the sidewalk for donations. I took the cable car down Powell Street and at the end of the line got out and helped turn the car around on its turntable for the return trip. At noon I met John Beckett, an army guy that I had known at DLIEC. He was back in San Francisco, his hometown, on inactive duty, I supposed. He regretted that he had only his lunch hour off from his job at a bank to show me around town. This was a disappointment for him because he genuinely loved San Francisco and often bragged about the city, denigrating Washington, D.C., in comparison to it. After several months, though, he conceded that Washington did indeed have a lot to offer culturally.

Sometimes during lunch breaks at DLIEC I talked with Beckett about various subjects including wine and literature. I think that at the time I was reading George Saintsbury's book on wines and was beginning to acquire a slight knowledge of how to appreciate fine wines. I mentioned that I had enjoyed sampling certain wines from New York, but Beckett, understandably, maintained that in America the finest wines came from California. One day during the lunch break he was trying to solve a puzzle in *The Saturday Review of Literature*. The puzzle asked for the name of a French writer of maxims, and Beckett thought of La Rochefoucauld. The number of letters, though, did not match, so I suggested he might try Vauvenargues. When he wrote in the letters for the name, he realized that was the answer and was amazed that I knew this writer of whom he had never heard. I was aware of the name because in my eighteenth-century French literature class at Georgia Southern we had read a few of his maxims.

As Beckett and I walked around downtown San Francisco, he took me to an outdoor exhibit of sculptures by Benny Bufano. All I remember about the sculptures is that they were colorful, smoothly rounded stone pieces that reminded me somewhat of large babushka dolls. Then Beckett had to return to work. I also regretted that we did not have more time to talk because he knew much more about art and high culture than I did and could have given me a wonderful tour of the city that he loved.

I walked around central San Francisco and visited Haight-Ashbury, noted for its hippie counterculture. Later that afternoon I took the ferry to Sausalito. A wedding party was on board. The bride in her wedding gown and the groom in his black tuxedo drank a champagne toast, surrounded by well-wishers, plus a flock of sea gulls following the ferry, emitting cries while hovering almost motionless in the air. I looked intently at Alcatraz as we passed, remembering Burt Lancaster in *Bird Man of Alcatraz*. It was a beautiful sunny afternoon on the bay. Upon returning from Sausalito, I went to Ghirardelli Square and then Aquatic Park. That evening I ordered Eastern Oysters Rockefeller and a glass of Chablis for supper at a Fisherman's Wharf restaurant. As the fog rolled in, I walked along Grant Avenue through Chinatown and then past City Hall. By then it was late. Fog covered everything as I made my way back to the YMCA. The window in my room opened onto an airshaft. During the night I occasionally woke up and heard the distant dinging of bells and foghorns of ships in the harbor. The whole night seemed to be adrift in the fog, and these sounds were soothing and relaxing.

The next day I went to the Greyhound station to catch the bus to Travis Air Force Base. While I was stowing my sea bag in the luggage compartment, someone called my name from an open window in the bus. It was Brandon Stokowski. It was good to see him and realize that I would not have to fly alone across the Pacific. Going to the other side of the world with a friend was not so bad. At Travis we had a six-hour wait for our flight. Both of us were tense about our final day in America. We ate two greasy meals we did not need and drank too much overdone coffee.

It was twilight before our plane, a Flying Tigers jet, took off. It banked, and I caught a glimpse of the lights sprinkled around San Francisco Bay, the last sight of the U.S.A. mainland for a while. The plane turned west and continued ascending. This part of a flight always made me a bit nervous. After a while the captain came on the speaker and announced that we were flying at thirty thousand feet and would briefly overtake the twilight glow over the Aleutians near Shemya, Alaska. That is when Stokowski poked me with his elbow and told me that Gerald, our sunbathing friend at Fort Myer, had been assigned to Adak, and I suggested we should perhaps send him a bottle of suntan lotion from the Philippines. We both laughed at the irony and felt a sense of relief after all the tension of the day. A flight attendant was already taking orders for drinks.

Every seat on the plane was occupied. Across the aisle a Japanese woman rocked a baby in her arms. Her husband, an Air Force sergeant, held a rattle over the baby's tiny hands and occasionally leaned over and rubbed his nose against the child's stomach, saying, "I'll get it. I'll get all that sugar there!" The baby gurgled and sputtered happily, kicking his feet.

Up the aisle a Navy captain relaxed with a drink in his hand next to his companion, a beautiful Vietnamese woman wearing a white silk áo dài. A little girl began kicking the back of Stokowski's seat, singing "Mary Had a Little Lamb." She cheerfully emphasized each "lamb" with a kick. Stokowski rolled his eyes and said, "This I've got to put up with for 11,000 miles!"

That was one of the longest nights I have ever spent—eighteen hours en route in darkness all the way. Every few hours we were served a meal, but I finally got tired of eating and just wanted to get there. We stopped in Anchorage, Alaska, to let military dependents off. Everyone had to deplane for a while, and in the waiting room I walked around and around a stuffed Kodiak bear standing on its hind legs. That is the only time I have been in Alaska, although I would fly over it additional times in crossing the Pacific. We landed at Yokota Air Base near Tokyo, letting off some additional personnel and their dependents and taking on more. It was the middle of the night, and I strolled around the terminal, where young Japanese men in black suits were selling cameras at a counter. Upon takeoff, I admired Tokyo's lights, extending as far as I could see out the window.

We landed at Clark Air Base in the Philippines about 7:30 a.m. and deplaned according to military protocol—dependents and their sponsors first, officers next, and finally, enlisted men. The first thing I saw at the door of the plane was a tall mountain that appeared to be an extinct volcano. In 1991 another nearby "extinct" volcano, Mount Pinatubo, erupted and forced the closure of the base. Outside the terminal Stokowski and I waited for the bus that would take us to San Miguel Naval Communications Station. A large red box had a sign that stated, "All persons with explosives, please drop them in this box. No questions will be asked, no action taken." When the bus arrived, it had metal mesh over the windows, obviously placed there to protect it from thrown rocks. I began to wonder about the safety of the place where we had arrived.

The four-hour trip through the mountains to San Miguel on the coast of the West Philippine Sea was memorable since this was the first time I had traveled to another country. The narrow road was rough and marked with potholes, curving frequently, uphill and downhill, with occasional steep drop-offs on one side and mountain slopes on the other. The traffic was heavy with buses, jeepneys, and military vehicles. At one point we were behind a flat-bed truck loaded with huge artillery shells, bound, I supposed, for Subic Bay. We passed by nipa huts with people working nearby in the rice paddies. Water buffaloes (carabaos) were pulling plows in the fields, and at one place a boy was splashing water over a water buffalo standing in a water-filled-ditch. Naked children were bathing in tubs in their yards, and men were taking a leak with their backs turned to the road. In one village we had to stop for a funeral procession. A small wooden coffin painted silver was borne on the shoulders of pallbearers; acolytes dressed in their surplices, one carrying a crucifix, preceded the coffin; and behind came a train of mourners dressed in somber clothes, in turn followed by teen-age boys in jeans, shoving one another, joking, and laughing, out for a lark. We passed along narrow streets lined by shops for woodworking, guitar making, ceramics, wrought iron work, shoe repairs, and sewing. The smell of burning trash came through the windows sometimes, and occasionally, there were hogs feeding on garbage. Walls surrounding houses in the barrios were topped with shards of broken class. Graffiti on the walls of some buildings said, "Yankee, go home!" I knew, of course, that these words referred to all Americans, but as a southerner, I could not help smiling, realizing that some of my ancestors would have agreed. Behind one nipa hut on the hillside was a huge billboard with a picture of Santa Claus drinking a Coca-Cola. Beneath the picture were the words, "Things go better with Coke!" I appreciated the situational irony. In the distance were misty-blue mountains spotted with the shadows of clouds. By the time we reached the gate at San Miguel, I was exhausted from jet lag and culture shock.

CHAPTER 6

San Miguel, Philippines

The Naval Communications Station at San Miguel, in Zambales Province about twenty miles north of Subic Bay, was in some ways like a tropical resort. The base included nice housing for military personnel and their dependents. These homes were surrounded by yards with hibiscus flowers, rubber plants, and palm trees. The base included a beach on the West Philippine Sea, as well as an exchange, a movie theater, library, and chapel. Beautiful mountains surrounded the station, and on one of them a waterfall was visible against the foliage after a rain. About two miles off the beach there were three small islands, called the Capones, surrounded by clear aquamarine water and coral reefs. The largest of these islands had a beach ideal for swimming and snorkeling over the reefs. In greeting us, the commanding officer reminded us that the station seemed like a paradise to the people living in the nearby villages and said that we should appreciate our advantages and show respect to the local people. We should also remember that sometimes intruders crossed the perimeter fence and stole things. The most dramatic example of this occurred on a sunny afternoon when thieves stole one of the station's fire trucks. The thieves were clever. They drove at high speed towards the gate with the sirens blaring and the red lights flashing. The Marine guards waved them through, thinking there was a fire in the nearby brush. About three weeks before we arrived at San Miguel, there had been an earthquake, which left a crack in the floor of the base library. I was a bit nervous that another quake might shake the base, but this never happened during my stay.

A detachment of Marines with guard dogs provided security for the station, and on the first morning after our arrival, Stokowski and I were assigned to unload sacks of dog food off a truck at the kennels. That was hot work, so occasionally, we took a break. At one point we lay down on our backs on the grass and watched the clouds sail across a blue sky. Most of the time, though, the duty at San Miguel was not difficult. For the first few days after our arrival, we were placed in X Division with frequent guard duty. One night I was assigned to guard the armory, a small structure a short

distance in front of our barracks. I had a walkie-talkie to report any incidents to the OOD. Rather than standing in front of the armory, I hid under
a large bush not far from it. There I had a good view of the surrounding
area. I sat under that bush most of the night and watched the stars unreel
over Mount Maubanban. Shortly before daybreak, it became a bit cool, and
I heard a rooster crow from the neighboring village. On another night, I
was assigned the first watch at the fire station, and I sat at a desk in the
office with my feet propped up, reading a book and watching geckos crawl
on the wall.

Before going out to the kennels on that first morning, I was surprised
to wake up with a bunch of Filipino men surrounding my bunk loudly
talking and gesturing, each one trying to persuade me to let him be my
houseboy. I had never had a servant and did not like the idea of having
one, but some of the other sailors said that, in not choosing one of them,
I would be depriving the local people of some needed income. Moreover,
they would continue to plead with me, hounding my steps, until I selected
one of them. Some of the supplicants were thin, middle-aged men, and I
suspected they might be a little too clever for my pleasure. I noticed a teen-
age boy who appeared to be about fifteen or sixteen, and I asked him to
be my houseboy. Angelo was quiet and unobtrusive, and he never disappointed me. I placed my dirty clothes in two duffel bags hanging from the
post of my bunk, and they disappeared for a day or two and then magically
reappeared, neatly folded and smelling as if they had been dried in the open
air and sunshine. I forget how much I paid Angelo, but he never seemed
displeased. Older houseboys sometimes importuned their employers for
cigarettes from their ration cards, but Angelo never did this. I was grateful
for his quiet, efficient service.

At San Miguel I consented to go to Da Nang for flight duty. When
the division warrant officer and chief welcomed Stokowski and me, they
were surprised that several of the Vietnamese linguists who were with us
at Goodfellow Air Force base had been assigned to Fort Meade. They were
desperate for linguists to go to Da Nang because several members of the
det were finishing their tour. They inquired about the linguists in Texas,
and before Stokowski could finish explaining, placed a call to ensure that
the next class was not assigned to Fort Meade. I wrote as follows to my
friend Jackson, a DLIEC classmate and one of those who went to Fort
Meade: "Guess what I am most likely going to be doing? Well, think of
what I most did not want to do, what I vowed that I would not volunteer
for, and did not volunteer for, and you have it. They are so short of people
that they sort of 'herded' me along." Even though I was afraid of flying in
reconnaissance aircraft in a combat zone, I did it anyway. I did not think of
myself as a courageous person, but in looking back at my decision in later

years, I understood that courage sometimes involves doing what you most fear.

The main duty of CTIs at San Miguel was linguistic training for duty either in Da Nang or aboard one of the ships in the Gulf of Tonkin. We attended classes at the Receivers Building next to the beach about a mile north of the main part of the base. Bobby, who had served as a linguist in Da Nang and maybe aboard a ship in the Gulf of Tonkin, was our instructor, and he played tapes of activities by the North Vietnamese Air Force. There were only a few of us in the class, and Bobby worked patiently with us. Overall, he was somewhat laid back and a time or two ordered lum pia for us from the Crossroads, the community near the gate. We used old headphones, black with round earpieces, and listened to various kinds of activities, including attempted shoot-downs of American aircraft, practice GCIs (Ground Controlled Intercepts), and routine formation flying. Sometimes it was hard to discern what was being said because there was so much static on the recording, and Bobby let us know that, when we assumed our duties, we should expect radio transmissions often to be difficult to hear because of the static. We learned to recognize code words for altitude, headings, afterburners, and targets acquired. He told us that, in monitoring a real activity, we would be expected to keep a running transcript of what was being said so that the evaluating officer aboard the plane or the ship could know what was happening and when bandit warnings needed to be issued. Understanding what was being said on the tapes was frequently difficult, and I wondered if I would measure up to what was expected of a TacAir linguist.

On Christmas Day 1970 I went to the Capones Islands with two friends. We hired a local man with a banca boat, a motorized canoe with one outrigger, and had a thrilling trip out to the islands. The sea was unbelievably blue, a rich royal blue with small crests of foam breaking on the waves. Near the shore of the main island the water was emerald green and crystal clear. We beached the banca boat and then went into the water of a cove bound by rocky ledges with stratified layers of rock slanting upwards out of the sand. Coral reefs extended a great distance into the water, and I could wade out a long way on them until they suddenly dropped off into deep water. My friends had a snorkel mask and fins and let me borrow them. The water was wonderfully clear with rainbow colors playing back and forth over the coral and the sandy bottom. There were all kinds of tropical fish, some phosphorescent blue or gold with black stripes. We had a broom handle, and we took turns giving each other a tour of the coral reefs. To do this, two of us grabbed each end of the broomstick, while the third man simply held on, wearing the mask and enjoying looking down into the water. While we swam and snorkeled, our banca boat driver sat on the

Herb Shippey on one of the Capones Islands about two miles from the beach of the San Miguel Naval Communications Station on the west coast of Luzon Island in the Philippines. I went out to the Capones with friends two or three times. I believe this photograph was taken on Christmas Day, 1970.

beach with other drivers who had brought groups out for the day. They smoked cigarettes and ate coconuts, hacking them open with a machete.

We climbed to the upper part of the island, not the main peak, which was too steep, but a level area, or plateau, which was about a hundred feet above the sea. On the landward side rocky ledges, covered with tall grass, sloped down toward the water. Walking here was treacherous since large rocks were hidden in the grass. There was an unoccupied lighthouse and cabin in the center of the plateau. It was pleasant to stand on one of the promontories and look across the sparkling water of the cove and the open sea beyond. From my perch I could see footprints along the beach, where the banca boatmen laughed and smoked, and beyond them the communications station, small and insignificant in the immense panorama of coastline, palm groves, and mountains. The view from where I was standing was one of the most spectacular and beautiful that I have ever seen.

On our return trip the waves were high and being in the canoe was like riding a bucking horse. We rose high on the crest of each swell and then dropped down into the trough between waves. The outrigger rose into the air after a high wave and then crashed down into the water with a spray of foam that wet us all. Occasionally, a flying fish leaped out of a wave and sailed several feet before plopping back into the water. As we approached the beach, the driver tried to run straight in, timing the incoming waves so that he could place the prow of the boat safely on the sand without a sudden jolt. But just as we were about to land, a big wave came and lifted the back end of the boat high into the air, causing the prow to dig into the sand and shudder. We were swamped with water and had to hold on tight to avoid being thrown out. In spite of our rough landing, it was an adventuresome and pleasant day, certainly a different way to spend Christmas.

The dining hall at San Miguel served excellent food, and according to a menu I saved, Christmas dinner on the day my friends and I went to the Capones Islands featured Tom turkey, Virginia baked ham, prime rib of beef, cornbread dressing, snowflake potatoes, buttered green peas, whole kernel corn, Parkerhouse rolls, tossed salad, Waldorf salad, pumpkin pie, pecan pie, chocolate cake, and fresh fruit. Many times at evening meals we could fix an ice cream sundae for dessert with a multitude of toppings at a side table. For breakfast the cooks scrambled or fried eggs the way the men wanted them. In addition to baked beans, American fried potatoes, SOS, bacon, sausage, toast, and pancakes, there was always fruit that included pineapple, mangoes, and papaya. In fact, everywhere I was stationed, the Navy had good food, even when we were in the air flying on missions off the coast of North Vietnam.

One afternoon I walked by myself along the beach most of the distance between the main part of the base and Receivers, the heart of the communications station, which was about a mile north. At one point I waded into the water and splashed around for a while. Then I noticed a Filipino man standing on the dune above the beach observing me. He was wearing a broad straw hat and held a machete in one hand. Apparently, he had been cutting some of the tall grass that bordered the beach. I got out of the water, and he kept staring at me in a way that did not seem friendly. I then recalled what I had heard about Huks, communist guerrillas who operated in Central Luzon. There were stories about American servicemen who were captured and held hostage by the Huks. Also, there was an account about piano wire strung across a road where motorcyclists traveled. I did not know whether this man was a Huk or not, but I realized it was unwise to walk away from the base by myself since not all Filipinos were pleased with the American presence in their country.

I did not go down to the Crossroads near the base to join in the drinking and carousing to check out what Borawski had told us in San Angelo, but occasionally, I took a Victory Liner bus to Olongapo, which had a reputation as sin city of the Orient. A similar label, however, might be attached to any city adjacent to a large American military base overseas. A Victory Liner bus or van came every fifteen or twenty minutes. Moreover, it was possible to catch a Victory Liner bus most anywhere and to travel all over Luzon Island, if one did not mind the frequent stops and occasional flat tire. In the villages along the route to Olongapo, people with live chickens and produce boarded the bus. At some stops local people ran to the bus to try to sell papaya, guavas, strawberries, and vegetables. Passengers on the bus handed money for their purchases through the open windows. The strawberries looked lush and delicious, but I did not dare buy any of them because of rumors that the local gardeners used human feces as fertilizer. Some of the bigger buses had a conductor who took up the fare after the bus was underway. On one of my trips a middle-aged man wearing a suit coat sat down beside me, and I noticed that he had long, yellow fingernails that were curled and twisted. His nails must have been two inches in length. I wondered if he let his nails grow to show that he was upper class and did not do any manual labor.

One afternoon Bobby, two other guys, and I took a Victory Liner bus to Olongapo. As we walked along the sidewalk after our arrival, jeepney drivers kept pulling up beside us and hollering, "Hey, Joe! Change your dollars to pesos?" We smiled, shook our heads and kept moving. The street that ran from the gate to the Subic Bay naval base wound through the city like a snake and was lined with almost door-to-door bars. As we walked, bar maids came onto the sidewalk and tried to entice us into the bars where they worked. Some draped their arms around sailors as they walked by, attempting to lure them into their establishment. Bobby led us into one of the bars, and we sat down at a table. Since it was mid-afternoon, the bar was empty, except for us. Promptly, one of the bar maids sat in my lap and wrapped her arms around my shoulders. I did not like this kind of attention but did not want to be rude. Bobby, seeing my discomfort and also knowing my moral convictions, spoke sharply to her: "Get off his lap, bitch!" She got up and sat in a chair at the table, and we all then had a reasonably pleasant conversation after San Miguel beers had been ordered. Bobby insisted that the beers be opened at the table. After a few minutes he led us to one of his favorite restaurants that served good lumpia, the Philippine version of Chinese spring rolls. While we ate, we sat by a plate glass window with a good view of the busy street. Looking at this street, I was reminded of Vanity Fair in John Bunyan's *The Pilgrim's Progress*.

On another occasion David Mullis and I, along with another friend, went to Olongapo on a Victory Liner bus. David was a friend who had good morals and was pleasant to be with on an outing. He might have been one of the guys who went with me out to the Capones Islands on Christmas Day that year. We went our separate ways in Olongapo but agreed to meet again at the bus station, a large dirt parking area. I think I probably walked to the base at Subic that day. To do this, I had to cross a bridge over a river filled with all kinds of trash, dead animals, and sewage. Sailors gave this river an appropriate name. Sometimes I went to the library or the exchange at Subic. The USS *Enterprise* was in port, and I saw its misty-blue profile at the entrance to the harbor. Late that afternoon I returned to the place where the buses pulled up and boarded the bus that would go to the Crossroads. I did not see David or our other friend on the bus or anywhere nearby. The driver started the engine, preparing to pull out, and from the back seat I yelled, "Teka moni!" in a bungled attempt to say "Wait" in Tagalog. The middle-aged woman across the aisle laughed at my mangled Tagalog and then asked me where I was from. Her son, about nine or ten years old, was sitting beside her. We had a pleasant conversation as the bus traveled north towards the base. She was a kind, courteous woman, very different from the Olongapo bar maids. We talked until it was time for me to get off the bus at the Crossroads near San Miguel.

On the base, as well as other places that I visited in the Philippines, I met Filipino women who were, like this woman, decent and respectable. One who worked in administration at San Miguel always greeted me humorously whenever I went to send a money order home or to inquire about my records. She would say, "Oh no. Not you again, Shippey. What is it this time?" This was a standing joke between us because I did not pester her or the other administrative people with questions and was always polite to them. In February of 1972, I went to Baguio for three days of liberty at the John Hay R and R Base. Three Navy officers from San Miguel reserved a van for the trip, and since they had space for one more person, I was allowed to travel with them. While I was strolling in the park near the cathedral, a well-dressed middle-aged woman asked me where I was from. When I mentioned that I was stationed at San Miguel, she said, "Zambales! I too am from Zambales," readily accepting me as if I were a Filipino and that were also my home province. After talking with me briefly, she continued walking with her friends around the park. There was openness and lack of guile in these kinds of greetings, and I found that refreshing and felt at home in the Philippines.

For over a month after my arrival at San Miguel, I had a bad cough. In training sessions at Receivers, when I and other guys were practicing listening to and translating tapes of the North Vietnamese Air Force, I sometimes had coughing spasms, and Bobby, looking concerned, would ask me if I was all right. On New Year's morning 1971, I went to sick bay, and the PO1 hospital corpsman who examined me chewed me out for having the audacity to get sick on what should have been his day off. I wanted to say that I would not be there if I could help it, but I kept quiet and let him be grumpy while he examined me. In looking back, I think I probably had bronchitis.

Time passed quickly after New Year's, and I continued my training at Receivers, wondering if I would understand Vietnamese well enough to do my job properly when I arrived at Da Nang. Occasionally, I had all-night duty at Receivers, and then at dawn I and the other men on duty walked out to catch a jeepney back to the main part of the base. For ten cents we could go anywhere on the station. We all crowded onto the jeepney, some with their feet hanging off the back; someone yelled "Sige na" ("Go ahead") to the driver; and we were underway to breakfast at the cafeteria. Along the way we looked out over the tall grass towards the waves breaking on the beach. Beyond that was the open water of the West Philippine Sea and then the South China Sea with Vietnam on the other side.

CHAPTER 7

Arrival in Da Nang

Near the end of January 1971, Stokowski and I finally received orders for Da Nang. Officially, we were going on TAD assignment, but in actuality, Da Nang was our primary duty station. We traveled by Navy bus to Clark Airbase, where we spent part of the night. After midnight we went to the airfield and boarded a C-141 StarLifter. The jet made strange noises during the flight across the South China Sea to Da Nang. Pipes, wires, and straps crisscrossed the fuselage interior in a Gordian knot of intricacy. The seats in which Stokowski and I sat were facing the rear of the aircraft. "Just like the military," I thought, "bass-ackward." I had out my paperback copy of Tolstoy's *Anna Karenina* but was too worked up to read it. To this day, I am ashamed to admit, I have still not read the novel. An Air Force sergeant came back, swinging from seat to seat, and told us to fasten our seatbelts; we were beginning the descent into Da Nang.

It was still dark when we stepped off the plane, and I was surprised by the cool temperature. I had thought Vietnam would be warm, but it was cooler than South Georgia on a fall morning. Then I realized the air just seemed cooler because I had become acclimatized to the Philippines. I wished we were back in the P.I. lounging on the beach at San Miguel. I picked up my seabag to go through processing and wondered if I would have a hernia by the time I got out of the Navy.

The duty driver for the detachment picked us up and drove us through the pre-dawn darkness along a road cluttered on both sides with coils of concertina wire, stacks of oil drums, CONEX units in rows, rusted pieces of vehicles, and shacks with low tin roofs. "Welcome to beautiful Da Nang," he said and offered his hand. "I'm Chuck Ferrell, and that's the detachment compound ahead on the right. Home, sweet home!"

On our left a long hill brooded over the base. Lights led up the side, spot-lighting a red clay road. A star shell floated over the summit. Low clouds lay in dark, heavy slabs across the sky. "Is that Monkey Mountain?" I asked. "No, that's Freedom Hill," Chuck replied and swung the truck through the gate into the compound. The guard waved us through, and we passed down a line of dark two-story wooden barracks interspersed with sand-bagged bunkers. Even in the uncertain light I could see grass and fern leaves growing from the sides of the bags, some of which were split open. Chuck stopped the truck and pointed down the line of barracks. "The barracks ahead on the right is the Det home. Just carry your stuff upstairs. There's a mess up there with a bar and a pool table. Your quarters are in the room behind the mess. I've got to make another run. I'll be back in a few minutes, and we'll go to breakfast and after that down to the workspaces." Brandon and I went up the stairs and walked through the empty mess to our room. There were four bunk beds. I chose one on top and put my things into a locker. This would be our temporary quarters until we were assigned rooms downstairs. Through the screen windows lining the top of the room, I could hear the roar of F-4 jets taking off, and in the quiet intervals the chopping of helicopters moving across the countryside behind the base. That night I went to bed on the top rack, but about 2:00 a.m. the light clicked on, and I woke up to see Steve White in his camos at one of the other bunks getting ready for bed. He was one of the SAM (Surface-to-Air Missile) "I" beats with whom I often flew. I later learned that he was also from Georgia.

The Barracks

Our barracks at Da Nang was an unpainted wooden structure. From a little distance, it resembled an old Georgia poultry house with two floors. Most of the enlisted men's quarters were downstairs. Upstairs in the front was the mess, a large room that doubled as a bar and game area with a poker table and pool table. There was also a TV mounted on a shelf where the men could watch AFVN (American Forces Vietnam Network). In the back were quarters for the NCOs. The officers were in a different barracks.

There were no glass windows in frames that could be closed. Instead a screened-in window ran down the length of the two sides downstairs and most of the length upstairs. An overhang prevented most of the rain from coming in but did not keep out the fine mist and moisture of the rainy season. In the room to which I was finally assigned, paperbacks lined the ledge next to the window. Previous occupants had left them, and some of them had swollen and mildewed pages from water damage, but they were a nice legacy anyway. I read several of the books and even brought a few of them home. I particularly recall reading *Act One*, the autobiography of the playwright Moss Hart, *Anti-Memoirs* by Andre Malraux, *The American Challenge* by J.J. Servan-Schreiber, and selections

The Big Look Spooks barracks, Da Nang. Men of the detachment often gathered on the steps and upstairs landing to talk. On the second floor there was a mess where drinks and snacks could be purchased (photograph by Tim Yerdon).

from a collection of East Asian literature that included poetry by Mao Zedong.

I had more than one roommate, although only one at the time. Sometimes my roommate and I stacked the bunk beds to have more space. Occasionally, we placed both bunks on the floor. I had a mosquito net but did not always use it. I hung my trousers at the end of the bed so that, if a rocket attack occurred, I could grab them as I ran by on my way to the bunker. There was also a table with a lamp on it, where we listened to radio and music tapes and wrote letters home. On the floor there was a reefer, a small refrigerator, where we kept cokes and orange juice. A cardboard box near the door served as a trash basket. One of the det dogs, Spook ("Spooky" as I called her) slept in it after she and I became friends. She looked like a red fox curled up in the box. Beggar, her grown puppy, was another Det mascot. She was black with rust-colored markings. These dogs often ran with us to the bunker during a rocket attack.

The Spook Mess, the bar upstairs, was a popular hangout in the evenings. One of the PO1s, Bayne, whom we called Sarge, served as a quarter master and kept it well supplied with whiskey, beer, cokes, juice, and a variety of snacks, such as peanuts, potato chips, pork skins, Hungarian goulash, beanie-weenies, and Vienna sausages. Johnny Walker, Jim Beam, Jack Daniels, and Mateus Rosé were available on a shelf back of the bar. Each whiskey bottle was capped with a chrome-plated shot pourer. San Miguel, the favorite det beer, was kept in a refrigerator. There was also a ship's bell hanging near the doorway. If anyone walked in and forgot to remove his cap, someone rang the bell, there was a shout of universal joy, and the victim had to buy drinks for everyone in the room. It was nice to sit on a stool at the bar in the late evening after a flight and eat a can of goulash heated on the hotplate.

The bar was on one side of the entrance to the mess area, and a bulletin board was on the other. Here is where one of the CTA's posted the flight bill each evening for the planes going up next day. The list included those with duty on the EA-3Bs and either the EP-3B or the EC-121. The one with duty driver for the day was also posted. The men gathered eagerly around this list when they came in to see which flights, if any, they had the following day. Some glanced at the sheet and let out obscenities; others accepted the assignments with quiet resignation. Occasionally, one announced, "Damn right! I'm on the A-3 tomorrow!" The TacAir CTI position on the A-3 was in the canopy, right back of the pilot, and offered a spectacular view. Much of the time, the CTIs had two or three days of flight duty followed by one day on the ground as duty driver or duty in the work building, translating the many tapes that accumulated from each flight.

On the wall just beyond the flight bill, there was the *Playboy* pinup for the month, dutifully updated by someone in the det. A water cooler dispenser was against the wall opposite the bar. Sometimes when I went to get a drink from this cooler, the water in the bottle was yellowish with particles swirling about in it. I would exclaim, "Can't go that route," and order a coke or orange juice from the bar instead. Eventually, I grew tired of sweet drinks and wanted something that would satisfy thirst. As a result, I bought some Coors beer from the exchange near Freedom Hill and stored the cans in a cardboard lid under my bunk, and I kept one or two cold ones in the reefer. I did not regard myself as a beer drinker, but the beer satisfied my thirst on hot days when the water in the dispenser in the Spook mess appeared unsafe to drink.

Often men not on duty preferred to sit outside on the second-floor porch or the steps leading up to it. Here is where we talked about returning home to the world, as we called it. Some of the men smoked, and I could see the points of lighted cigarettes swinging up and down in the night. There

The cantonment where the Spooks and VQ-1 barracks were located with a row of heads to the left. Unidentified men in the photograph with one guy on the ground taking a photograph. Da Nang, 1971–1972 (photograph by Tim Yerdon).

was also the murmur and occasional laughter of other men sitting outside at their barracks up and down the line. I recall Barney one evening joking about a woman he had once dated: "She was so ugly she looked like her face had chased a fart through a keg of nails, and a long keg at that." He drew a thoughtful drag on his cigarette. Someone chuckled and said, "Barney, you sure come up with some good ones." Some of the men shared dear John letters they had received, and everyone either remained silent in commiseration for a while or laughed outright if the sentiments expressed in the letter were unusually naïve: "I just know that the two of you [the present boyfriend and the former one] are going to be great friends when you get back home." That dear John letter went into the detachment quote book. Dillon, one of the PO1s, would greet each new arrival with some statement such as this: "Well, if it isn't Piotrowski of the world's most powerful nuclear Navy!" And someone else would ask, "Piotrowski, did you kill a commie for Christ today?" Irony and humorous sarcasm were the rule. Except for a few diehards, there was a general dislike of the war itself and much talk about why we had decided to join the Navy. One man might say, "I joined to keep from having to go to Nam," and everybody would laugh. At regular intervals the talk was drowned out by the roar of an F-4 taking off on the nearby runway. The bombing continued day and night, making Da Nang at times the busiest airfield in the world.

The Firing Range

On our second day in Da Nang, I and Rudy Cole, a friend from San Miguel, were scheduled to stand the night watch at a bunker behind the detachment work building. When LCDR Kent Pelot,* the commanding officer, asked about our experience with the M16, I explained that in recruit training at Orlando I had instruction on the M16 but had not actually fired the weapon. Since the training center was within the Orlando city limits, it was against the law to fire weapons, even for the military. All we did was aim the M16 at a target and then click the trigger with no ammo in the chamber, an exercise that seemed rather useless to me. When he learned that I had never fired the M16, Mr. Pelot gave an order to LTJG Nat Benchley: "Organize a range party. I won't have men standing the bunker watch who have not fired the M16." Several of us climbed into the back of the detachment truck, and we traveled west of the base to the firing range back of Freedom Hill. I realized while we were riding to the range that we were beginning to get some distance out into the countryside. When the truck stopped, we were on elevated ground on the south side of Freedom Hill. The base and the shantytown bordering it could barely be seen. We climbed out with M16s in hand. Mr. Benchley was wearing a holster with a Colt 45 as a sidearm. I looked to the south and saw rice paddies and fields stretching away to the jagged mountains in the distance. Bushes and low trees lined the elevated space where the range was located. I glanced around apprehensively, imagining a volley of shots suddenly coming from the bushes, and asked Mr. Benchley, "Are we in dangerous territory here?" He replied that it was indeed potentially dangerous. Then I asked if he were perhaps kin to an author with the same last name, and he said that he was related. That piece of information gave me a little bit of comfort by reconnecting me for

---

*Later in his Navy career Kent B. Pelot attained the rank of captain and served in the Naval Space Technology Program.

a moment with the world of literature.* Then I took my place on the firing line.

For over an hour we shot the M16s at metal drums about a hundred-fifty feet away. First, I tried shooting single shots and rarely hit the oil drum that was my target. Then I put the rifle on automatic fire and discovered that I could easily hit the target by firing a burp in its general direction. That realization was both comforting and scary. I could hit a sapper with that setting; likewise, he could easily take me out with automatic fire.

When the practice ended, and we returned to the truck, I realized I could hear hardly anything with my left ear. Too late, I learned that I should have worn earplugs. I mentioned this to Chief Holt when we arrived back at the workplace, and he said that, whenever he went to the range, he cut off the filters of two cigarettes and stuck them in his ears as plugs. I wished someone had suggested this to me. That night in my upper bunk I sat up and held my watch to my left ear. I could not hear it ticking. When I held it to my right ear, I could clearly hear the ticking. My hearing in the left ear gradually returned, but it was never quite the same. From that time on, I had trouble with that ear. Whenever I had a cold, it filled with fluid first and remained full long after the fluid in the other ear had drained. When I was in my late fifties, the hearing began gradually to diminish in that ear, and today, now that I am in my seventies, I wear hearing aids in both ears, even though I have never been in the habit of listening to loud music and do not like loud sounds of any kind. I wince whenever I see men using jackhammers on the street or blowing off sidewalks with a leaf blower and notice that they are not wearing earplugs. I want to run up to them and tell them that they need to protect their hearing.

While in Da Nang, I went to the firing range at least two more times. On one of these later trips, I tried firing the Colt 45 and discovered that it had a kick that made it difficult for me to hold it steady while firing. I had trouble hitting the target. I sometimes joked with friends in the det that with a Colt 45 I could not hit the wall of a barn, even if I were standing inside it. As a result of going to the firing range, however, I felt more comfortable carrying the M16 when I stood watch at the bunker outside our

---

*When I wrote to Nat Benchley to ask for permission to use his name in the memoir, he informed me that both his father (Nathaniel Benchley, 1915–1981) and his grandfather (Robert Benchley, 1889–1945) were authors. Robert Benchley, a humorist writer, was a founding member of the Algonquin Round Table in New York, and he is the one of whom I was aware through my American literature classes. Nat's father, Nathaniel Benchley, was a freelance writer and painter who wrote a biography of Humphrey Bogart, several novels, movie scripts, and a number of books for children. His novel *The Off-Islanders* was made into the movie *The Russians Are Coming! The Russians Are Coming!* Peter Benchley, the author of *Jaws*, is Nat Benchley's brother, and Nat himself is both a writer and actor.

Det Bravo Spooks at the firing range behind Freedom Hill, Da Nang, March 1971. This was the second time I went to the firing range. The first time was on the second day after my arrival at Da Nang in January 1971. LCDR Kent Pelot, our commanding officer at the time, ordered a range party when he learned that some men scheduled to stand watch had never fired the M-16. I cannot with certainty identify the men who were with me at the range that day (photograph by the author).

work building. I placed a clip in the rifle but rarely jammed it in, thinking I was more likely to shoot myself accidentally if I chambered a round than I was to have a need to fire at a sapper. Whenever I was duty driver, I wore a Colt 45 in a holster on my right thigh, but fortunately, never had to fire the weapon, except at the firing range. I wondered what friends and family back home would think of me, walking around with a pistol strapped to my leg—Herbert, the meek and mild young man with a loaded weapon.

CHAPTER 8

Standing Night Watch

Sometimes I had the midnight to dawn watch at Fire Point Thirteen, a sandbagged bunker back of our work building. The bunker was beside a wide drainage ditch filled with grass. The ditch made an L-shaped turn where the bunker was located, and a mixture of water and oil trickled along the bottom. I also suspected that agent orange might have been in that toxic mixture. Inside the bunker there was a field phone that I could use to call the OOD. The phone had a ring that sounded like the trilling of a loud cricket, and a small orange light on top glowed when it rang. After relieving whoever had stood the watch from seven o'clock until midnight, I called the OOD to let him know that I was on duty and Fire Point Thirteen was secure.

I paced back and forth in front of the bunker and occasionally circled it. Whenever I moved around the bunker, I held the M16 with the butt ready to strike. I had fears of a sapper with piano wire ready to loop it around my neck. There was a stand on top of the bunker with a 360-degree view of the surroundings, but I rarely climbed up there since I felt too exposed. Sometimes I stood still in the shadow of the paint shop located in front of the bunker. From there I could hide but still see the entire open area. I carried the M16 on my shoulder with the clip in, but I did not usually chamber a round.

Eight other guard perimeters lay between Fire Point Thirteen and the outer fence of the base. I knew that if a sapper survived this far, he would be desperate to reach the airplanes parked in their revetments and would not hesitate to kill me. I had heard stories of how in previous years sappers had managed to run onto the field, flinging their satchel charges. Sometimes our jets bombed enemy positions at the end of the runway. The noise level at the bunker was extremely high with F-4s constantly landing and taking off and C-130s and C-141s taxiing nearby. I could see the tails of the large aircraft above the revetments behind me as they moved into position for takeoff. The sand in the bags on the wall of the bunker made a hissing sound from the almost constant roar. I sometimes joked to myself that a unit of sappers could come marching along the ditch with a brass band, and I would never hear them until it was too late.

Occasionally, I was startled by a loud whoosh and thought a rocket was coming in, but then I realized it was only a star shell being fired by a neighboring watch. The whoosh was followed by a pop, and then the entire area was illuminated with a dim orange light as the flare floated down on a small parachute, leaving a zigzag trail of smoke. In the light of the flare, I could see stacks of oil drums and the concrete plant on the other side of the ditch.

A few times during the night the mobile security watch would swing through the area in a jeep, and then I would step into the light so they could see I was on duty. They waved in acknowledgment and swung back onto the street toward the hangars and the revetments. Sometimes I heard a stirring in the grass, but usually it was just the wind. There were also wharf rats moving around, and one night I glimpsed one as it gracefully leaped over the trickle of water in the bottom of the ditch. On another night, the guy on watch before me had killed a huge rat and hung it by a string from the concertina wire lining the ditch. All night the rat turned back and forth in the wind. Commander Lewis came out one time and told me that anything moving in the ditch was fair game. In other words, I had permission to shoot first and ask questions later.

My second night in Da Nang I stood the midnight to dawn watch at Fire Point Thirteen. That was a night I will never forget since it was the first time I came under indirect enemy fire. I went to midrats (midnight rations) in the dining hall and then walked to the bunker and relieved Rudy Cole, who had the sunset to midnight watch. I believe that was also his first bunker watch, and he reported nothing unusual had occurred. I walked back and forth in front of the bunker and cautiously circled it every few minutes. The night seemed long, and around 3:30 it turned cold. I had on my olive greens without a jacket. I noticed a flak jacket lying in the sand outside the bunker. I felt a bit foolish putting it on but reasoned it would help keep me warm. I had just finished fastening the last snap on the jacket when the first rocket hit about a block away. I dove for the bunker and lay there on the floor trembling while other rockets exploded in the distance. One of them hit a fuel dump, resulting in a huge secondary explosion that lit up the sky. I expected a rocket to make a direct hit on the bunker any second. Then I recalled it was my duty to report to the OOD that Da Nang was under attack, as if he did not already know. The field phone was outside, but I did not want to leave the bunker. I grabbed the cord to the phone and pulled it toward me. I wound the handle until the orange light glowed to report that Fire Point Thirteen was calling to let him know that Da Nang was under attack, but no one responded. I can still remember the dank, musty smell of the bunker and the sound of mosquitoes buzzing around my ears while I lay there still afraid to go outside after the explosions had stopped. Suddenly, the phone lit up, and the OOD apologized for not answering my call. He said he and the men with him had been in their bunker.

Outside I heard footsteps. Several men from inside the work building came rushing out with M16 in their hands to see if I was all right. I achieved some notoriety as a result of that night. Back at the barracks the detters wondered who was standing the bunker watch, and someone said it was the "nicky new guy," Shippey. Several men joked with me about the experience and slapped me on the back. That was the first time in several months that the Viet Cong had hit the base since, throughout the fall, Da Nang had been in the rainy season when rocket attacks seldom occurred. None of our Spooks were injured, but down the flight line a few steps from the work building, a rocket hit next to a hangar. It was apparently a dud since it did not make a big hole, but shrapnel pierced the aluminum siding, and I heard that a VQ-1 chief was injured while sitting on the john. I always wondered how he explained receiving his Purple Heart. Every time I passed that hangar at night I winced because the light from inside shone through many holes peppering the wall.

Those night watches seemed eternal. To pass the time, I sometimes thought about food, remembering the special dishes that each of my aunts brought to the Shippey family reunion. The M16 rifle chaffed my shoulder, and I sometimes carried it at port arms and recalled that my Aunt Elizabeth made the best biscuits I had ever tasted. Uncle L.P. insisted on homemade biscuits rather than the ones bought at the store. I could see him at the table with his bald head glowing from the overhead light as he said grace, surrounded by his wife, three daughters, my parents, and me, and concluded with a hearty amen, reaching for one of the warm biscuits wrapped in a red and white checkered cloth.

Sometimes an F-4 on strip alert across the airfield tested its engines in one quick blast. I passed from shadow to light and back to shadow, listening to the night wind rustling the grass in the ditch. Was it the wind? I waited and concluded it was only a rat. A white cat passed along the ditch on the other side, hunting for anything that might be hiding in the stacks of concrete conduits deposited there.

I continued my train of thought. Aunt Justine made the best baked beans with strips of bacon and sliced onions in a casserole dish. Aunt Geraldine brought a caramel cake each year for the reunion, and everyone wanted a piece. In my mind I saw the long serving table covered with deviled eggs, potato salad garnished with red pepper, pink congealed salad with chunks of pineapple, platters of fried chicken, slices of ham, pimento cheese sandwiches cut in triangles, green bean casseroles, sweet potato soufflé covered with melted marshmallows, pecan pies, yellow-layer chocolate cake, and brownies. Each aunt was a superb cook. How I missed being at home, but not for the food, as wonderful as that was. I missed all of my extended family. I missed the good times sitting around a table, drinking coffee and listening to them tell jokes and talk about the past while playing a game of setback.

With these thoughts the night passed more quickly, and I walked around the bunker again, stopping to listen. Then I was surprised that I could see the mountains through the morning mist. Behind me a C-141 taxied out with its taillight flashing, and I realized that it was dawn. I could go to breakfast at the mess hall. I squatted beside the field phone to call the OOD and secure the bunker watch for the night. I stood the night watch several more times while I was in a Da Nang, but none of those watches was as exciting and memorable as that first night.

CHAPTER 9

Flight Duty

At Da Nang I flew reconnaissance in three types of aircraft: the EC-121, a converted Super Constellation such as airlines used in the 1950s, often referred to as the Connie; the P-3, a turbo-prop used by the Navy mostly for submarine detection; and the A-3, a two-engine jet, fondly referred to as "the Whale," the largest plane at the time that could land on and be catapulted off an aircraft carrier. All of these aircraft had been modified to include a radar dome and an abundance of electronic surveillance equipment. Technically, the P-3 was known as an EP-3B, and the A-3 was known as an EA-3B. The aircraft were flown and maintained by the VQ-1 crew, home based at first in Atsugi, Japan, and later in Guam. Big Look was the name for the reconnaissance operation, although the term Wee Look was sometimes used for the A-3 track over Laos. My flight duty was about equally divided on the three types of aircraft. Normally, the "I" beats like me flew two or three days and then stayed off a day or two to translate tapes brought back from the missions or to serve as duty driver for the detachment. Also, when we came off a flight, we were expected to do translation work right away, especially if there had been a CRITIC, an urgent situation involving the shoot-down of an American plane. Word about a shoot-down was supposed to reach the desk of the President in ten minutes, so an "I" beat monitoring an air activity over North Vietnam or its vicinity had to be absolutely sure that a plane had actually been shot down. I never declared a CRITIC, but I came close to making this decision one day, as described later in the section "All Hell Breaks Loose Day."

What I share about our missions is written from my perspective as a TacAir op. I had little knowledge of other types of intelligence gathered during our flights since I had no need to know. I was involved with COMINT (communications intelligence). For TacAir ops this term referred to intelligence gained through radio communications of the North Vietnamese Air Force. Other terms that applied to reconnaissance during the Vietnam War include SIGINT, designating all signal intelligence derived through air, sea, and ground-based reconnaissance; ELINT (electronic

EA-3B Skywarrior, fondly referred to as "the Whale." Da Nang Air Base, 1972. A huffer is attached to start the engines. Many times, the other crew members and I entered the A-3 through the lower hatch with the huffer still attached and engines whining. During the Vietnam War, the A-3 was the largest aircraft that could be catapulted from the flight deck of an aircraft carrier, hence the name "the Whale" (photograph by Harry Lange).

intelligence); TELINT (telemetry intelligence); and IMINT (imagery intelligence). In short, I was part of a skilled team working in various ways to protect our planes and ships in the war zone.

The planes flew two tracks, one over the Gulf of Tonkin and the other over Laos. These tracks, as I understood, were triangular in shape. The EC-121 was unpressurized and flew at an altitude of around 10,000 feet. Often after a flight on one of the Willy Victors, as we sometimes called this type of plane, I had sinus issues and drank a mug of hot coffee when we landed to bring up the yuck. The P-3 flew at an altitude of about 20,000 feet and was pressurized, as was the A-3, which flew at 30,000 to 35,000 feet when we were on track. Since I sat behind the pilot on the A-3, I had certain duties as a crewmember. During takeoffs and landings, the overhead hatch was kept open as an emergency exit, should the plane crash. It was my job shortly after takeoff to close the hatch, and then the pilot pressurized the cabin. The air whooshed in with a loud rush, and for several minutes I could not hear well. Then my ears adjusted to the new pressure. As we approached the field while landing, the pilot told me at a certain point to open the overhead hatch. Once we were on the runway, I had to tell him if the drag chute had opened full or was streaming. If it did not open properly, he had to take counter measures. In the daytime this was easy since I sat facing the tail of the aircraft. Night landings made this job difficult because I could not see the chute, so I learned to fix my eyes on the strobe lights at the end of the runway, and when those lights suddenly blackened out, I announced, "Chute, open and full." As we turned onto the taxi strip, I was charged with standing up in my seat with my head and shoulders outside of the hatch. The pilot wanted me to do this to let him know if the drag chute was drifting to port or starboard and likely to become entangled in the lights lining the taxi strip. I would tell him, "Drifting to port, sir," and he would gun the engine on that side to straighten the chute out. I also was to watch for anything that might pose a hazard on the taxi strip, a stray dog, perhaps, or possibly even a sapper who had managed to get past the guard perimeters and run onto the field with the intention of blowing up the plane. I notified the pilot through the plane's intercom system, which was connected to my helmet. As we approached the revetments near the VQ-1 hangar, one of the ground crew directed us with red-tipped lights to our position and then signaled the engine shut-down. Other members of the ground crew opened the hatch in the belly of the A3 and put the wheel chocks in place. As I unstrapped from my seat, the wings of the plane folded with a slight jolt.

The first mission I flew was on the EC-121. About midway through the

EC-121, the Willy Victor, as this aircraft was called, on the tarmac in front of the VQ-1 hangar at Da Nang Air Base, 1971–1972. The Det Bravo Spooks flew in these airplanes piloted and maintained by the men of VQ-1, home based in Atsugi, Japan, and later Guam (photograph by Harry Lange).

mission, I needed to urinate, so I walked to the tail of the plane, where three VQ-1 crewmen were talking and drinking coffee. I saw what looked like a small urinal on the bulkhead at the rear, but it was covered with a red, white, and blue lid with the words "U.S. Mail" painted on it. I was confused, so I asked the VQ-1 men where the urinal was, and one of them asked, "You want to send a letter to Hanoi?" Another man pointed to the small urinal and said, "Go ahead. Mail a letter to Uncle Ho!" I felt a bit awkward lifting up the lid and realized that the drain for the urinal connected directly to the outside of the aircraft. I was, therefore, sprinkling the Gulf of Tonkin.

The tail fin of the P-3, the second aircraft in which I flew, was painted black, and on it some VQ-1 wag had painted a white Playboy bunny. There was a cylinder on this aircraft for urination, and a small portable john for bigger jobs. This pot was referred to as the "honey bucket." During a mission everyone postponed using this pot for as long as possible because whoever went first had to empty it. Finally, some unlucky crew member could wait no longer, and the pilot announced over the intercom, "The honey bucket is open." After that, others freely dumped on the first user. As a low-ranking crew member, several times I had to empty the urinal pot after a flight. I lugged the heavy, sloshing thing down the ladder of the P-3 and across the tarmac to a head in the hangar to empty it, usually spilling some of it along the way. To this day, my flight suit has some of the odors of those christenings.

During takeoffs and landings on the EC-121 and the P-3, we had ditching stations. On the P-3 my station was at the table in the galley, which was in the tail of the aircraft. Mick Schwartz, another "I" beat, sometimes shared this ditching station with me. We had interesting conversations while sitting in the galley. Once we talked about Shakespeare's plays, and he mentioned that he did not like Shakespeare. I asked him why, and he said he did not appreciate the way Shakespeare portrayed Jews since he was Jewish. In particular, he objected to Shylock in *The Merchant of Venice*, and I had to admit there was some justice to his claim. In the same way African American students in my classes over the years have sometimes told me they do not like the novels of William Faulkner or Mark Twain because of their use of the "n" word. I do not recall if I tried to reason with Schwartz that Shakespeare, like Faulkner and Twain, was himself not necessarily prejudiced but simply realistically depicting the biased attitudes and language of the characters during the time of the setting. Schwartz, though, like my African American students, probably would not have agreed with this reasoning. He was a good-natured guy who was easy-going on every other subject we discussed.

Sometimes we also had to sit at our ditching stations if we did a practice dive toward the ocean as if we were going to crash land in the water.

Willy Victor PR-27 in the revetment preparing to depart with men from the VQ-1 ground crew looking on. One of the EP-3Bs in which the Spooks flew is in the background. Da Nang Air Base, 1971 (photograph by the author).

The pilots periodically performed these drills so that everyone on board would know what to do in an emergency. On these occasions Schwartz, removed his cap and ran his fingers through his hair, saying, "I hate this. Oh, how I hate this," because the steep dive with the pronounced fish-tailing of the aircraft where we were sitting made him nervous. While preparing this memoir for publication, I learned from Schwartz the reason the dives affected him in this way. He said that he was not worried about crashing or the structure of the aircraft coming apart. Rather, he was anxious that he would throw up during one of the dives. He shared that he had a history of motion sickness when he was younger and, as a result, worried about having this kind of episode while flying on a mission. He revealed that every day, when he went out to board one of the planes, he looked up to the sky and thought about a line from "American Pie," a song by Don McLean, "thinking this will be the day that I die," and prayed, "God in Heaven—please don't let me barf!" Reading this, I recalled that Schwartz once showed me a barf bag that he carried in a pocket of his flight suit. He confided in a member of the det whom he trusted to maintain confidentiality to learn if there was anything he could take to mitigate the effects of his condition. He received this reply: "No way you are going to be able to take anything and do the kind of job you do. If you do try it, you will run the risk for all those with whom you fly." Since Schwartz wanted to do his job well and become a senior TacAir op, he realized he would just have to deal with his condition, no matter how bad it became. And deal with it he did. He eventually became a senior op and remained in Da Nang longer than I did, flying numerous missions. Like others of us in Det Bravo, he overcame a significant personal obstacle to do what he needed to do, and, in the process, showed true courage and determination.

On landings, I would look at Schwartz and say, "I wonder what treat we're going to be served tonight." One of the P-3 pilots, a middle-aged man, prided himself on braking the plane hard so that he could make the second turn-off from the runway onto the taxi strip, a feat most pilots did not attempt. On those occasions, something often came loose in the galley and flew through the air towards Schwartz and me. One night, it was a canister of dill pickles that came at us, turning end over end, flinging pickles and juice everywhere. When these objects became detached, Schwartz and I dodged as best we could and laughed. It was good to see him laugh since flying made both him and me nervous.

Being a CTI on a reconnaissance flight involved multitasking. I sat at my position and monitored air activities on two radio receivers, each of which had a panoramic scope to show the spikes of radio signals from North Vietnamese pilots and ground controllers. I wore a set of headphones with a different channel going to each ear. I kept a log of what was said on a yellow legal pad, which I divided into two columns. I was supposed to mark the time at regular intervals on the log. In addition, there were two reel-to-reel tape recorders linked to the two radio receivers. I had to change tapes whenever one ran out. Moreover, I had to keep the evaluating officer informed of what was happening at all times. On the EC-121 and P-3 there were two TacAir CTIs, one of whom was the supervisor of the other, and this senior "I" beat had to check periodically with the junior one to see what air activities he was monitoring. On the A-3 jets there was only one TacAir CTI, who sat in the cockpit immediately behind the pilot, facing the tail of the plane. There the "I" beat had a clear view of everything that was happening in the aircraft, the surrounding airspace, and the ground or ocean below. The view was spectacular and exciting, in fact, sometimes a little too exciting for comfort.

Typically, missions on the EC 121s and P-3s lasted about eight hours, but sometimes they extended on busy days to ten hours. A-3 missions took four to four and a half hours. During most of the time in flight on the big planes, I had to sit at my position, although I could get up to use the bathroom or even to eat if it was a slack day. Much of the time, though, we were busy monitoring what the North Vietnamese Air Force was doing, so I had to sit at my position all day. Meals were served at our positions, so in addition to the other tasks, we had to fit in occasional bites of food or sips of coffee. The food was not bad. One of the VQ-1 chiefs or petty officers cooked the meals in flight in the galley of the larger planes. For breakfast, we often had steak and eggs scrambled with cheese. For lunch we might have baloney sandwiches with slices cut off a long roll, which the NCOs referred to as "horse cock." The pleasant smells of steak pieces and onions frying in a pan created a strange domestic atmosphere while I was listening on a typical day to a practice ground-control intercept (PGCI) by MiG-21s out of Phuc Yen airfield or formation flying by MiG-17s out of Kien An airfield near Haiphong. I could almost imagine myself back home with my father cooking an early morning breakfast before a fishing trip, but the occasional hiss of a MiG-21 mic and the "Nghe rõ" ("Roger") of the pilot acknowledging ground controller commands brought me back to the present reality. At intervals, a pilot in a practice GCI might say "Mục tiêu phát hiện, hai rưỡ cây số" ("The target appears, two and a half kilometers"), and I had to be sure this was just a practice target and not a real one because I was aware that what appeared to be a routine activity could quickly change into an attack on our aircraft or other American planes. The officer evaluator, though, was also aware of what the electronic surveillance positions were monitoring, so he knew if a MiG-21 had gone "feet wet" (out over the water) or not. Moreover, a cruiser known by the designation "Red Crown" provided additional electronic surveillance. It was stationed just off the coast of southern North Vietnam. During part of the time I was at Da Nang, the USS *Chicago* was "Red Crown."

In addition to monitoring the practice ground-control intercepts and formation flying, we also sometimes listened to cargo plane flights from one airfield to another, but we paid special attention to any MiG-21 which transited from Phuc Yen to an airfield further south, such as Bai Thuong or Vinh, because this meant that the North Vietnamese Air Force was getting into an advantageous position to try to shoot down B-52s or other aircraft. MiG-21 transits were included in the daily frag reports presented to the evaluating officer for each mission. Most importantly, we monitored actual ground-control intercepts or attacks against American aircraft, and the evaluator sent out bandit warnings. Occasionally, I heard the Russian language and realized these transmissions were Russians training Vietnamese pilots. A time or two I also picked up Chinese and assumed that these signals were coming from planes operating out of an airbase on Hainan Island on the north end of the Gulf of Tonkin.

In listening on the radio receivers, CTIs had ways of recognizing MiG-21s. Sometimes when a pilot landed, he would announce to the ground controller, "Bốn mươi lăm đô, tốt" ("Forty-five degrees good"). This referred to a forty-five-degree wing flap setting and was a clear indication that the plane was a Fishbed-F, an upgraded version of the MiG-21. CTIs could also discern a MiG-21 by the unique sound of its mic. Moreover, any GCI that we intercepted was almost certain to be a MiG-21 since the North Vietnamese Air Force used its most advanced aircraft in attempted shoot-downs. The MiG-21 was a lightweight, versatile interceptor, and experienced North Vietnamese MiG-21 pilots were formidable adversaries skilled in quick hit and run attacks. As a result, we TacAir CTIs had to be extremely alert in sitting at our positions.

BARCAP (Barrier Combat Air Patrol)

Occasionally, while we were on track, the BARCAP jets joined us. Two F-4s would come alongside the P-3 and hover just off our wing tip. The pilot and his radar man would wave and flip the bird, and some of our crew would return the greeting in kind. At times one of the planes flipped over and flew upside down beside us. Navy fighter pilots were known for their capricious humor. To match our slow speed, the F-4s sometimes lowered their landing gear. After flying with us for a few minutes, the F-4s would suddenly peel off or bank and then go into a long curving dive until they were just tiny silver specks against the blue sea. They might also do a victory roll while zooming out of sight. The mission of the BARCAP jets was to provide a protective barrier for the Seventh Fleet and Navy aircraft over the Gulf of Tonkin. I felt better knowing they were out there somewhere, but if they were at one end of the track while we were at the other, sometimes a distance of two-hundred miles, there was danger that a MiG-21 out of Vinh airfield could go feet wet and shoot us down before BARCAP could intervene.

On one mission, when John Shipman was the other "I" beat under my supervision, we were informed by the fleet that we were the only aircraft over the Gulf of Tonkin. In other words, we had no BARCAP protection. I turned to Shipman and said, "It'll be OK as long as we remain the *only* aircraft over the Gulf." He lifted an earphone up and nodded. It was late in the day, almost time to go off track. The sun had set, and the twilight glow was visible through the P-3s' portholes. No air activity was up over North Vietnam. I kept tuning up and down the frequencies, but got nothing, just a steady humming or static in my headphones. Then gradually I began to hear a weak signal, with the distinctive hiss of a MiG-21 mic. I could faintly hear "Nghe rõ" over and over. A MiG-21 pilot was responding to ground control commands in what seemed to be a practice GCI. The pilot acknowledged a heading of ninety degrees. That meant he was flying due east. This caused me some concern since we had no BARCAP. For almost five minutes I did not hear the pilot because the signal had faded, and I became increasingly nervous. I informed Mr. Shermer, the evaluator, that the last known heading of the plane was ninety degrees, meaning he was flying in our general direction. I realized that, since the signal was weak, he was probably far away in the vicinity of Phuc Yen airfield near Hanoi, but I wanted to be extra cautious, remembering the North Korean MiG that had flown 150 miles out to sea in radio silence and shot down an EC-121 reconnaissance plane like ours, killing everyone on board. I recommended that, if we were near the northern end of our track, we should perhaps turn south. A few more minutes passed, and I again acquired the signal. Then I heard words that froze my blood. The pilot suddenly said, "Locked on good," signifying that his radar was locked onto a target preparatory to firing a missile. I quickly told Mr. Shermer, who quietly told me to calm down and not become too excited. He informed the pilot, and we took a dive towards the deck, as we called the ocean surface. Later, I realized the MiG-21 was nowhere near us, and the electronic surveillance guys in the P-3 showed that no MiG-21 radar had been engaged. But to be on the safe side, we took a dive since no BARCAP jets were airborne to protect us.

Attempted Shoot-Downs of B-52s

From what I understood in "I" beat training, the MiG-21 was specifically developed by the Russians as a counter measure against American B-52s since they could climb to high altitudes, fly at almost Mach 2, and theoretically launch heat-seeking missiles from as far away as eleven kilometers from a target, although the preferred distance was much closer. To achieve high altitudes to match the flight paths of B-52s, MiG-21 pilots did a zoom climb, which involved going up rapidly several thousand feet, leveling off, flying level for a while, and then climbing several thousand feet again, executing a series of stair-step maneuvers to reach the desired altitude. On rare occasions our surveillance monitored zoom climb practices by the North Vietnamese air force, clearly indicating that they were preparing to shoot down Arc Lights (B-52s).

One night my friend Stokowski returned from an A-3 mission over Laos. He had tracked an attempted shoot-down of a B-52 by a MiG-21. I do not recall most of the details, but from what Stokowski said, the MiG launched at least one missile at the B-52, which exploded in its vicinity, resulting in some damage but not causing the plane to crash. B-52s were equipped with electronic counter measures. This attack, however, greatly alarmed the pilot and crew, who had expected no attack at the altitude at which they were flying over the Ho Chi Minh Trail. I remember thinking that Stokowski tended to be airborne when the most exciting things happened. On one of his A-3 flights he saw tracer shots from anti-aircraft fire streak past the plane. A tinge of envy crossed my mind, but then I checked myself, realizing that I did not really want to be the only "I" beat on track when something dangerous like the attempted shoot-down occurred. The weight of responsibility rested heavily on me and all of the "I" beats who flew on the missions out of the Da Nang detachment. We understood all too clearly that, if we were not good enough in our understanding of Vietnamese or if we were somehow careless and overlooked an important detail, the lives of American pilots, sailors aboard ships stationed off the coast, and crew members on the planes in which we flew might be lost. This realization placed great stress on us, making us intently alert while flying but also sometimes creating nervous disorders that affected us throughout our tour of duty and, in some cases, like mine, for many years afterwards.

Not long after Stokowski's experience, I had my own ordeal by fire. I also was on a night mission in the A-3 over Laos when I picked up the signal of a MiG-21. From what I remember, this plane might have been from either Bai Thuong or Vinh, airfields from which shoot-downs were sometimes attempted. We were especially on alert after any reception involving the transit of a MiG-21 from Phuc Yen, near Hanoi, to either of these airfields, both of which were further South than most of the air bases. Vinh, in fact, was on the coast just a few miles north of the border with South Vietnam. I believe it was this flight when I was especially apprehensive since a frequency change had just occurred in the North Vietnamese Air Force. These changes happened periodically in an attempt to foil American reconnaissance. The attack channels were changed, as well as the channels for routine practices and transits. Moreover, code words for commands involving altitude, air speed, afterburners, missiles, pilot billet suffixes, and designations for hostile aircraft also changed, making a CTIs job more difficult. In a sense, right after a frequency change, we were flying blind and deaf, but within a day or two we had cracked the new channels and code words. Although any channel could be used as an attack frequency, the North Vietnamese preferred a set channel, which we soon learned. It might, for example, normally be 127.5 megahertz. On this night, I watched carefully for any signal to pop up on the panoramic display for my two radio receivers since I had no idea which channel might be reserved for an attack. As soon as a signal appeared, I tuned up or down and then listened. In a real attack the commands and acknowledgments were not at first steady, so patience was required. Then the signal appeared again, and I knew this was a MiG-21 being vectored towards an enemy target. My concern was whether we or someone else was the target since the plane was directed to assume a

270-degree heading with slight variations afterwards. In short, he was flying towards Laos, where our track lay.

The ground controller at Hanoi Bac Mai told the pilot that the "white pig," the new code word for an American aircraft, was straight ahead, seventy kilometers; however, I thought he said "thirty kilometers." The reason for this is understandable since the Vietnamese for seventy kilometers is "bảy mươi cây," and the term for thirty kilometers is "ba mươi cây,"* wording that might sound similar, considering the noise of the A-3 engines and some static in the signal. It was better for me to place the MiG closer to his target than he was rather than further away since this made the response time to warn our aircraft all the more urgent. Often, if we had a MiG coming in our general direction, I first alerted the pilot, whose seat was directly behind mine, and he communicated the information to the evaluation officer in the back of the A-3. This officer in turn broadcast a warning. He might announce, for example, "Bandit, bandit, one blue bandit, vicinity of Squid."

Our evaluator gave the bandit warning, and I continued to monitor the activity but heard no evidence that the MiG had gone into attack mode or launched missiles. If an attack was proceeding, the ground controller would continue to order successively higher altitudes, if this was a zoom climb. As the MiG moved closer to the target, he might say, "Nơi gió!" ("Windy place!"), meaning "Turn on afterburners," followed a short time later with the command to drop the auxiliary fuel tank. Sometimes the pilot himself let the controller know he had already released the auxiliary tank. The controller might then direct the pilot to check to make sure his weapons switch was working properly. If all of this went smoothly, the last command before the attack might be directions for a new heading after the missiles had been launched. For example, the controller might say, "When the attack is finished, break off at 360," to which the pilot would reply, "Nghe rõ," acknowledging that he understood. Then there was usually radio silence while the attack was in progress. If a hit was made, the pilot sometimes became very excited, exclaiming, "Chết rồi!" ("Dead!"). "They are burning; they are falling!" If there was no clear indication of a hit, the controller might ask, "Uống bia chưa?" ("Have you drunk beer yet?"), code for "Have you launched missiles?" to which the pilot might say, "Tôi đã uống hai chai bia!" ("I have drunk two bottles of beer"). Since I heard no evidence of an attack, I assumed the MiG had broken off for some reason.

Once on the ground that night, I sat up late with Mike Farmer,

---

*The term for "kilometers" is "cây số," but I do not remember ever hearing the "số" part of the term. Perhaps a shortened form was used by the ground controllers, or maybe what I heard pronounced was the letter "k" used as an abbreviation for "kilometers."

listening to the tape. He was the best TacAir translator in the detachment and often helped with important or difficult tapes. For all translations, the "I" beat sat at a typewriter and listened to the tape, replaying difficult parts repeatedly and then typing the translation onto a six-ply sheet, with at least one copy to go to NSA at Fort George Meade, Maryland, or as we sometimes said, "Daddy DIRNSA," Director of NSA. Listening to the tape that evening with Farmer, I heard information that I could not clearly distinguish while we were in the air. At one point the controller told the MiG-21 pilot, "Nó đang đi một trăm năm mươi" ("It is going at 150"). The pronoun "nó" ("it") is not normally used for people. Instead, it refers to animals, objects, or enemies. From our training, we knew to add two zeroes to 150, making it 15,000, the altitude of the target aircraft. Since this figure was in meters, the target was at an altitude of approximately 49,000 feet, the height at which Arc Lights might fly. In other words, the target was clearly a B-52.

During some bombing activities, the forward battle commander for the U.S. Air Force was positioned in a helicopter somewhere near the border between Thailand and Laos. As we later learned, the battle commander on that particular night aborted the B-52 mission after hearing the bandit warning and ordered an F-4 to the intended destination, where it encountered a MiG-21 orbiting, ready to attack the bomber. The F-4 chased the MiG back into North Vietnamese air space but, under the rules of engagement at that time, was not given permission to shoot it down. A few days later two Air Force officers visited our commanding officer, LCDR Purring, to thank our unit for preventing a shoot down of the B-52. Mr. Purring invited me, among others, to meet the officers in his office. I do not remember if on this occasion the detachment received a Bravo Zulu from the commander of the Seventh Fleet, but occasionally, our team did receive commendations for their good work.

On another evening, when I was flying on the P-3, we were expecting an attempted shoot-down of a B-52 because we knew that a MiG-21 had transited to Bai Thuong airfield the preceding day. The other TacAir CTI and I, along with the electronic surveillance guys, were sitting on ready, when we heard Hanoi Bac Mai order the plane to scramble. We kept track of the headings and altitude changes given by the GCI controller. At first, I was afraid that we might be the target, but instead of flying east, where we were over the Gulf of Tonkin, the MiG was ordered to go west in an attempt to shoot down the Combat Apple reconnaissance aircraft, which was airborne over Cambodia. Combat Apple was the Air Force equivalent of the Navy's Big Look, only they had an RC-135, a huge jet rather than a propeller or turbo-prop aircraft. I could hear the radio communications between the pilot and the ground controller as the MiG kept trying to close on its target. This attempt made me nervous because, since the VPAF (Vietnamese

People's Air Force) was targeting the Air Force reconnaissance plane, they might be planning to go after us as well. Fortunately, the MiG was not successful. After we returned from the mission, I saw the flight path of the Combat Apple jet plotted by our radio trackers and was amazed by the maneuvers taken to avoid the MiG. The track zigzagged for a considerable distance over Cambodia, and I marveled that Combat Apple had not been shot down.

All-Hell-Breaks-Loose Day

During the middle of December 1971, perhaps on the 18th, I sat at my position on the EC-121 during one of the most trying days of my tour. On that day four American fighter jets went down over North Vietnam. As we were flying north over the Gulf of Tonkin from Da Nang to go on track, I was listening on my receivers and already aware that something was wrong. There was a lot of activity on the airwaves. At first it was a confusing mass of quick-fire transmissions, much of which I could not understand, but I gradually began to realize that an American airplane had been shot down in the north and MiGs were interfering with rescue by a Jolly Green Giant helicopter. Two men were on the ground in danger of being taken prisoner. Every time an American aircraft tried to go in, the MiGs converged and drove them off.

I was immediately faced with a problem. The shoot-down of an American aircraft meant that a CRITC had to be issued, and it was up to the "I" beat monitoring an activity to verify the need for the CRITIC. But I realized this shoot-down had already occurred, how much earlier I did not know. So I wondered if the "I" beat on the plane on track at that time had declared the CRITIC or if they had already departed from the track without issuing the CRITIC. As I continued to listen to my receivers, there was no doubt about the shoot-down, but I agonized over whether to tell the supervising officer that a CRITIC should be issued. If I made this decision, then the radio transmission of the CRITIC was supposed to be on the President's desk in ten minutes. I believe Stokowski was the lead TacAir CTI on the P-3 coming off track. Had he already verified the CRITIC or not? Finally, after much anguish, I decided not to call for the CRITIC, concluding that it had probably already been decided on by the evaluator aboard the P-3. As it turned out, I was right. There was no need for issuing another CRITIC report, but this decision was one of the hardest that I faced in Vietnam.

After arriving on track, we remained airborne the rest of that day and into the evening, over ten hours, and we accumulated eighteen reel-to-reel tapes of activity by the VPAF. The day was frenetic with dog fights and chases, along with attempted rescues by our helicopters. This was one of the few times I lost my cool and became angry with the North Vietnamese pilots, at one point yelling at them for preventing the rescue of the downed pilot and his radar man. From what I later heard and also learned from the tapes, F-4s tried to drive the MiG-21s off and gave chase to them. I never saw an official report, but from what I could understand, another American jet was shot down, and two more ran out of fuel chasing MiGs over the North. As a result, four American pilots and their radar men were captured and taken to prison at the Hanoi Hilton. It was distressing to listen to the activity and realize that we could do nothing about it. When we landed that night, I was angry and frustrated. My eyes were filled with hot tears. Moreover, I had several important tapes that needed immediate attention. Fortunately, Mike Farmer, with his cool, calm, hippie face, love beads and all,

The detachment work building, referred to as "the spaces." Entrance was by security code only. This was the center for secure communications and translation of tapes accumulated during missions. The CO's office and the administrative office were located here (photograph by Tim Yerdon).

was there to help. He seemed to enjoy translating badly garbled and diffi-cult segments of tape.

Flying with Mr. Andrews

LT Andrews was one of my favorite pilots, but sometimes he exasper-ated me when he tried to fly the A-3 as if it were a jet fighter. I think being a fighter pilot might have been his dream. One day, as we were coming off track over the Gulf of Tonkin, he decided to do a practice intercept on the EC-121, the aircraft that was relieving us. The clouds that afternoon were high billowing masses with occasional clear spaces. A few minutes earlier in a break between the clouds I had seen the EC-121 several thousand feet below us headed north. It was starkly white, small, and insignificant against the blue surface of the sea. I did not inform Mr. Andrews that I had already spotted the EC-121 since I was tired and just wanted to return to Da Nang. But he kept turning, descending and climbing, cutting through clouds and out again into clear sky, searching for the EC-121, discussing its possible location with the navigator. I sat behind him, rolling my eyes and saying to myself, "Please, let's just go home!" Finally, he had to admit defeat, and we headed for the base.

One night I had a mission with him over Laos. We flew smoothly up and down the track. At the end of each leg, a wing of the A-3 tilted upwards, and it seemed as if we were not turning but rather as if the ground were rotating below us. Then for a long stretch everything was smooth and calm, and I was intent on my radio receivers. At one point we passed above Nak-hon Phanom, Thailand, and I could see the blue and amber lights of the American airfield there. A dark space extended between Nakhon Phanom on the Thai side of the border and the town on the Laotian side. Although I could not see it, I knew that this dark gap was the Mekong River. The glow from Savannakhet, another Laotian town, was visible further south down the river. Here and there a star shell floated over the dark landscape, and I wondered if these flares marked the sites of American, Laotian, Pathet Lao, or North Vietnamese units.

We flew with our running lights off. As I later learned, that is why this track was called Black Track. Once in a while, though, Mr. Andrews turned the lights on briefly when another aircraft with its red and green wing lights and flashing taillight was coming in our direction at a lower altitude. I watched the approaching plane carefully to see if it turned on an afterburner. Even though I had no hostile activity up on my receivers, I was always sus-picious of a trick by the VPAF. I assumed Mr. Andrews had radio contact to discern that the aircraft was friendly, probably returning to base in Thailand.

On this track we flew west of the Annamite chain of mountains. During the rainy season the land east of this mountain range was often blanketed with clouds while the skies to the west were clear. One evening we had to recover in Thailand since Da Nang was socked in with clouds and rain. If we landed there, we would have to catch the wire with our tail hook, a maneuver that was, I assumed, a tricky business at night, maybe not even available, although we sometimes did this on rainy days. This procedure required men on the side of the runway managing the wire. We turned west, and while we were still over Laos, I noticed flickering lights on the ground on our port side. I asked Mr. Andrews if he knew what those lights were. He replied, "Anti-aircraft fire." I hoped we were high enough to be out of its range, and I wondered if the gunners were trying to target us or another plane at a lower altitude. My eyes remained fixed on those flickering lights until they were far to our rear. Always I was a bit nervous over Laos since it was possible the North Vietnamese might have secretly established SAM sites near our track. Presumably, the CTI at the SAM position could monitor the missile site chatter and the electronic surveillance guys in the back of the A-3 could detect the FAN SONG radar that guided the SAMs, if it were turned on, but this knowledge did not relieve my anxiety.

As we approached the airfield at Ubon,* Mr. Andrews threw the A-3 into a steep, curving dive. The G force pressed me back into my seat so that I could not move. I am not sure how many G's we pulled or how many thousands of feet we dove, but the force was greater than any I had previously experienced. Then Mr. Andrews pulled the plane out of the dive and made a low pass over the field. We zoomed down the runway at an altitude of maybe twenty-five to thirty feet at 200-plus miles per hour, and then he pulled the A-3 up in a steep climb, leveled off, banked sharply so that I was looking straight down at the ground, flew a quick box pattern, and landed. When I climbed down from the belly of the A-3, I felt like kneeling and kissing the tarmac.

Even though Mr. Andrews sometimes scared me with these fighter pilot tactics, I trusted him. If a MiG-21 had ever tried to intercept us, our chance of surviving the attack would have been better if he were the pilot since his quick, jerky movements, could perhaps have surprised the enemy pilot.

---

*The airfield could have been either Ubon or Udorn. Our planes sometimes recovered at both bases in Thailand.

CHAPTER 10

Flying Dangerously

Flying on a mission out of Da Nang involved dangers other than those posed by MiG-21s. Errors in navigation, mechanical or electrical problems, and bad weather often put us in danger and sometimes caused a mission to be aborted. We were all aware of the crash of an EC-121 at Da Nang on March 16, 1970. PR-26 was landing at Da Nang on a flight from Tainan, Taiwan, with one engine feathered when, in an attempt to veer off and go around again, the aircraft banked too sharply, hit a revetment hangar, and broke into three pieces, two of which burst into flame. Of the thirty-one VQ-1 personnel on board, there were only eight survivors. No Spooks were on the flight, but this crash was a reminder of what might happen to us when we flew, whether on the EC-121, P-3, or A-3.

Several times on the EC-121 the pilot had to feather an engine. In other words, because of a problem with one of the four engines, he had to shut it down. This usually did not affect the mission; the plane could fly effectively on three engines. But on some flights two engines had to be feathered, and at that point we had to abort the mission and return to base. If this occurred early in the flight, that meant we had too much fuel in the wing tanks for a safe landing, so we had to dump fuel over the Gulf of Tonkin. This was always a dangerous process because fumes built up in the cabin, and even the slightest electrical spark from any of the equipment could have blown the plane up. I was always nervous while fuel was venting. I could look out one of the portholes and see a long white trail, resembling a contrail, stretching behind us. I wondered how dumped fuel affected the Gulf of Tonkin environment, especially the fishing on which many coastal residents of both North and South Vietnam depended.

One night when our EC-121 was on the track over the Gulf of Tonkin, the pilot called the navigator to the cockpit and asked why he was seeing lights on the horizon ahead where there should be no lights. The pilot realized that he was looking at the lights of Haiphong harbor, the major port of North Vietnam, where there were MiG-17s at Kien An airfield as well as SAM sites. Our track should not have extended that far north. He then

EC-121 Willy Victor departing from the VQ-1 tarmac, with an OV-10 observation and light attack aircraft in the background. Da Nang Air Base, 1970–1971 (photograph by Mike Farmer).

thoroughly chewed out the navigator for his error. The electronic surveillance guys noticed that the SPOON REST acquisition radar at the SAM sites had already begun to track us. We made a quick turn south to the proper track and out of immediate danger.

Another time I was monitoring bombing practice over the sea off Haiphong harbor by Ilyushin 28s. These were small Russian bombers with two jet engines. The activity was routine, long, and somewhat boring to listen to, but at one point I heard the ground controller tell the pilots, "Chú ý phía nam. Có địch ở đó" ("Pay attention to the south. The enemy is there."). I wondered if we were getting too close on our track or if the ground controller was perhaps referring to the BARCAP fighters.

Even during typhoon weather, we sometimes went up on track. On one P-3 mission we were over the Gulf of Tonkin as a typhoon approached Da Nang. On that morning we did not get above the clouds as usual; we were flying through opaque grayness the entire time. Visibility was almost zero. I heard the pilot through my earphones talking to ground control in Da Nang. He asked if they had us clearly on their radar scope because, he said, "An F-4 just came screaming by my wing." The plane vibrated roughly, moving suddenly up and down and yawing back and forth. Sitting at my position, I kept rocking forward, backwards, and sideways. Finally, realizing the futility of continuing the mission, ground command ordered us to return early.

One beautiful afternoon while we were returning to Da Nang on the A-3 after coming off track, one of the two engines shut down. It made a sickening groaning sound as it died. The pilot tried first one thing and then another while barking orders to the aircrew in the back, telling them to hit the alternate electrical circuit. We were only a short distance from the base, just north of the entrance to Da Nang Bay, but we were steadily losing altitude. At one point I looked straight out of the cockpit and saw that we were halfway down the side of the mountains that flanked the north side of the bay. I knew that those mountains were approximately two-thousand feet above sea level, so that meant we must have been about a thousand feet above the sea surface. I saw rocky outcrops in the sea below us with waves breaking against them. It looked as if we were going into the drink, and from what I had heard, no one knew what would happen when an A-3 loaded with electrical equipment hit the water. Would it sink like a rock or stay afloat long enough for the crew to escape through the overhead hatch near my position? I wondered if the radios and tape recorders on the metal frame in front of me would break loose upon impact and crush me. I looked out the cockpit and saw the sea steadily coming closer. I was both scared and immeasurably sad, afraid that I might not survive the impact or be trapped in the sinking plane but also sad at the profound grief that my death would cause my mother and father. I was their only child, and sadness for them dominated my mind, even over the fear. Fortunately, the alternate circuit caught, and the engine restarted, so we were able to proceed to base and make a safe landing.

Another night I was flying with Mr. Andrews, and the officer in the navigator's seat was Mr. Walters. Somewhere over the Gulf of Tonkin while we were on track, the starboard engine made a groaning sound and then died. Mr. Walters turned around to me and told me to flip the switch for the alternate circuit. As an "I" beat, I had not been trained in the instrumentation of the A-3 or the procedure for dealing with various types of emergencies; therefore, I did not know that the plane had A and B electrical circuits. He became angry with me because I hesitated and asked him where the switch was located. Fortunately, one of the men from the rear of the plane came forward and flipped the switch for the "B" circuit on the panel just forward of my position. The engine caught, and we began to climb again and continued with the mission. When we landed, however, Mr. Walters chewed me out for not responding immediately, but I had no way to respond since I knew nothing about the electrical circuits of the plane. I realized that it would have been good if VQ-1 had scheduled some sessions with those of us who were part of the flight crew to tell us about some essential features of the different planes in which we flew and what we should do in certain types of emergency situations. We also needed instruction on how to bail out of the aircraft. Sometimes we had bail-out drills on the P-3, but I did not really know what to do, other than to yank the metallic handle on the left side of the parachute harness. During one of these drills, after we were lined up ready to exist the plane, not knowing if this were just a drill or the real thing, the NCO in charge blessed out one of the aircrewmen. He had put his Mae West life preserver on over his parachute rather than under it. As a result, had this been a real bail-out, there would have been no way for his chute to open.

There was another pilot, besides Mr. Andrews, that I admired. He was a thin but wiry middle-aged man, a solid no-nonsense pilot, career military. I felt safe flying with him because he did nothing extreme; everything he did was practical and according to common sense. He is the one I chiefly remember who would tell me when to open the overhead hatch on the A-3 as we prepared to land. I recall asking him one cloudy afternoon if I should go ahead and open the hatch as we were approaching Da Nang from the south, and he told me to wait. The flat terrain below us looked like a moon-scape because of numerous old bomb craters, except grass and water were in the craters rather than bare rock. We were landing earlier than sched-uled since we had to abort the mission because of some electrical problem, and I was a bit nervous during the return flight. Finally, with the end of the runway in sight, he told me to open the hatch. Fortunately, I did not know the extent of the danger. After we had landed, I was in the work building unpacking my tapes and other materials, when I overheard him talking to Chief Holt. He said that he had to work hard to keep the A-3 airborne because one system after another was failing and that it would have been easier to tell the crew to step to the hatch and bail out. I realized then how close we had come to crashing, and I was thankful for his skill as a pilot.

In returning off track in the P-3 late one afternoon, our pilot announced that he had seen a jet refueling plane crash into the sea ahead of us. We flew to the spot and then orbited it until a rescue helicopter could arrive, but in looking out the open door and the windows of the P-3, our crew could see no debris from the crash, not even an oil slick. The pilot directed a VQ-1 crewmember to drop a radio beacon to mark the site for the helicopter, but it fell short of the place where the pilot wanted it, and he cursed the crewman for his mistake. Everyone was upset because noth-ing came to the surface, except, finally, a single Mae West. We continued to orbit the site of the crash for over an hour and then returned to base. We later learned that the pilot of the downed plane was about to complete his tour. In fact, he was scheduled to go home the next week and, as I heard, attempted to do a victory roll to celebrate.

One morning we were in the P-3 getting ready to taxi. I was at my ditching station in the galley and was looking forward at all the other men

PR-32 in a revetment at Da Nang Air Base, 1971. The Big Look Spooks flew reconnaissance on two specially modified Lockheed P-3 Orions (PR-31 and PR-32) maintained by VQ-1. The revetments were designed to protect the aircraft from shrapnel during rocket or mortar attacks, but they also provided protection from our own aircraft that occasionally crashed during takeoffs and landings (photograph by Tim Yerdon).

sitting at their positions. I remember looking at Jeff Buckingham, who was sitting a short distance from me with his cap on. All of a sudden, his face turned rosy red, and the interior of the plane lit up with a red glow. I was thinking, "What in the—?" when I heard a loud explosion, and some of the guys at the door began shouting, "Holy Christ! Get out! Get out!" All of us scrambled for the hatch, expecting the airplane was about to burst into flames. We scampered down the ladder and ran under the wing of the P-3 onto the tarmac at the entrance of the revetment. I saw flaming parts of an aircraft strewing the taxi strip and the runway. Further down the field there were three places where black smoke was ascending. VQ-1 men came running from the hangars in our direction. Lieutenant Commander Pelot and some of the guys from the det ran onto the tarmac from our workspace. Mr. Pelot saw me and shouted, "Stay calm, Shippey! Stay calm!" I realized that he was perhaps saying this for himself, as well as for my benefit. It was obvious that an aircraft had crashed. We learned that a jet fighter, fully loaded with missiles and bombs, had crashed just after lifting off the runway. Fortunately, the pilot was able to eject and apparently survived. The explosion occurred almost even with the revetment in which the P-3, fully loaded with fuel, was located. If even one piece of that burning plane had come across the wall and hit the wing of the P-3, it could have exploded, killing all of us. The force of the blast blew the larger pieces of the jet forward further down the field, and that is where I saw the black smoke billowing upward.*

One night, in returning from a mission, we were delayed in landing at Da Nang. A crash had occurred on the field, and it took a while to remove the debris from the runway. When we finally landed, I went to the work building to unpack my bag and stow my gear. Chief Holt, sitting at his desk, told us to leave as quickly as we could, not to remain and listen to tapes as we often did. He said the plane that had crashed was an F-4, and it was still armed with a missile that had not been fired. Moreover, the jet and the missile were both pointed at our workspace, and the missile at any second could fire in our direction. We hurriedly unpacked and asked if he was staying. He replied that the work area had to be occupied by personnel at all times since it housed classified materials. As we left, I saw him still sitting at his desk, bent over some paperwork as if it were a normal evening.

---

*"Stevie Wonder" was on the P-3 mission that morning and was in a better position to see the crash: "I was standing at the top of the stairway in the door of the P-3 when that happened. The straight scoop on the event was that, as the jet left the runway and began climbing, it began a slow roll to the left, which was in our direction. The left wing hit the ground just to the left of the runway, and it cartwheeled down the runway while exploding. All of the debris looked like it continued down the runway past us. I looked back up the runway and saw a parachute floating toward the ground. At about this point, the hatch over the wing was removed, and men began exiting over the wing. I was nearly trampled by my crewmates trying to exit through the door. The ground crew showed up with a tractor and towed the P-3 away from the runway. The story that I heard later was that the aircraft had just left maintenance and lost hydraulics during take-off" (from Steve White's editing notes on the manuscript for this memoir). I thought the jet that crashed was an A-4 Skyhawk, but White remembered it as either an A-7 Corsair or an F-8 Crusader. In searching the Internet, I could not find any information about this crash.

CHAPTER 11

Daily Life in Da Nang

In the early morning when everything was quiet in the barracks, when the only visible movement was the gentle fanning to and fro of the sheets hung as curtains across the doors of the men's sleeping quarters, Bà Tao came, a middle-aged woman dressed in black slacks. She placed her conical hat on a nail in the maids' room upstairs, took up a short broom made of elephant grass, and went to sweep the dirt from the front steps. Then, bent over, she moved steadily down to the first-floor hall. The sunlight streamed in shafts through the dust raised by her broom as she advanced, sweeping in arcs, bringing back the reality of day. The other maids arrived, and the chattering began, punctuated with sudden shouts of "Oi!" and "Đừng nói láo!" followed by giggles. This was a morning routine. My second morning in Da Nang one of the young maids entered my room, climbed on top of my bunk, which was the upper one, and standing over me in her black slacks in an authoritative pose, shouted, "Oi!" motioning me out of the bed. She took no notice that I was dressed only in my skivvies and a tee shirt, but I did not argue the point with her. Then she stripped the sheets and put on clean sheets tying them around the ends of the mattress. At noon from the maids' room came the odor of cooked rice and fish steeped in nước mắm sauce, along with much talking and peals of laughter. Sometimes on those early mornings, a thin elderly man with a wispy beard also worked his way along the sidewalk past the line of barracks, spearing trash with his pointed stick and stopping to probe through our garbage cans for anything usable. He had a sad, solemn face.

The Vietnamese women who worked in the compound moved freely around the barracks and the heads, where the washing machines and dryers were located. Once while I was sitting on the john, two middle-aged maids, wearing conical hats, came into the head to retrieve clothes from the washing machine at the other end of the room. There were no stalls, just a line of commodes, so I was rather embarrassed, not knowing what to do. They took no notice of me, working as if I were not even there. I pulled up my trousers as best I could, and when they left with their baskets of clothes, I quickly finished up.

91

One afternoon while I was duty driver, I went to the other side of the airfield to pick up Bà Ho, who was one of the bartenders in the Spook mess. According to Morrison's detachment history, her husband was in the South Vietnamese Air Force, so she lived in base housing. When I arrived at her address, I went to the door to let her know I was there, and she asked me to wait while she finished getting ready. I returned to the truck and sat down. After a few minutes three or four young Vietnamese boys, maybe five or six years old, began picking up pebbles from the street and tossing them at the truck. I was a bit nervous about this but not alarmed since the boys were not throwing large rocks. Bà Ho came out and said, as she climbed into the truck, that the children meant no harm; however, I was not too sure. I saw how things might possibly escalate. Seeing Bà Ho in the truck, the boys stopped, and we traveled back to the west side of the base.

Bà Ho nicknamed me "Hạnh phúc," "Happy," a name that I appreciated since it seemed to imply that she had a good opinion of me, although, in looking back, I am not certain that it applied most of the time since I was often nervous and stressed out. She and the other women who worked in the Spook mess and cleaned the barracks did good work for us. One of the young women married Patrick Butler, a member of the det, and returned with him to America to live. I do not know what happened to the other women when the war ended, but I hoped they and their families survived and did not experience terrible hardships. According to a reminiscence by one of the detters, the men closing down the detachment took furniture and appliances from the barracks, including reefers, tables, chairs, and bunks, and sold them to benefit those who had taken care of us rather than see these items go to some government surplus warehouse.

A Morning in Da Nang: From My Journal

A typical morning in Da Nang. I emerge from the barracks and plod towards the head with a towel around my neck, stumbling in my flip-flops. I stand at the urinal half asleep, staring stupidly at the cigarette butts and chewing gum thrown into the bowl. Sparrows chirp from the eaves of the head. I look out the screened-in window and am suddenly surprised by the splendor of the morning. The dawn sky is scarlet. Double-barred utility poles between the rows of barracks are black crosses of Lorraine against the eastern sky. Wires sag between the poles like the empty bars of a musical score waiting for the notes to be added. For a moment I am lost in reverie, thinking about the beautiful sunrises I have seen at home or at college when I was up early and walked to the cafeteria for breakfast. The flushing of a commode brings me back to reality. In the building next to the head, I hear the high-pitched chatter of Vietnamese housemaids already washing clothes. Through the window I see wet purple and green *áo dài* dripping from the clothesline, bright patches of color against the drab barracks and bunkers crouching beneath the resplendent sky.

I turn on the faucet, and a long sucking, gurgling sound emerges. No water. I curse to myself. The Air Force has already turned off the water from the other side of the base. I have to dry shave again this morning. In the distance I hear the brief burp of M16 automatic fire. An F-4 roars down the runway. Outside the head a jeep pulls up with a spray of gravel, and two dogs rush out barking from beneath the steps of the VQ-1 barracks. The Marine driver, stepping out of the jeep, gives one a swift quick. The dog yelps once and slinks back beneath the steps while its companion keeps barking loudly. I hear the heavy crunching of the Marine's boots as he walks to one of the barracks. I think, "A new day in beautiful Da Nang," and attack my chin with the razor.

Early One Sunday Morning

I had been up most of the night translating air activity tapes in the work building and returned just before dawn to the barracks. Two friends were still up drinking beers at the bar and talking quietly about life back in the world. I heated a can of beef goulash on the hotplate and then sat on a stool eating it from the can with a plastic spoon. Someone was inevitably playing pool. The fluorescent light hanging low above the pool table cast a dim, undersea luminescence over the Spook mess. Spilled beer cans and cracked potato chips littered the floor. I twirled around on the stool, enjoying the warm goulash. On that day I did not have to fly. The previous night as the A-3 took off over Da Nang Bay and I looked down at the string of lights rimming the shore all the way around to Red Beach, I for a moment envied the people who could remain on the ground, even though their daily lives were difficult. But I did not have to fly for a day and sat listening to the clack of the billiard balls.

I walked to the head to brush my teeth. The gables of the barracks on either side pointed darkly toward the sky in the last blackness before dawn. Walking on the cracked sidewalk in my flip-flops, suddenly, I heard the clangor of bells coming from outside the base perimeter. I paused, wondering, "What in the world," and then I understood. They were ringing from a Catholic church on the outskirts of Da Nang, and it dawned on me that it was Sunday morning and I did not realize it. One day ran into another without distinction in the war zone. The only distinguishing feature of Sunday was that it was the day the housemaids did not come to work. Back home it was early Sunday evening. If I had been there, I would have gone to church with my mother that morning. A Phantom jet roared off the runway. The war went on as usual, and I continued to the head to brush my teeth before going to bed for a little while.

Funny Money

Those of us serving in the armed forces in Vietnam were paid in Military Payment Certificates (MPCs) rather than dollars. I am not sure of all the rationale for this, but part of the reason was to prevent black market exchanges involving U.S. dollars, to avoid flooding the local economy with dollars, and to keep dollars from falling into the hands of the VC. In Det Bravo we referred to MPCs as funny money or monopoly money. We were not allowed to take leave in the city of Da Nang, and there were only a

few places on the base where we could spend our MPCs. Since those of us involved in air reconnaissance received both hazardous-duty pay and flight pay, in addition to our regular pay, we accumulated a good bit of money. On one occasion, when several of us were relaxing on the steps of the barracks, Barney O'Feild remarked, "This is a hell of a note. To have all the money in the world and no place to spend it." Occasionally, I went to the base post office and mailed my mother a money order, which she deposited into my account so that I would have funds to

Military Payment Certificate, front and back. The Spooks called MPCs "funny money" or "Monopoly money." This is how we were paid in country. We exchanged the MPCs for American dollars whenever we went out of Vietnam (photograph by the author).

go back to graduate school or use in other ways when I returned home from the Navy.

Z-grams

Occasionally, FleetSupDet (Fleet Support Detachment) received Z-grams, messages about new personnel policies from Admiral Elmo Zumwalt, Chief of Naval Operations. The men in the det referred to him as Zummie. One morning when I arrived at the workspaces, a Z-gram was posted on the bulletin board near the door. It gave permission for Navy men to have neatly trimmed beards, moustaches, and sideburns. Chief Holt, however, made it clear that no official document allowing this policy change had been received. I do not know the point when permission became official, but I recall that some men had moustaches. Barney, in particular, grew a long, handlebar moustache with twisted ends. His moustache reminded me of the horns of a Texas Longhorn. Today, Admiral Zumwalt is remembered for many directives that modernized the Navy and gave more equal opportunities for women and minorities.

Barbershop

There was a barbershop in our compound, and occasionally, I went to have my hair cut, although the chiefs and officers in Det Bravo were not overly strict about hair length. Many of us also did not polish our flight boots, and some of us wore love beads and other unauthorized apparel. The barber was a short middle-aged Vietnamese man who wore a white barber's tunic. He was quick and efficient with his clippers and did good work, but on my first visit I was surprised when, after finishing cutting my hair, he grabbed the back of my head and gave my neck a sudden pop. I felt better after this manipulation, but I realized how easy it would have been for him to snap my neck. I wondered if he might be a VC, one of those who went up into the hills behind the base after dark and launched rockets. At that time, I was not aware of joint popping and massages as a traditional part of a visit to a barbershop in the Far East. Later, I learned that the expected routine involved washing the hair, getting the haircut, a second shampooing to wash out the loose hair, and depending upon the level of service desired, massaging and joint popping, including popping the joints on each finger. If one had to wait for an open chair, tea was served. When my wife and I visited China many years later, I had a haircut in a shop where there were male and female barbers. After the haircut and shampooing, the women suggested that I should then go to the back room for a message. I quickly replied, "Bu yao, bu yao!" ("Do not need, do not need!"), and they kept insisting, "Yao, yao, yao," and looked disappointed that I did not get the full service that went with the payment. When I walked by the shop on another day, the women recognized me and cheerfully waved. I humorously thought of them as sirens trying to lure me to come in. A photograph in the Big Look Spooks gallery shows that the barbershop in our compound was damaged by one of the typhoons that struck Da Nang, and I wondered what had happened to this barber, especially after the U.S. withdrawal from Vietnam.

Reprimand

One morning I received word that Lieutenant Commander Purring wanted to see me in his office. When I entered, he invited me to sit down. I was a bit anxious, wondering if he was about to reprimand me, but I could not remember anything I might have done wrong. He remained silent for a few seconds and then loudly commanded, "Shippey, write your mother!" I was surprised at what he said but also knew that he was right because I had not written a letter to my parents in three weeks. I was also amazed at the power of a concerned mother to set the bureaucratic apparatus of the Navy in motion. Somehow, she (or some official at her request) had called up the chain of command until she reached someone, probably in Navy BUPERS, who then made a series of calls until he reached Mr. Purring and ordered him to order me to write my mother. After barking out his order, Mr. Purring relaxed and said, "Shippey, they worry about us if they haven't heard from us in a while. They read in the newspapers about rocket attacks on Da Nang, and they see things on TV and worry. Every time we have an attack, I write my wife, even if it's just a brief note, to let her know I am all right. So write your mother." After that I made it a point to be more regular in my correspondence home. I had even greater respect for Mr. Purring and marveled at the tenacity and power of my Navy mother.

Initiations

In Da Nang we did not have any initiations like crossing the equator for the first time on a Navy ship. There were, nevertheless, some rites of passage for new guys. One of those was being called a "nicky new guy." One had to be there for a while before being fully accepted by the seasoned detters. This involved flying many missions, becoming skilled at one's position, and experiencing several rocket attacks. Newcomers might not have a room immediately assigned to them in the barracks. They sometimes were billeted for a time, as I was, to the upstairs room that had four double bunk beds. This room was rather noisy since it was right behind the Spook mess, where at night there was the clack of billiard balls and the sound of the TV. There was also loud music. It seemed that someone was always playing music by Santana or, less frequently, "Lucy in the Sky with Diamonds." Moreover, the housemaids' room was across the hall, and during the day there was often the sound of talking in Vietnamese and giggling.

One of the initiations for newbies was the funnel trick. In the Spook mess in the evening, one of the veteran detters would ask a nicky new guy if he had the skill to balance a coin on his forehead and then drop it into a funnel inserted in the waistline of his trousers. The newbie would think that this was not too hard, so a detter would place a nickel or a quarter on his head so that he had to look at the ceiling to balance it before bringing his head forward, supposedly to let the coin drop into the funnel. But as soon as he tried to balance the coin while looking up, one of the detters stepped forward and poured a beer down the funnel. If the victim were brassy enough, he chased the perpetrator around the mess and poured beer over his head. Sometimes the duo fell on the floor and tussled, with everyone laughing at these antics. Occasionally, a new guy, especially after he had drunk a few beers, would be challenged to walk a straight line, following the floor tiles, with his left hand extended and the right hand on his hip. When he began walking, the detters standing around him burst out singing, "A pretty girl is like a melody...." On some nights in the Spook mess, the Polish guys, or "Skis," as they called themselves, lined up with linked arms and sang and danced, while doing high kicks like the Radio City Music Hall Rockettes. I recall in particular how Ken Piotrowski, with beer in hand, enjoyed these hijinks with his companions. This was an amazing and amusing sight to newcomers. It was obvious that the detters knew how to work hard and play hard, extracting what merriment they could from being in the war zone.

For newly arrived young officers, especially ensigns, there was the deep six initiation. This involved throwing the officer into a mud puddle and then rolling him in sand. I believe that both officers and enlisted men participated in this initiation. Soon after his arrival Ensign Robert Gordon, nicknamed Flash Gordon, experienced the deep six ritual. I did not participate in his initiation, but I recall seeing him covered in sand with his hair in disarray and his glasses awry on his face as he came up to the Spook mess one evening after being deep sixed. He was a good-natured young officer who took the initiation like a sport, and as a result, the men liked him. Many years later Mr. Gordon informed me that he was a Mustang, an enlisted man before being commissioned as an officer, and that he had previously served on a submarine.

I recall joking with one of the new young officer evaluators. Before going up on mission in the morning, we would gather in the work building to review information we might need to know about what had happened overnight. The officer assigned as evaluator of the radio and electronic positions received a satchel that contained reports that were called frags, or fragmented accounts of air activity over the North. I recall handing the reports to the courteous young officer and telling him that there was a frag for him in the satchel. This, of course, was an allusion to another kind of frag, namely, attempts by soldiers to frag their supervising officers or NCOs, in other words, to blow them up with a hand grenade or shoot them and make it seem this had occurred as a result of enemy action. The officer knew that I was joking, but fragging was a serious concern of the military during the war. In fact, we heard that a Marine officer stationed at the other end of the cantonment where our detachment was located had been fragged. I do not recall if the officer died as a result of the incident.

Night Patrol

Members of our detachment stood bunker watches near our work building, but we did not go out on night patrols. Marines quartered at the north end of our cantonment, however, went out on patrol every evening. I sometimes saw trucks passing out the gate with the men sitting in the rear on benches along the sides. Through the open slats in the wall of the truck bed they all looked the same, like olive-colored clones wearing helmets and flak jackets with the muzzles of their M16s pointing towards the sky. Throughout the night star shells floated over rice paddies in the direction of the mountains behind the base. Choppers scurried urgently over the dark countryside, disturbing the fetid air with their heavily beating blades. Occasionally, a red tracer shot arched upwards against the stars, and there was a brief sound of M16 fire far away in the immense Oriental night.

At breakfast we saw them in the mess hall standing in line, dog-tired and muddy. They had metamorphosed back into individual human beings. Once more they were smooth-faced young men with red eyes and tousled hair, half-heartedly joking with the Vietnamese serving women, whom they addressed as "Mamasan." Occasionally, though, one of the men would say something that the serving women did not like. I saw one of them throw a serving spoon at a Marine.

A petite middle-aged woman wiped down the tables where I and other detters ate. She was obviously out of place there, but the deprivations of war made it necessary for her to work in the mess hall. She was a respectable, quiet-spoken woman who should have been in a nice home surrounded by her children. My friends and I spoke in a respectful way to her in Vietnamese, addressing her as "Thưa bà." Whenever she was on duty, she stopped by our table and conversed briefly with us. Once she said that she appreciated our talk with her because we were not like some others, glancing in the direction of the men standing in the chow line. My heart went out to this woman and others like her who worked on the base. They, like us, were trapped by the war, but our tour of duty would end after a short time while they faced a difficult and uncertain future. Many of them had lost family members. A middle-aged woman who cleaned our barracks told me that the VC had killed her husband. She had suffered much, yet she worked and endured and at the same time kept a quiet, respectful demeanor towards others. I wished there had been something I could do for this woman and the others like her. All I could do, though, was listen and reply with kind words.

CHAPTER 12

Vignettes

After being in Da Nang for several months, I had flown many missions, and sometimes I just wanted to get away from the war, from the stress of flying almost daily in potentially dangerous situations. I longed for some place peaceful—the beach at San Miguel, the fields of the Old Merritt place where I had lived as a child, my parents' living room on a typical night, any peaceful place, even the steps of the det barracks in the morning sunshine. But every day we had to go out and do our duty. In thinking about this years later, I remembered a particular day when I had this kind of longing.

As I recall, I walked out to the flight line with two or three other members of the crew. It was a bright, windy noon with small, ragged clouds floating across the sky. Our baggy flight suits flapped in the breeze. The airfield was unusually quiet; only a single F-4 with its brown and olive camouflage taxied on the other side. The huge antennae on the side of Monkey Mountain stood out against the misty blue slope behind them, pointing their white dishes at the sky like broken mushrooms. They were unreal in the Oriental noon that seemed tranquil and domestic, with fried rice and boiled fish being served in a thousand hooches behind the base. Somewhere out there across the jumble of rusting CONEX units and the tangle of concertina wire lining roads, palm fronds were turning languidly in the breeze beside a garden wall, and an old woman in a conical hat and a silk blouse was trotting quickly homeward beneath a shoulder yoke with two water buckets sloshing on either side.

But I realized that this illusory tranquility with its small beauties was not for me. Ahead, backed into its corrugated revetment, the P-3 loomed in stark black and white like a huge bird of prey. The large four-bladed propellers tipped with red stood with awesome immobility. The crewmembers and I passed around the wing tip and ascended the narrow ladder. I paused on the top step to take one final glance at the jagged blue mountains in the distance, the column of smoke from the rubbish heap at the end of the field, and the shadow of the P-3's wing on the tarmac. I turned and went quickly into the dark interior of the fuselage and took a seat at my ditching station.

Sometimes after spending the first part of the night translating tapes in the det office, I had some time to myself before going to bed. Usually, I sat on the steps of the barracks with a Coke in one hand and a warm can of Hungarian goulash in the other, eating and drinking greedily, not for the food but for the time of quietness allotted for enjoying such simple pleasures. As I ate, I stared across the orange and blue lights of the airfield and thought of home, wondering what my mother and father might be doing.

I remember one such evening. It was quiet, except for the barking of a dog down the line of dark barracks in the compound. I could see the tips of cigarettes where other men were enjoying the quietness before going to bed. The lights on Monkey Mountain shimmered against the night. They seemed to float in space above the brightly illumined base on one side and the black emptiness of the South China Sea on the other. A profound longing and sadness welled up inside me.

An F-4 streaked along the runway, deceptively quiet at first, peaking to an ear-splitting roar, its sound washing against me like ocean waves. The afterburners glowed blue, like the flames of a Bunsen burner, and the plane lifted abruptly from the field at a sharp angle. The wingman quickly followed. The sound echoed off the aluminum buildings and wooden barracks with a reverberating roar and an undertone of hissing, as if a sandstorm were blowing against the walls. The fighter bombers became two orange points against the night. They turned smoothly to the right and back again, heading due north. The afterburners went out, and there was only the sustained roar, gradually diminishing, rumbling between the mountains and the sea that embraced Da Nang.

Then the night was still again with puffs of wind like gentle fingertips touching me on my face, neck, and hands. My hair lifted in the breeze, and suddenly, it was good to be a young man, eating Hungarian goulash, musing on the imponderable, unutterable things waiting out there in the night in the mountains behind the base and in the sky, where a few stars twinkled coldly. I even felt ready to fly again in the morning, but that night it was good simply to sit and listen to the barking dog.

Another occasion. It is a little before midnight, and some detters sit on the second-floor landing of the steps at the front of the barracks. Some sit on the bench, some on the steps, and others on the porch rail, talking quietly while smoking or drinking a beer. F-4 jets occasionally roar down the runway with their afterburners on. We watch as they lift off, fast and low, and then follow the tail flames arching to the left, finally fading as they climb. Dark figures pass along the sidewalk below, VQ-1 men returning from the hangars to the barracks, tired and weary, ready to have a quick beer and then go to bed. Frogs croak in the ditch out back. A star shell lights up and floats languidly over the south end of the airfield. A dog down the line of barracks barks, and then all is quiet, except for the frogs.

The men talk. "That's goooood," drawn out by one of my friends in response to something said. "That's what I want to do. I don't know, maybe return to Utah for a month and then visit a friend in Maine."

"So you're not going to go to the university in Manila after all?"

"I don't know; I might. It's just that back home in the World.... Christ! That place is so uptight. I could easily see living for a while in the P.I."

"Things are tight, all right," Barney remarks.

"How tight are they, Barney?"

"Tighter than a frog's ass, and friends, that's water-tight."

One of the approaching figures turns off the sidewalk and climbs the stairs. A detter greets him: "Well, if it isn't Baby Pooh!"

"Of the world's most powerful nuclear navy!"

Shane joins us, clomping up the steps in his flight boots. "Guys, I thought you would be out seeing some action, and here you are just sitting around like a bunch of old maids complaining about the mosquitoes."

"Where the hell you gonna get any action around here?" Barney asks. "It's scarce, friend, mighty scarce, scarcer than lips in a poultry house."

"Christ, Barney! You come out with some!"

Barney flips a cigarette onto the sidewalk, and it breaks into a dozen sparks and dies.

"Think we'll get hit tonight?" Shane asks.

"Might," Barney replies. "It's overdue, that's for sure. It's almost three weeks now, and it's early Monday morning, one of their favorite times to lob them in."

Shane steps inside the Spook Mess for a beer. A bell clangs, and a huge whoop goes up.

"Free beers for everybody! Shane forgot to take off his cover at the bar!"

"Freaking A!"

"Shane, you guppied into that one!"

"There it is!"

"All right, guys," Shane says. "Beer for everyone on me. Sarge, put it on my tab."

Shane takes it like a sport, and someone inside passes bottles of San Miguel spilling with foam to the men on the porch.

An F-4 revs its engines and then streaks down the runway with a deafening roar. After the noise fades, I hear a helicopter chopping its way across the base in the direction of Freedom Hill. The frogs continue to croak.

Sarge (Bayne) liked to rib me. One evening I walked into the Spook mess, remembering first to remove my cap. Sarge was sitting on a stool at the bar. At my entrance he twirled around and said, "Shippey, you're going to have to behave yourself. This is a nice, clean bar, see, and we don't want any trouble, see, or we'll have to call the bouncer. No cussing, spitting, or fighting, see." He always kept us entertained. Sarge was a true artist in the way he ran the mess. There was never a lack of supplies behind the bar or in the fridge. He occasionally rounded up those of us who did not smoke or drink, or drank only occasionally, and took us to one of the exchanges so that he could use our ration cards to stock the mess with cigarettes, beer, and liquor. I recall riding in the back of the det truck with Sarge to the exchange near Freedom Hill. We returned with the truck bed loaded to the gunwales. Quite likely, he is the one who arranged for a flight by one of our planes to bring the detachment a load of San Miguel beer from the Philippines. I remember helping to carry the boxes from the truck to the mess upstairs. He was the master in charge of the amazing detachment Christmas celebration in 1971. More about that later. Occasionally, he arranged for a stag movie to be shown in the mess. I did not attend these movies, but I remember glimpsing one as I passed through on the way to the area back of the mess. Sarge was standing up front, making comments. There were occasionally other movies. I suppose it was Sarge who arranged for a screen to be set up in front of the barracks one night so that we could watch *Tora!, Tora!, Tora!* Although I had previously seen this movie about the Japanese attack on Pearl Harbor, I watched it again with great interest from the perspective of one who had been on many flight missions. I also think Sarge had something to do with the performance of an all-girl Korean band one evening in the Spook mess. I do not know what he did during the rest of his career in the Navy, but he would have made a great manager and host for some exclusive club, although his down-to-earth sense of humor might have been a drawback. Sometimes, though, people who are members of such clubs appreciate a man who does not put on airs but instead jokes and creates an atmosphere of bonhomie. Sarge would probably have made fun of me for using that last word.

PO1 Haley displeased some men in the detachment because of remarks he sometimes made. These men also had some issues with him concerning his administrative work for the det, but I never had any problems with Haley. In fact, he spoke pleasantly to me whenever we met or had occasion to talk. My chief memory of him relates to an event that occurred one evening in the work building. A few other men and I were working on sorting and translating tapes when Haley walked by us from the administrative office, carrying a Colt 45 in his hand. He headed for the door and told us that, if we heard a shot when he got outside, it would be because he was clearing a round stuck in the chamber. Suddenly, a loud bang made all of us jump. The pistol had fired before he reached the door. Fortunately, the barrel was angled downwards, and the shot went through the bottom half of the door. Later that night a new entry appeared in the detachment quote book, which was a loose-leaf notebook filled with numerous entries about humorous sayings and interesting events in the detachment. As best I recall, the entry read as follows: "Take that, you blankety blank door! Funeral services for the front door will be held tomorrow at 10:00 a.m."

Hal Gamble's room was on the ground floor at the back of the barracks. It was a favorite gathering place because Hal had a good sense of humor and often sat on his bunk strumming on his guitar, talking about his girl back in the world. His tour of duty in Da Nang was growing short, and there were various jokes about being short. I remember during a gathering in his room one evening Hal said, "I'm getting short, guys; I'm getting short! In fact, I'm so short I can sit on a dime and have room to swing my legs." One afternoon someone looked into Hal's room and saw him walking around in a circle carrying a duffle bag and asked him what he was doing. "Practicing," Hal replied. "Just practicing."

Sometimes at night I stood on the back steps of the barracks and listened to the sound of out-going artillery fire. First, there was the heavy thump of the shot, followed in two or three seconds by a flash in the hills behind the base, an orange flower silently blossoming against the night sky. In looking at these explosions, I thought of *Les Fleurs du Mal*, a collection of poems by the nineteenth-century French poet Charles Baudelaire. These were true flowers of evil for the VC entrenched in the hills. Following the flash, there were a few seconds of silence and then the rumbling report, like distant thunder. After the report silence again rushed in to fill the vacuum left by the shot, until the next thump of out-going fire. The process seemed unreal, a surreal drama, a grim strophe and antistrophe in the darkness beyond Freedom Hill. Finally, the firing ceased, and there was only the mystery of the Vietnamese night, the base and the shanty village of Dogpatch behind it sweltering in the fetid air beneath an overcast sky. The hills and valleys beyond the base perimeter seemed to be waiting, suspending breath in an agony of unending suspense, the expected cataclysm still not arriving. Anything would have been a relief—a flash of lightning, a thunderstorm with rushing wind and rain squalls—anything, even a rocket attack.

CHAPTER 13

Rocket Attacks

And eventually there was another rocket attack. We had about a dozen attacks while I was in Da Nang, some on a distant part of the base or one of the outlying areas of the surrounding city and some that were uncomfortably close. For excitement nothing that I had previously experienced could match a Viet Cong rocket attack, and the position of the detachment barracks near the tarmac and taxi strip made us a prime target. I developed the habit of staying up late, rarely going to bed before 2:00 a.m. because, if they were going to hit us, it would likely be before that time. I was nervous sometimes about the possibility of a hit. When I lay down on my bunk at night, I wondered if we might have a direct hit. If that happened, I realized I might be crushed by the pool table crashing down on me from the Spook mess upstairs. The irony of possibly dying that way produced a grim sense of humor. Strangely, if things were quiet for too long, I began almost to wish for a rocket attack, something to break the monotony and liven things up. Every evening when I returned from the head after showering and brushing my teeth, I passed by the dark line of unpainted barracks looming over me as I plodded along in my flip-flops. Their pointed gables pointed ominously towards the night sky, and I wondered, "Tonight?"

I waited each night, expecting an attack, and inevitably it came when I had given up thinking about it, say on a Sunday evening when I sat at the bar in the Spook mess pouring a coke over a cup of ice. Suddenly, *KA-WHOOM*, with a vibrating concussion, followed by wailing sirens, and someone in the mess yelling, "Holy Christ! Incoming! Let's go!" The sound of feet moving towards the door and then the door open and a flash of light with a cracking explosion, shaking the barracks so that even the nails seemed ready to pop out of the boards. All of us momentarily confused, not knowing whether to stay inside or run for the bunker, afraid of red-hot shrapnel flying through the air, the sudden sting and stunned awareness that you were hit, my God hit, or the near miss smashing into the boards, throwing splinters past your head. Then another *KA-WHOOM*, the siren wailing all the time—me expecting death any second, seeing nothing,

Det Bravo barracks where the Big Look Spooks and VQ-1 were quartered at Da Nang Air Base. This is an early photograph of the compound. The barracks were heavily damaged in the July 15, 1967, rocket attack and had to be rebuilt. In his history of the detachment, Robert Morrison states that the damage was not done by a direct rocket hit but by the explosion of a nearby ammo dump. The new barracks eventually had a double row of sand-filled metal barrels around the ground floor to protect them from shrapnel by rocket explosions. Also, larger, more substantial bunkers were built between the barracks (photograph by Aron Cook).

hearing nothing, knowing nothing, except the explosions. Deciding to run, stumbling down rather than descending the stairs, maybe twisting an ankle, arriving at the bunker entrance, everyone shoving, yelling, "Hurry up! For Christ's sakes, get in!"

Then we all sat silently, ranged along the benches, the beams of the bunker overhead, bare light bulbs suspended from them, gravel underfoot. Some men wearing nothing but their skivvies, some in trousers only, someone soapy and wet from the shower with a towel around his middle, one guy in a flak jacket and a helmet, all of us just sitting, breathing hard, slapping at mosquitoes, looking at the ground and listening to the booms still going further down the field. Like a South Georgia thunderstorm passing overhead, I thought. Then everybody is relieved, and we laugh and joke, telling where we were when we heard the first rocket hit. One guy is wet with beer he spilled all over himself, and another sits, calmly smoking a cigar, still holding his poker cards and claiming he had the best hand he'd ever been dealt right before the first one hit.

Bunker between the Spooks barracks and the VQ-1 barracks, Da Nang Air Base, 1970–1971. Several times while I was in Da Nang, we ran to this bunker. Sometimes VQ-1 men with M16s stood guard at either entrance in case of a ground attack (photograph by Bill Dillon).

Indeed, there was nothing like a rocket attack for excitement. After an attack I felt keenly alive and glad to be alive but looked forward to one day returning to the world, where I could sleep easy at night with no explosions and no sirens, except maybe for an ambulance or a fire truck in the distance.

While I was at Da Nang, none of the men in the detachment was killed or injured, but some on the base were not so fortunate. One night we ran to the bunker, even though the hits were not close by. After the all-clear, we emerged and saw flames shooting up from the Air Force compound on the other side of the field and knew that some significant damage had been done. The next day I was in the work building when Mr. Purring returned from a visit to the Air Force side of the base. He said that a rocket had made a direct hit on a barracks and killed some men. He mentioned seeing a burned torso in a flak jacket.

One evening Danny Scoggins and I were listening to reconnaissance tapes in the work building. We wore earphones and replayed parts of the tapes that were difficult to hear, rewinding the tapes frequently and typing our translations onto the multi-ply paper in our typewriters. I heard something like a distant thud and removed my earphones. I looked at Scoggins and said, "You know…. That sounded like it might be a rocket." Suddenly, there was a thundering explosion that shook the whole building. We nodded at each other and both exclaimed, "Yep! Rocket attack," and dove under the table. Several loud explosions followed. Fortunately, nothing in our compound was damaged, although it sounded as if one of the rockets exploded on the airfield not far from our building. After I had left Da Nang, I heard that one of our guys was on bunker watch at Fire Point 13 one night when an attack occurred. According to what I remember, he stepped to the side of the bunker to urinate while drinking a cup of coffee. At that point a rocket hit nearby, and he threw the coffee cup into the air, diving for the bunker. He was not injured but never found the cup.

One night I went to a head that was a little further from the barracks than the one I usually used. On this evening I wanted a little more privacy since I needed to sit on the john. I finished, flushed the commode, and walked to the door ready to return to the barracks. At that instant, I saw an orange flash to the north and west of our work building. There was a loud cracking report followed by other explosions. Rocket attack! I considered running to the nearby bunker, but the explosions were coming so fast that I realized I might be safer remaining in the head. I crouched down among the toilets, which offered some protection from shrapnel that might penetrate the wall if a hit occurred nearby. I thought, "How ironic. Maybe to die while hugging the white porcelain of one of the toilets." I recalled the chief who had been injured while sitting on the toilet during an attack shortly after my arrival in Da Nang.

When I began my duty at Da Nang, I at first wore contact lenses, but after a rocket attack or two, I returned to wearing glasses. There was no time to insert contacts during a rocket attack. It was easy to reach for my glasses on the shelf above my bunk, grab my trousers hanging at the end of the bunk, and run, still in my skivvies, for the bunker. One night during an attack I did this, but my wallet fell out of my pants pocket. I squatted down and fumbled for the wallet in the dark, and my ration card and MACV card, along with other papers, fell onto the floor. I was trying to gather them up but heard bare feet rapidly approaching and realized I was about to be trampled by other men running for the bunker. I left my cards and papers and retreated, pants in hand, ahead of the oncoming feet. After the attack I returned and gathered up what I had dropped. I prided myself on my fleetness of foot in running for the bunker, but I was outdone by our mascot dogs, Spook and Beggar, who had learned to run fast whenever we ran.

The base had a radar system that was supposed to detect incoming rockets and sound a warning siren, but most of the time the first warning of an attack was an explosion followed by the wailing siren. Several nights while I was at Da Nang I was awakened by the sound of distant explosions.

Sometimes they seemed to be walking towards us, like a giant stomping his way up the airfield. If I was in the barracks, I took cover in the bunker. Sometimes VQ-1 men stood guard with M16 rifles at the two entrances in case the rocket attack was accompanied by a ground attack. There was always the possibility that sappers could have broken through the perimeters. Some men who had been at Da Nang for a long time took a fatalistic approach and did not bother to get out of bed and go to the bunker. They reasoned that, if it was not their time, they would be ok, and if it was their time, running for cover would not help.

Our barracks was surrounded by a row of metal drums filled with sand to serve as a barrier against shrapnel from rocket or mortar attacks. At first there was only one level of barrels, but one day I worked with other guys in the det to fill a second level of oil drums with sand. That was hot, gritty work. Some men worked with their shirts off, and I could hear the clinking of dog tags as we scooped the sand and shoveled it into the top drums. Drops of sweat tickled as they ran down my torso. A few men complained about the heat, but to me it seemed no worse than the hot, humid days of South Georgia that I was accustomed to. After that extra level of shrapnel drums was added, I felt a bit more secure when I lay down at night. The disadvantage of that additional row of protection was that, when Typhoon Hester struck the base in October 1971, the wind picked up the sand from the top of the barrels and slung it through the screens, plastering the walls of our rooms and covering our bunks with wet grit.

At the beginning of 1972, shortly before my tour in Da Nang ended, Bob Morrison was my roommate for a while. I recall that he was reading J.R.R. Tolkien's *Lord of the Rings.* I realized that I too wanted to read the trilogy, but nearly forty years passed before I finally read it in a marathon reading session. Then I regretted having deprived myself of this treat for so many years. Bob put up a mosquito net around his bunk, but this was a luxury I decided to forego because during a rocket attack lifting the net and disentangling myself from it delayed me in running for the bunker. While Bob was rooming with me, the base was hit by another rocket attack. One of the rockets hit nearby in our cantonment. The next morning, we went to examine the crater, which was across the street from our mess hall. The hole the rocket had made was about two yards wide and two feet deep. On the pavement next to the crater was a bloodstain, showing that someone had been injured or killed by the explosion. We stepped down into the hole for a closer look and found a piece of shrapnel. Merely touching the sharp end of that piece of metal with the tip of the finger was painful. I could not imagine the damage of hundreds of pieces of such shrapnel ripping through human flesh when a rocket exploded. Many years later Bob wrote on the *Big Look Spooks* website that he kept the piece of shrapnel for a long time but

Rocket damage to the bunker between the Spooks barracks and the VQ-1 barracks, Da Nang Air Base, 1972. The rocket did not explode. Fortunately, no one was killed, but one VQ-1 member was injured (photograph Max Mercer).

eventually lost it. He also wrote an excellent history of the detachment that included reminiscences by men who served with Det Bravo.

Towards the end of 1972, after I had left the detachment, rocket attacks increased. On December 26 of that year a rocket struck in front of the Spooks and VQ-1 barracks, overturning the det truck and creating a huge hole that was large enough for several men to stand in at the same time. A dud also struck the bunker between the two barracks, knocking part of it down, and throwing some shrapnel through the ground floor of the VQ-1 barracks, injuring one man. Fortunately, no one in the det or VQ-1 was killed during these attacks.

Nothing brings reality into focus more clearly than the realization that you might die at any moment. That was what I comprehended clearly as a result of the rocket attacks I experienced in Da Nang. I realized that life is complicated, filled with all kinds of problems and contradictions, but at the same time beautiful and precious. I realized that awareness of death prompts awareness of beauty and meaning in life. These experiences reaffirmed what I already understood as a follower of Christ.

CHAPTER 14

Typhoons

Looking back after nearly fifty years, I cannot recall many details about typhoons that struck the Philippines and South Vietnam during the time I was there. If I remember correctly, I experienced four typhoons during the 1971 season, two in the Philippines and two at Da Nang. One of the latter, I can identify as Hester because it was so destructive. I do not, however, know the names of the other three.

I returned to San Miguel from SERE training in late August. I wanted to go on to Da Nang to resume my duties, but there was a delay of about two months because the officers in charge of the Fleet Support Detachment were considering at that time possibly discontinuing reconnaissance flights out of Da Nang and basing them instead on aircraft carriers. This latter possibility worried me because this option seemed more dangerous than flying from the airbase at Da Nang. At any rate, I could not immediately return to Da Nang. During those two months, at least two typhoons crossed over or near Luzon. I kept a journal sporadically, and below is an edited version of what I wrote on October 6 about the typhoon passing somewhere near San Miguel:

> Today, a typhoon passing over the Philippines has dominated my thoughts. Rather, the waves created by it have occupied my attention. Three times today I went down to the beach to stare in amazement at the sea. The waves were coming in at a furious pace, ten or fifteen feet high, curling far out with foam moving along the crests, throwing off streamers of white spray up and sideways like the mane of a wild stallion flying in the wind. Near the beach the water was all churning, moiling foam, one layer scudding in on top of another layer. The whole sea as far out as I could observe was tossing and heaving towards the sky. Occasionally, rain drove in hard gusts and obscured everything except the crashing foam. In the distance the waves looked frightening, as though they would easily come in over the shore and inundate the station. For a while this morning, the sun was out, and mist from the waves created a rainbow low over the beach.

While I stood on the beach observing the crashing waves, the mist in the air clouded my glasses and left a taste of salt on my lips. I do not recall that the typhoon did any damage to the communications station, but it was, never-theless, impressive.

On another occasion that fall, I went to the beach to see the effect of a typhoon passing nearby. That afternoon the waves were heaving and toss-ing as before. I noticed a freighter a little way out headed towards the larg-est of the Capones Islands. The pilot realized the danger and turned hard to starboard, heading straight out into the West Philippine Sea. I remember seeing the stern of the ship rocking back and forth as it moved away from the land.

During the rainy season in the Philippines, I wrote to Judy Shippey, a cousin, telling her that the rain did not come down in buckets but in wash-tubs. At home in South Georgia, we sometimes had heavy rain, but it was not so prolonged as the torrential downpours in the P.I. I bought umbrellas from the exchange to avoid getting soaking wet, especially when I walked from the barracks to the chow hall, but sometimes when I went to retrieve my umbrella, left near the door while I ate, I discovered that someone had taken it. It is interesting that someone who would perhaps not steal your wallet would, nevertheless, take your umbrella if it is raining. I bought white shoe polish and put designs on my new black umbrella to mark it clearly, but it too was taken by some sailor desperate not to get soaked.

Towards the middle of October, I was finally able to return to Da Nang. It was a bit strange. In stepping onto the tarmac at the Fifteenth Air Termi-nal, I was glad to be back. It seemed almost like coming home. I returned to flight duty, and I remember one day aboard the P-3 when a typhoon was passing somewhere close by. The plane yawed back and forth. While I sat at my position with earphones on, I kept rolling back and forth and sideways with the motion of the plane. For some reason I was not afraid. The rocking of the P-3 was somewhat soothing. After being on station for a while over the Gulf of Tonkin, we were ordered to return to base.

On October 23 one of the most damaging typhoons to hit Vietnam passed over Da Nang and Hue. From accounts on the web, I learned that this was Typhoon Hester. Many of the aircraft were evacuated ahead of the storm, but most of the men remained. The day Hester hit I was duty driver. I remember that the wooden covering on the back of the truck was bang-ing up and down in the wind and about to blow off. Several of the guys came out from the work building, and we tore the structure off. As I drove down the street by the hangars towards our barracks, pieces of tin twirled through the air like frisbees. At the barracks the wind was ripping tin off the roof, and men were up there placing sandbags on the sheets. Some of us filled the bags and handed them up to the guys on the roof. Wearing my poncho, I joined the line of men carrying sandbags to one of the detters on a ladder, who in turned passed the bags to men on the roof. The rain was coming down sideways and stinging when it hit my face. The wind must have been gusting at a hundred miles per hour or more, and we had to lean into the wind to walk. Several inches of water flooded the ground floor of the barracks. While standing at the back door of the barracks, I saw the wind collapse a vehicle repair shed across the road. Some of the barracks in our compound had most of the tin blown off the roof, but thanks to the hard work of our men, the roof of our barracks remained largely intact. At one barracks down the line, the upper floor was torn loose and twisted around over the lower floor. Planks were blown away on some of the other barracks, and part of the roof had caved in. Sand from the top of the metal drums that surrounded our barracks as a protection from shrapnel of rocket explosions was blown through the screen windows and plastered the walls and bunk covers. After the typhoon had blown over, I walked around the compound taking photos of the damage with my Asahi Pentax camera, but the camera was new, and I had not secured the film properly to roll on the spools. As a result, I lost the photos.

After the typhoon had passed, I had an opportunity to visit China Beach. The sea was dirty, and limbs and tree branches were being cast onto the beach by the waves. We were fortunate that the storm did not take any lives on the base, but the Vietnamese people along the coast were not so lucky. I wondered how much damage was done to the ramshackle hooches in which many people lived in the areas surrounding the base. Many people were refugees from their homes, cast up by the storms of war around the presumed safety of the area near the American airbase. They built their makeshift shelters out of whatever was available, including tin, packing crates, cardboard, random pieces of lumber, and cement blocks. Old tires were sometimes stacked in front of the dwellings to serve as a barrier to protect the inhabitants from the shrapnel of rocket attacks. When we drove through these areas, my heart went out to the people. I saw children standing at the doorways of these structures scooping rice out of a bowl into their mouths with chopsticks. Elderly women wearing their conical hats sat in the doorways, their mouths black from chewing betel nut. Garbage strewed the roadside. In places wooden stands covered with canvas were set up to serve as open-air markets. Scooters and bikes crowded the road. Even though I wanted to identify with the local people, I knew that there was always the danger of a thrown hand grenade or a sniper attack, so I kept a sharp lookout as we passed through these village areas. The duty driver was issued a Colt 45 pistol. I felt a bit foolish wearing the weapon since I had never been a gun fancier, but I strapped the holster for the 45 to my thigh, realizing I might need the protection. I wondered what family and friends back home would think if they saw me—Shippey, the "war hero." Yeah, right!

Repairing the roof of the Spooks barracks after the October 1971 typhoon. Left to right: Mick Schwartz on the ladder, Ken Piotrowski below him, and Robert Sluter near the door. The typhoon heavily damaged some barracks, but the men of the detachment minimized the damage to our barracks by placing sandbags on the roof (photograph by Tim Yerdon).

Flights Diverted to Thailand

Sometimes when we returned from a mission in the A-3, we could not land at Da Nang, perhaps because a crash had occurred on the field, bad weather was passing through, or the controllers were just too busy with air traffic to take us. On those occasions we diverted to a base in Thailand. I recorded one of these diversions in my journal. I cannot recall which air base it was, perhaps the one at Udorn. When we landed, it was a beautiful day with a blue sky, different from the cloudy weather at Da Nang during the rainy season. Our pilot taxied to a temporary parking apron at the side of the runway. F-4 Phantoms used this small stretch of concrete to release their drag chute after landing. An Air Force ground crewman made sweeping motions with his arms towards our parking position. The strong wind blowing across the field made his uniform cling to his body and reveal its shape as if he had been soaked in water.

Our pilot pulled the A-3 into position, and the hatch below me opened. Sitting right behind the pilot in the canopy, I watched his gloved hand on the thrust lever, listening to the high-pitched whining of the engines, waiting impatiently for him to pull it back to kill the engines so that I could climb out and savor the warm sunshine that I had not enjoyed now for many weeks. Outside I carefully removed my helmet, with some difficulty as usual, hurting my ears as I pulled it off. Then I stepped out of my torso harness and took off my flight gloves, relishing the freedom of having on nothing but my flight suit and the olive-green uniform beneath it.

We had to re-pack our own drag chute into its canvas casing. I did not know how, but I helped the VQ-1 crewmembers as much as possible. First, we secured the tip of the chute beneath one of the wheels to hold it while we untwisted the cords. Then gradually we pulled in the straps, folding them back and forth on themselves into the bag, fastening each fold with snaps, which would automatically undo the next time the chute was released. We simply folded up the silk any way and packed it in by sitting on it and bouncing up and down. The cloth was dirty gray from long use and was frayed all over. One of the VQ-1 guys lay down on his back beneath the chute recess in the tail and pushed the pack into the slot with his feet after securing it. Then he simply closed the two small doors over it, leaving a piece of the silk sticking out through the crack, but that did not affect the effectiveness of the chute.

During all of this time, F-4s continually taxied up and parked briefly while a ground crewman checked the aircraft and then motioned the pilots to continue to the tarmac. The jets came rolling up with a tremendous rumbling sound, like a volcano preparing to erupt. The twin tailpipes issued a trail of hot smoke and gaseous fumes that made the buildings and palm trees on the opposite side of the field dance and shimmer in a haze. The canopies for the pilot and his radar man were both raised on hinges, and the two men pulled off their oxygen masks at this point. The pilot gave a slight blast with the engines, and the yellow, slitted drag chute, extended in full blossom behind the jet, suddenly released and blew to the rear, crumpling into a limp piece of silk skimming across the concrete while a man chased after it, retrieved it, and hastily folded it into his arms.

Jets took off continually, roaring almost directly over us, and we had to put our fingers in our ears. I watched each plane as it passed overhead and swooped into the sky, the orange fire in its twin exhausts twirling round and round, propelling the jet out of sight towards its target in North Vietnam.

Our pilot stepped to the edge of the concrete and urinated, and I did the same, watching the red clay darken in the spot where the urine fell. A

EA-3B with the drag shoot open after it had landed. The pilot had already folded the tail and the wings (upper left of the photograph) as the plane taxied to the VQ-1 tarmac. These procedures are necessary for planes based on aircraft carriers, where space is limited. This photograph was taken from an open hatch above the TacAir position in the cockpit. The dark spot in the foreground is an air vent for cooling the interior of the fuselage. Da Nang Air Base, 1972 (photograph by David Gilbert).

wave of homesickness passed over me because this clay reminded me so much of the red clay of Georgia, now thousands of miles away on the other side of the earth. The wind stirred the palm trees lining the fence, and stepping-stone clouds floated across the blue sky. I realized it was the wee hours of the morning back home.

We sat down by the nose of our plane and waited for the Air Force crew to bring a fuel truck and a huffer so that we could be on our way back to Da Nang. The lieutenant JG evaluator sat on the top of the plane by the overhead hatch with his legs crossed. The sun moved slowly down the sky, and finally, a yellow fuel truck detached itself from the buildings in the distance and headed our way.

On another occasion we diverted in the P-3 to U-Tapao, a Thai airfield, used by the U.S. Air Force during the war. As we approached the field, I could see several B-52s lined up along the tarmac. This was obviously where some of the Arc Lights that bombed the Ho Chi Minh Trail were based. We went to a hotel in town to spend the night. This was my first visit to Thailand, and I regretted that there was no time for sightseeing. That evening I went down to the hotel restaurant and, while eating, listened to background music playing on the radio. The music and what I could see of the town seemed to be heavily influenced by Indian culture. Stepping outside, I was entranced by the warm oriental night and the exotic odors and again wished we could stay longer. The next morning on the van back to the air base, we passed along narrow streets. It was early, and Buddhist monks dressed in their saffron robes and sandals were out begging for their breakfast at the food stalls and shops in the market. Each one carried a small iron pot for the food. I later understood that, according to their religion, the people giving food to the monks acquired merit for this benevolent act.

Another night we again diverted to Thailand, landing this time at Ubon. I remember folding my dirty blue cap into the leg pocket of my flight suit as we passed through the lobby of the hotel where we spent the night. Once in my room, I stripped down to my boxer shorts and then noticed myself in the mirror, the first time I had had an opportunity to do this in some time. I was appalled at how much weight I had lost. My ribs clearly showed, and my face was thin and haggard. The constant tension and difficulty I had experienced eating and swallowing as a result of stress had taken their toll. It was good to sleep in the hotel bed that night and forget about the war for a few hours.

CHAPTER 15

Stress

"Never a dull day in Da Nang" was a true saying. Life moved at a rapid pace with dangerous or exciting events frequently happening. The stress of flying, rocket attacks, jets crash landing or blowing up on takeoff, and just the daily routine of being in a war zone produced stress in one form or another in most of us, and I also experienced it, especially during the rainy season. During this gray period, my days were a succession of hollow-stomached mornings in anticipation of the afternoon and evening flights on the A-3. I was so keyed up that I could not easily swallow food at meals. It seemed to stick in my throat. For weeks I lived off soup, mashed potatoes, beanie-weenies, Hungarian goulash, and cokes. Anything with particles, like rice or the granules of hamburgers, choked me. At breakfast I sometimes started up from the table, spilling my coffee, and ran gasping for air to the entrance of the mess hall to spit out the mass of unswallowable food. On those rainy mornings, I stood outside in the bleak, gray light of dawn, coughing and spitting, cursing to myself in frustration.

I had a row of paperbacks on the windowsill of my room, but at night when I tried to read, the books that had once pleased made me restless. If I sat down to read and try to relax, I became antsy after only a moment and laid the book aside, preferring to sit on the steps of the barracks, watching the jets take off and listening to the talk of friends remembering girls back in the world. I discovered that only Sarah Orne Jewett's *The Country of the Pointed Firs* calmed me, and I read it in small increments, only two or three pages a day—that was all I could endure—taking a month to complete it, although it is a short book. The tranquility of the Maine seacoast village that she described, the lore about garden herbs, and the sturdy but eccentric characters depicted gave me some relief from my anxiety. I still have the book, and Jewett's beautiful writing continues to hold a special place in my affections.

Every morning before a flight, I became anxious, and a strong sense of helplessness came over me. The hollow sensation in my stomach returned, and I seemed to be choking on my own saliva. Sometimes I would clench my teeth and say in angry, hushed words to myself, "One day! Just one lousy day on the ground! Just one time when my name and number do not appear on the flight bill. That's all I ask! One lousy, stinking day!" Then the next day when the CTA posted the flight bill, there was my name again with my social security number stretched out below it like a printed scream.

During this desperate period, I was awakened one night with a flashlight in my face. It was the duty driver. He had come to take me to the workspaces because the A-3 on track had developed a problem and had to return to base. Chief Holt was planning to send a replacement plane on track over Laos in the middle of the night. I assumed Arc Light bombing runs were in progress. When I arrived at the work building, though, I learned that the only A-3 available did not have any working radio receivers at the "I" beat position. At that point I lost it. I exclaimed, "What am I supposed to do? Go up and hang my head out of the cockpit so that I can perhaps hear them coming? Maybe I could toss some rocks at them!" I was angry at being awakened in the middle of the night for an impossible mission. Going up to sit at my position in the A-3 seemed an exercise in futility. After some deliberation, the Chief decided that he would not send a relief plane aloft, and I was able to return to the barracks. Later, I felt abashed about becoming so angry and vocal because the Chief himself was under orders and simply doing what he had to, and I knew him to be a conscientious, fair-minded, good man. But the sustained stress took its toll and made me vocalize what I would ordinarily have kept to myself. The Chief understood these occasions and made allowance for them, cutting us all some slack from time to time while simultaneously upholding standards, and for that I had great respect for him.

During those months it rained endlessly, dripping from the eaves of the barracks in maddening monotony. Everything was damp. The towels mildewed, my underwear was cold and clammy when I put it on each morning, and the paperback books on the window ledge became soggy and warped from the continuous fine mist that drifted through the screen. At night crawling in between the damp sheets on my rack was, to my mind, like lying down inside a live oyster. The rain was never-ending. At midnight the frogs croaked in cacophony in the puddle outside the barracks. I imagined them praying demonically for yet more rain. The tin roof drummed with the steady pour, and ponchos hanging on nails along the hall dripped puddles onto the tile floor. Each morning I awakened to the swish of jeep and truck tires on the wet road behind the barracks. When hardly anyone else was awake, I paced the hall end to end in quiet desperation, pausing at the back door to stare at the ragged clouds that obliterated the mountains behind the base, reducing everything to a uniform grayness. The sky was gray, the rain was gray, the barracks in the compound were a darker shade of gray, I was gray, everything was gray! Grayness was consuming the world.

Then my mind would do a flip-flop. Suddenly, the thought of flying brought relief. At least at thirty-thousand feet in the A-3 there was sunshine, brilliant sunshine pouring into the canopy, blinding in its brilliance as it reflected off the masses of clouds below. And there was blue sky, not this grayness. It would be a consolation to ascend above the rain in the A-3, even if for only four hours, even if I became anxious again there, staring in desperation at my consoles. I was caught like an animal in a trap. Life was a choice between two kinds of despair.

On those mornings I frantically rummaged through the papers on my table, searching for *The Country of the Pointed Firs* again, like a wino digging in the trash for his bottle, and then, finding it, sitting down to read a page or two, waiting for the duty driver to come in the gray truck to take me to the workspaces to get ready for my flight.

The rainy season got to other men, too. I remember Charlie Capes lying one evening in the huge mud puddle beside the entrance to the barracks. He lay there wearing only his skivvies, propped up on his elbows, quietly smoking a cigarette. We could not help but notice him and shake our heads at his odd behavior. He lay there a good part of the evening, and several of the detters who passed by made remarks at his expense. Salkowski, an "I" beat from Chicago, took note of Charlie: "Look! It's the lung fish in the process of evolving, just before it emerges from the water and crawls up onto the land!" Salkowski had the look of a Bolshevik intellectual with his curly hair, thin face, and wire-rimmed glasses. He continued to expatiate on Capes, who paid no attention to him, calmly enjoying his cigarette. I felt for Charlie. He was a good ole' boy from Georgia, stocky with red hair and freckled arms, who loved a good time, and to some extent I felt I understood him, even though our characters were totally different. He was dealing with stress his own way, even though Salkowski joked about his atavistically reverting to an earlier stage of evolutionary development. I admired Charlie's aplomb. Even though we were very different from each other, we had a few things in common other than being from Georgia. We both loved dogs. One night he and I stayed up late, sitting outdoors in folding chairs not far from the mud puddle in which he had reclined, talking about dogs our families had owned. He loved hunting dogs, and so did I, even though I had rarely gone hunting. We both agreed that we had no use for little yappy ankle-biters or spoiled lap dogs wearing jeweled collars. Men's dogs—that's what we admired. We must have talked three or four hours without becoming bored. While working on the manuscript for this book, I learned from Rudy, a friend we had in common, that he had died. My heart became heavy when I read that e-mail, and I grieved for him as I have done for every deceased detter who was with me in Da Nang during those days of stress, depression, anxiety, and hilarious, crazy fun, those days that changed all of our lives forever and left their indelible mark on what we became.

CHAPTER 16

Men of the Fleet Support Detachment

According to the roster for the detachment, 773 men served over the years with Det Bravo in Da Nang. As of July 2019, 155 had passed away, leaving about eighty percent still living, ranging in age from sixty-seven to eighty-four. I do not know the number of men serving in the det during the ten months I was in Da Nang, but at some point, I flew with most of them. I knew all of them by name, but became friends with only a few, although I got along well with everybody. As mentioned elsewhere, we were in some ways like a family. Whenever I was at San Miguel in the Philippines, I also had a chance to get to know other men who were stationed aboard ship in the Gulf of Tonkin or at Phu Bai. A few of these men also spent some time in Da Nang.

Tim Barczak was one of the men I enjoyed talking with while I was at San Miguel. He was married and deplored the fact that some married men in the war zone were unfaithful to their wives. He and I both wondered how these men would feel if they learned that their wives were unfaithful to them while they were away.

Rusty Harrison was one of my roommates in the barracks at Da Nang. He was an "I" beat like me and good at what he did. His family owned a steel plant in a small Indiana town, and his wife, a beautiful woman according to the photos Rusty showed me, regularly sent him care packages, which he shared with me. We often sat up late into the night talking about all kinds of things, Rusty reclining on his bunk with me sitting cross-legged on mine. From his treasure box from home, he took out canned rum babas and Edelweiss cheese and offered some to me. He loved classical music, as did I, and he had a stereo console that was a tape player and a radio. While we snacked on the babas, we listened to Beethoven, Schubert, Tchaikovsky, and Chopin. We both enjoyed good literature and discussed some of our favorite authors. We also both liked art, and I told him about visiting the galleries in Washington and New York. To decorate our room, he ordered canvas prints of great works. Two that we stuck on the walls were Vincent Van Gogh's *Starry Night* and Claude Monet's *Field of Poppies*, showing a woman with a parasol and a little girl beside her at the bottom of a hill covered with red poppies. These prints, like the paperbacks on the window ledge and the classical tapes, were our tenuous link with civilized life back home. How strange these artifacts often seemed in the midst of Da Nang, a giant machine dedicated to war.

Rusty's tour was up before mine, and when he departed, he left the stereo set and the tapes. I played Joseph Haydn's *London Symphony*, and remembered Rusty, thinking about him back in the states with his wife and small son, stationed at Fort Meade, Maryland. Many a night I listened to AFVN radio and thought nostalgically of my mother and father and our little house on Gordon Avenue in Albany. When they sent me tapes, I played them on the recorder that Rusty had left. I recall one in which my father told me how much they missed me and how they wished me a safe return. On that particular tape, my father forgot to turn the recorder off for several minutes, and I listened to the sounds of an ordinary evening at home—my mother washing the supper dishes in the kitchen sink, the TV in the background, the telephone ringing, and my father talking about a floor sanding job he was going to the next day, until he finally noticed the recorder was on and clicked it off. The message that they sent me was wonderful, but how precious were those ordinary sounds of home. Listening to them made my heart ache. I realized how valuable are those days of ordinary life that pass, for the most part, unnoticed and unappreciated, until we no longer have them, a truth that has especially been brought home to me in the years after the death of my parents. Because of Rusty's gift, I enjoyed these tapes from home and the classical music.

Sometimes late at night I tuned into a radio station from North Vietnam and listened to the propaganda programs. The station faded in and out, but I recall one program in which young women were singing about the homeland and the damage done by the American bandits. Sometimes Hanoi Hannah came on, and I heard her list American and South Vietnamese bases that were scheduled to be hit. What she said was accurate, but strangely, sometimes she ended her broadcast by saying, "But Phu Bai's all right," meaning that it would not be a target. This came to be a det saying—"Phu Bai's all right." When everything else was wrong and seemed to be going to hell, when we were stressed out and acted like maniacs, when rockets exploded on the base in the wee hours of the morning, after we were chewed out by the officers for some infraction, after we had almost crashed in planes that had electrical failures, we ironically reminded each other that "Phu Bai's all right," as if that one center of safety, dubiously promised by Hanoi Hannah, were an anchor in an otherwise shifting and uncertain world. Many years later I learned that one of the "R" beats had typed "Phu Bai's all right" on tape segments and plastered them in various places in the work building. They were found when the Spook mission was closing down and the building was being cleaned out by the last detters on the base.

I knew a guy, Andy Lentz, who was a linguist stationed at Phu Bai, which was located a few miles north of Da Nang. I am not sure if he was with me at DLIEC or if I met him in either San Angelo when we were in training or San Miguel while we were waiting to go TAD to Da Nang. While at San Miguel, he joined me and another friend on a trip by banca boat to the Capones Islands. I have a slide of him in his bathing suit on the big island. Occasionally, he came down to Da Nang for a day or two, dressed in his olive greens, and stopped by the barracks to visit with friends. He was from Harrisburg, Pennsylvania, where his father served in the state legislature. With his soft voice and kind, gentle ways, he seemed totally out of place in a war environment, and I was glad that he was there in Phu Bai if it was indeed all right. Rusty, with his dapper moustache and calm, cultured talk, also seemed out of place in Vietnam, as did I, but I realized that is the way war is. Did any of us really belong there? Except for a few gung-ho Marines attached to the det, we were all out of place and should have been back in the World pursuing our regular lives. The age of heroes was long past. We were not Achilles or Hector thirsty for glory. We were just ordinary young guys doing what we felt we had to do or could not avoid. On those nights I sat by the radio with its green light dimly illumining my room while F-4s roared on takeoff and helicopters moved over the village and countryside behind the base in the direction of the A Shau Valley. I heard the occasional burp of M16 fire. Whether we were willing or unwilling players, we had been thrust into this violent drama.

I kept the stereo console for over four decades. For several years after returning home, I listened to the tapes on the set, until it finally broke, and then I placed it on the back porch of my house. I eventually mustered up enough courage, when my wife and I remodeled the house, to throw the set away. But I still have the cassette tapes to this day, and every time I open the box in which they are stored, I think of Rusty, who passed away in the summer of 2017. I have read on the Internet that over the years he and his wife were generous benefactors of the music program at Indiana University, and I sometimes wonder if he occasionally thought about those times when we sat up until 2:00 a.m., listening to Tchaikovsky's *Symphony No. 6 in B Minor*, waiting to see if the VC were going to hit. Then early the next morning we got up, put on our flight suit and boots, and went out to the Willy Victor for another day over the Gulf of Tonkin.

Tyler was a good old boy about six feet tall with a medium build. I remember him in his olive-green flight suit with straw-colored hair sticking out from his cap. He occasionally flew with me on the Willy Victor or P-3 as my junior "I beat" and did a credible job. From time to time, I checked with him to find out what kind of air activity he had up on his receivers. I recall one day when he said he had MiG-17's out of Kien An doing formation flying. This kind of activity was enough to put anyone to sleep. It involved hour after hour of listening to "Right turn," "Roger," "Left turn," "Roger," along with changes in heading and altitude. I advised Tyler every now and then to check other channels on his second receiver to be sure that nothing more important or unexpected was up. I realized that the formation flying could be a distraction for an attempted shoot-down of an American aircraft. Tyler stuck with it.

I think for a while he might have gone off base on TAD missions, as did Steve White, who occasionally returned to the det, wearing camos and a black beret. Tyler, like some other men in the det, sometimes drank too much. One morning word went out in the barracks that Tyler was missing. We searched the entire barracks and checked at the work building. We went to the heads and the bunkers near our barracks but could not find Tyler. We were beginning to get worried that he had perhaps been abducted. But it occurred to me that, if he had been drinking heavily the night before, he might have gone to the head and then got turned around in the darkness. Some other guys and I went to search the barracks on the opposite side of the head. Some of them were unoccupied, and there on the second floor of one of the barracks we found Tyler sleeping like a baby. We shook him awake, and he was surprised to find us standing around him in a room full of empty racks with the morning sun streaming in through the windows. With his drinking he was coping with stress in his own way.

Bob Sluter had a quiet, understated sense of humor. Whenever I saw him, he seemed to be in a good mood, taking anything that came his way philosophically. We flew on some missions together, and he sometimes sat at the tape recorder and typewriter next to me when we were at work in the spaces translating air activity tapes. He always had something interesting and unexpected to share. One morning when he sat down at the typewriter next to mine, he said, "You know what is good for hemorrhoids?" He paused for dramatic effect. "Sex," he said. "Sex is good for hemorrhoids." I was not disposed to ask him to explain, but I could sympathize since I also sometimes suffered from the same ailment. He was an excellent "I" beat. Moreover, he was an expert on Jane's books of ships and planes and often had one of the volumes in hand. He remained in Da Nang longer than I did and was present a year later when rockets hit perilously close to the barracks. In preparing this memoir, I was saddened to learn that he had passed away from cancer.

LeBrun was an "O" beat who sometimes surprised us with what he said and did. The "I" beats referred to him as *hiep đồng la bàn*, "calibrate the compass," a command sometimes given by North Vietnamese ground control to MiG pilots near the beginning of a flight. The ID for LeBrun posted near the door to the workspaces was a newspaper clipping, instead of his photo, that read "The Beast." According to memories of detters posted many years later on Facebook, LeBrun sometimes wore a Colt 45 on a leather strap around his neck and one night accompanied some Marines on patrol with a Thompson submachine gun in hand and returned the next morning shaken by what he had experienced. On another occasion he hitched a ride with some Marines or Army guys to Phu Bai. These adventures were not part of our duties and could have placed him in serious trouble had they come to the attention of the CO. One afternoon LeBrun came into the workspaces with excitement on his face. Some of us looked up from translating air activity tapes, and he exclaimed, "They've got fig newtons in the mess hall!" I was amused, but now, in thinking about LeBrun, I admire the way he took delight in small things that many men take for granted. That perhaps was one of his ways of dealing with stress.

There were several other men in the det with whom I flew and knew to some extent. Mr. Lawson was a Marine captain who flew missions with us for a time. He was a capable evaluator but made no effort to be personable. He was rather strict, insisting on military protocol; in fact, he was a bit of a martinet. Yoshida, or "Yoshi," was in Da Nang for a while after I arrived. He had a sense of humor and was well liked by the men of the det. I remember one time when he came to the Spook mess with a towel still wrapped around his middle right after he had taken a shower. One of the chiefs was sitting on a stool at the bar, and his bald head was gleaming in the overhead lights. The men liked him because he was good-natured, and they teased him by calling him "the Chrome Dome." Walking past him, Yoshi planted a kiss on his bald head to annoy him and then ran off. He was one of the guys who sometimes wrestled on the floor of the mess just for the fun of it. Nick Gutierrez was one of the "O" beat Marines who flew with us. I often saw him around the barracks and the workspaces but did not get to know him well. I think he was one of those involved in the "Tiger Security" paint job mentioned elsewhere. I enjoyed talking with him at the third Spooks reunion in Charleston, South Carolina, in 2017 and was amazed to see that he had not aged much. He, like me, had brought his son to the reunion. Don Tremain occasionally stopped by my room to talk. He told me that some time ago he had contracted malaria and periodically had relapses with fever and chills. Malaria was a concern in Da Nang since mosquitoes were everywhere. I sometimes slept beneath a mosquito net, but during a rocket attack I was delayed from running to the bunker by disentangling myself from the net. Much of the time I simply pulled my sheet up to cover most of my head. I believe there were quinine tablets available in the workspaces, but I do not remember taking them. Many years later I thought of Tremain when my wife and I had to take anti-malaria capsules while traveling in southern Africa. Gaskins, also a radio man, is mentioned in my account of a bennie trip to Manila. He was among those who did not run to the bunker during a rocket attack. He had a fatalistic outlook and preferred to remain in bed, assuming that, if it was not his time, going to the bunker was not necessary, and, if it was his time, being in the bunker would not help.

Chuck Ferrell was another "I" beat in the det. He was the duty driver the morning Stokowski and I arrived in Da Nang. He roomed down the hall from me and had a collection of Beethoven's symphonies. He had a small moustache and laughed by grinning and blowing air from the corners of his mouth. He returned once from an A-3 mission excited that he had monitored a MiG that expended all of its fuel and crashed. I recall listening to a tape about a North Vietnamese pilot out of fuel who was told by the ground controller, "Anh giữ bình tĩnh" ("You remain calm"), because it was possible to land an aircraft with no fuel if air speed could be maintained. The problem, though, was the pilot got only one chance in approaching the field. Understandably, the pilot sounded nervous but kept acknowledging decreasing altitude and speed. Then suddenly he said, "Ô trời ơi!," an expression the equivalent of which in English might be "Oh my God!" but that translation does not convey the fear, desperation, and hopelessness in that pilot's voice. Afterwards, there was only the controller's voice repeatedly calling the pilot's billet number. This might have been a tape of the same activity Chuck monitored that day. He was dressed in his flight suit and torso harness, still holding his helmet and gear while relating the event. He became enthusiastic about other things as well. He came back from a bennie trip to Bangkok elated that he had been robbed on the street by a gunman. The stolen money did not seem to matter; he relished the experience of being robbed. He went on a flight to Hong Kong and returned with a box full of books. It did not bother him that some of the pages were upside down or not in sequence; he was pleased to have the books. Many years later I had a similar experience with books published in Hong Kong. Chuck did his TacAir work well, and he was there with the rest of us in the bunker during rocket attacks in the middle of the night when the explosions seemed to be walking up the airfield towards us.

After Chuck had returned to the states, he had an automobile accident that left him paralyzed below the neck. This was tragically ironic. He flew scores of missions in danger of being shot down or crashing from airplane failure and survived several rocket attacks only to return home, where he was supposedly safe, to be permanently injured. After I had finished my tour in Vietnam and the Philippines, I was assigned to the Navy detachment at Fort Meade, Maryland. I heard that he was in a Baltimore hospital. Several times I went on liberty into the city, but I am ashamed to say that I never visited him. I later learned from the *Big Look Spooks* website that he remained in his wheelchair the rest of his life but, strangely for a quadriplegic, felt pain in his body. Over four decades later, I looked Chuck up on the web and found that he had died when he was fifty and was buried in a cemetery near his home in Tennessee. Even though I did not get to know him well, Chuck had an obvious passion for life and seemed to make the most of every experience. Vietnam took its toll on all of us in one way or another. His name, like that of so many others who came back changed by the war, is not on the wall in Washington, D.C., but I sometimes think that maybe there should be an honor roll wall for those who continued to suffer in the years after the war. Although I never looked him up in the following years, I revere Chuck as a fallen brother because, even in death, he shares a bond with those of us who were also in Da Nang. This is a bond that transcends time and mere differences in personality, ideology, and background and that embraces all of the Spooks in a shared, ineffable experience, to be understood only by those who were there.

Sometimes, when I lie awake in the middle of the night, I seem to hear a voice in my head that cries out, "Were you there?" And without speaking out loud, I answer, "Yes, I was there." All of the Big Look Spooks were there. There is also a sense in which the whole nation was there since the news on TV every evening featured video tapes of combat and other atrocities taking place in Nam. The shots of helicopters with the wounded being loaded onto them, the units on foot patrol in tall grass, and jets roaring off aircraft carriers were in living rooms throughout the country. This was the first war that brought the reality of combat vividly into every home every day. The nation was all there because war, whether officially declared or not, becomes to some extent the responsibility of all citizens, whether they agree with it or not. The pilots bombing the North and the men slogging through the jungles, as well as the protestors marching down Pennsylvania Avenue or shouting in front of the Pentagon were all part of it. We were all there in one way or another. But some who were in Nam, although they returned from the war, were never truly at home when they came home. This included some of our friends in the detachment.

Randy Bennett is one of those who perhaps was never really at home when he returned home. For several years, the men of the detachment have diligently searched for information on Randy's whereabouts to let him know about the det reunions and just to stay in contact with him, but unfortunately, as I write these words, we have been unsuccessful in our search. We found where he graduated from his high school in Mississippi, and we located an address where he had once lived in San Diego. From what we heard, he had become a street person, not settled down in any one place. A female cousin who grew up with him in Mississippi and named her son after him corresponded with us, hoping that we could locate him.

Randy was stationed with me at the det in Da Nang, but I did not get to know him well there. When we were both at Fort Meade, however, he became a friend. Often, we went to the canteen on the base and simply talked while drinking our cokes and listening to the music that was playing over the radio on the overhead speakers. I remember "It Never Rains in Southern California" and "Leaving on a Jet Plane" in the background as we talked, and I associate these songs with him. We discussed all kinds of topics. Sometimes I went to his room in the barracks to talk, and sometimes he came to mine. One night in my room we talked about religion half the night. He explained what he as a Roman Catholic believed and practiced, and I explained my beliefs as a Baptist. At times, I am afraid, we became rather loud in voicing our opinions. Early the next morning when I woke up, I heard a sailor through the wall of the neighboring room ask his roommate, "Did you hear those guys arguing about religion last night?" I was mortified. I realized we had indeed become loud and probably sounded foolish. Randy and I were from the South, and we both took our faith seriously. After that night, though, I realized that arguing about religion is not a wise idea, and since then, I have attempted to refrain from such arguments.

Disagreeing on points of the Christian faith did not, however, damage our friendship. Randy and I joined other friends stationed at Ft. Meade on outings to Laurel, Maryland, and Washington, D.C. One night a group of us went to the drive-in movie in Laurel. I do not recall what the movie was about. Mainly, I remember Randy talking on the way to and from the movie. At one point in the evening the group talked about sex, and I recall that Randy said, "You know, I think that during your lifetime you are allowed a certain number of ejaculations, and when you have reached that number, you die." It is strange that I remember nothing else that was said.

President Johnson died while we were at Fort Meade. Late one night a group of friends and I decided to ride down to Washington to view the casket of the President lying in state in the Rotunda of the Capitol. Randy was part of the group. After traveling down the Washington-Baltimore Parkway, we parked somewhere on the east side of the Capitol around 1:00 a.m. Even at that hour, the end of the line was about two blocks long. In the distance we could see the dome illumined against the night sky. We waited for about two hours. I assumed that, when we finally reached the Rotunda, we would pass by the casket in just a few seconds, but as we entered, the line was halted, and the changing of the guard occurred. As a result, we were able to stand still for several minutes as the relief watch came on duty. The casket was directly beneath *The Apotheosis of Washington*, resting on the Lincoln catafalque and covered with the American flag. Guards representing each branch of the service were standing around the catafalque. As the relief guard entered, everything was silent, except for the squeaking of shoes on the floor. The servicemen marched slowly, carrying their rifles at present arms. They assumed their places and then stood at attention with their rifles at order arms. The relieved guard marched quietly out of the Rotunda. Several times I had seen the changing of the guard at the Tomb of the Unknown Soldier, but this ceremony around President Johnson's casket in the wee hours of the morning was truly impressive. My friends and I said little on the return trip to Fort Meade.

In Da Nang guys from our det sometimes visited an orphanage at China Beach. This was always a special occasion for those who went. I made the trip only one time, but I think Randy might have gone more than once. There is a photo in the detachment files that shows him holding a little girl wearing a blue sweater. She is laughing with her hand to her mouth, and Randy is smiling. This photo beautifully expresses Randy as I knew him. It reveals him as a man with kind eyes and a compassionate heart. I am reminded by this photo of the times when I visited his room and he sat on his bunk, discussing literature with me. As I recall, we talked about William Faulkner and Willie Morris, along with other writers from Mississippi and the South at large. He leaned back against the wall and spoke profoundly and somewhat wistfully about the meaning of life. After our time in Vietnam, there was a lot to talk about.

I smile when I think of Randy, but I am also filled with sadness about what he has experienced in the decades since I last saw him. So many came back from the war injured in either body or mind. I am reminded of a cousin, also a Vietnam veteran, who for some years before his death lived beneath a bridge, enduring the heat and cold, as well as the bugs and thefts by other vagrants, but he chose to stay there, even though there were places in his town where he could have obtained lodging. Perhaps he found peace in being alone beside the constantly flowing river while the passing cars and trucks rumbled overhead. He, like Randy, chose his own path that seems strange to the rest of us. As I write, Randy has friends in the det who care for him deeply and hope that one day they will locate him and that he then will truly be home from the war.

I cannot name all of the men who were with me in Da Nang because I did not get to know some of them well since their time overlapped mine only briefly. I flew with most of the men who were there at the same time I was and probably spoke with all of them to some extent. I knew Jim Felts by sight and probably talked with him a few times but actually got to know him only forty-four years after being in Vietnam. He was, in fact, the first det member I saw after leaving active duty in the Navy in 1973. He traveled to Tifton, Georgia, where I lived, for a reunion on his father's side of the family and, along with his parents, visited with my wife and me at our house. Then we went out to eat at a local restaurant. On a trip to Tifton the next year, he met us at Zaxby's, where I enjoyed talking with him and his father and mother. It was interesting to hear his father discuss being in World War II. He had been a cook for the Army, and I shared my father's experiences as an Army cook during World War II. Over the years Jim has been good at connecting with other members of the detachment. Matt Floyd was a CTA while I was in Da Nang and was one of those who went with me on the bennie trip to Manila, which I discuss in the next chapter. Dean Clark and I probably spoke occasionally. Not long ago he shared on a Facebook post that he recalled I was the one on watch at Fire Point Thirteen when the rockets hit on my second night in Da Nang. He and others back at the barracks wondered if I was maybe trying to dig my way back home to America after that bang of a welcome to Vietnam. From photos on the *Big Look Spooks* website, I remembered Chuck Saberton, a TacAir op, who also sometimes went out to the orphanage at China Beach. Charlie Capes, Bill Dillon, Jim Felts, Duane Mann, Tom O'Brien, and Terry Sharp were six of several CTRs who were part of the Det. David Gilbert, Jim Inks, Max Mercer, Ken Piotrowski, Steve White, Michael Leroy Will, and Tim Yerdon are a few of the SAM ops. Several of us were TacAir ops. CPL Nick Gutierrez and LCPL John Wayne McFee are two of the Marines who flew with us on the planes and joined with the Navy guys for good times in the Spook mess. Some of the officer evaluators with whom I flew include LTJG Robert A. Cornett, Jr., Ensign Robert Gordon, LTJG David B. Marshall, LTJG Nat Benchley, and LCDR William B. Shermer. LTJG Joseph D. Burns, who was an evaluator with the det before I arrived, later became an Admiral in the Naval Security Group.

Some of the men who served with the det before and after I had departed include Mike Barnowski, Patrick Butler, Dean Carstens, Mike Farmer, Jim Felts, David Gilbert, Jim Inks, Duane Mann, Max Mercer, Robert Morrison, David Mullis, Gary Nelson, Tom O'Brien, Mike O'Feild, John Phipps, Ken Piotrowski, Dan Scoggins, Mick Schwartz, John Shipman, Bob Sluter, David Thomas, John Vogt, Ralph Webb, Tim Yerdon, and Chief DeCourley, who took Chief Holt's place when he left. Several of these men were also present while I was in Da Nang. Patrick Butler married one of the young women who worked in the Spook mess. All of the men in the detachment admired her because of her beauty and good personality. I met and talked with Gilbert and Barnowski at the third Spook reunion in Charleston. Mann joined Don Tremain in moderating the Facebook group *Friends Who Like Big Look Spooks Danang*. Nelson was with the det when operations closed down in Da Nang and the planes flew out of Cubi Point and off carriers.

I wish I could have had the opportunity to get to know all of the men with whom I flew, along with those who were in the detachment during its early years.* I have eagerly read posts by many of them on Facebook and in *the Big Look Spooks* website. It was an honor to serve with them in the detachment whether they came before, during, or after my time in Da Nang.

---

*Many men who were with me in Da Nang are not mentioned in the memoir since I could include only the names of those who gave me written permission to do so; however, all of the men are recorded on the roster in the *Big Look Spooks* website. Also, it would have been good to get to know more of the men in VQ-1 since that squadron maintained and flew the aircraft that made it possible for the Spooks to carry out their mission.

CHAPTER 17

Bennie Trips

Occasionally at Da Nang, we were able to take bennie trips that did not count as official leave time. We had the opportunity to travel to Manila, Bangkok, and Korat. Also, we were able to have some brief time in other cities in Thailand, such as Ubon, Udorn, and U-Tapao, if, after completing a mission, our flight could not for some reason return to Da Nang.

On my first bennie trip to Bangkok, we stayed at the Florida Hotel, and early the next morning, before we had to leave for Don Mueang Airport to return to Da Nang, I took a taxi to the Temple of the Reclining Buddha. The traffic was heavy, and I was a bit worried that I would not get back in time for the flight, but I could not resist the chance to see one of the interesting sites of the city. I walked among the stupas scattered around the temple grounds. The immense reclining Buddha was impressive, but I also appreciated the huge stone figures that served as guards on either side of the gates. One of these statues resembled my father wearing a hat. On later trips to Bangkok, I visited the Emerald Buddha Temple, the Temple of Dawn, and the Golden Buddha Temple. The bright orange, tiered roofs of the temples in the morning sun were strikingly beautiful.

On one trip I wanted to go to a restaurant that served traditional Thai foods and featured classical dancing. At the hotel I got into the van that was to take me there, and then a bald-headed man a bit older than I was entered the van. In talking with him, I learned that he was an officer in the Royal Air Force stationed in Singapore. In fact, he was a dentist and had chosen to visit Bangkok when he had leave time. Since we were both headed to the same restaurant, we agreed to dine together. I attempted to engage him in conversation as we ate, but he was somewhat taciturn. Perhaps as an officer he did not relish the idea of dining with an American enlisted man but agreed to do so out of courtesy. The waiters brought us traditional dishes served in several small bowls. These were placed before us in a semicircle, and I enjoyed trying each one. I particularly remember a dish that featured vermicelli and some kind of sauce. While we dined, we were treated to various types of dances. At first there were folk dances from the countryside. Then we were entertained by dances set to scenes from the *Ramayana* or the *Ramakien*, as this long epic poem is known in Thailand. I had seen murals of scenes from the poem along the cloistered walkways of Wat Phra Kaew, the Temple of the Emerald Buddha. The musicians at the side of the stage played traditional stringed instruments and drums as the costumed dancers enacted a scene in which Rama and Hanuman, the monkey god, fought against Ravana, the demon king of Sri Lanka, to rescue Sita, Rama's wife, from captivity. The actors portraying Rama and Sita wore golden pagoda hats while the actor depicting Hanuman wore a mask and a white costume with a long tail. Ravana held a glass jewel in his hand, which he tossed into the air in the fight. Each time he tossed the jewel, the drums banged, representing lightning bolts and thunder. The movements were slow and stylized but graceful. I did not understand very well what I witnessed. It was only many years later, when I taught the *Ramayana* in my world literature classes, that I more fully comprehended what I had seen in the performance, as well as on the walls of the Temple of the Emerald Buddha. My companion, although somewhat dull in his conversation, seemed to enjoy the performance.

Touring Bangkok with Mr. Charley

On one bennie trip to Bangkok, David Mullis, Tom O'Brien, and I hired a local tour guide for the day. Mr. Charley, as he was called, had a classic 1957 red and white Pontiac. I forget how much we paid him, but he was worth every baht. That day he took us to Wat Phra Kaew (Temple of the Emerald Buddha), Wat Traimit (Temple of the Golden Buddha), Wat Arun (Temple of Dawn), Thonburi for the floating market, TIM Land theme park, and supper at a Mexican restaurant. The first stop was the Temple of the Emerald Buddha. Mr. Charley led us to the main chapel (Ordination Hall) of the temple complex, where people were worshiping. He instructed us to take off our shoes and place them in the slots of a shoe rack on the porch. Some people were purchasing small pieces of gold leaf, which they stuck to statues in the temple as part of the process of acquiring merit. I took photographs of a line of small gold-covered Garuda figures (part human and eagle) holding nagas (serpents) on a high relief frieze around the building. As we approached the entrance, Mr. Charley instructed us to step over the threshold and led us inside. We knelt on the red carpet and observed the interior of the hall. The worshipers were chanting certain words over and over. There were murals on the walls to our left and right, and I assumed that they depicted scenes from the life of the Buddha. The focal point, though, was the Emerald Buddha, a small jade statue, situated at the top of a series of raised platforms at the front of the hall. The statue was clothed in gold raiment beneath a seven-tiered umbrella. Mr. Charley informed us that the golden clothing was changed according to the season. After a while, we quietly departed from this hall and, putting on our shoes, walked around the cloisters of the temple to see the murals depicting scenes from the *Ramakien.* I was intrigued by the golden Kinnari statues, beautiful life-sized figures, part female, part bird, situated outside some of the buildings. At one place in the complex, there was a miniature model of Angkor Wat, the famous temple, in Cambodia. I hoped that one day I would be able to see this site, but at the time it was occupied by the Khmer Rouge communists. We walked by the front of the Royal Grand Palace but did not go inside.

Next, we visited Wat Traimit, the Temple of the Golden Buddha. As we went up the steps to the temple building, I paused to take a snapshot of monks in their saffron robes walking along the street. That is how I happened to have a slide photograph that also showed Mr. Charley's car. I had forgotten the type of car he drove, although I remembered that it was red and white. In comparing the car in the photo with images of classic American cars from 1957 on the Internet, I realized that it was a Pontiac. The temple building at that time was not impressive, just a rather small structure that lacked much ornamentation, unlike today's beautiful temple made of white marble. We were able to get close to the large seated statue of the solid gold Buddha. According to information on a placard posted near the statue, it had been transported from Ayutthaya, the old capital of Siam, to Bangkok. At that time no one realized the value of the statue because it was covered with stucco embedded with bits of glass. The stucco was perhaps applied to make it unlikely that the Burmese would confiscate the statue when they invaded Siam during the late eighteenth century. The statue remained in undistinguished quarters for a number of years, and its true value was realized only when it was dropped while being moved and part of the stucco broke off, revealing the gold underneath. The placard also mentioned that thieves had broken into the temple at some point and cut off one of the hands of the statue. Leaning nearer, we could discern the line where the hand had been reattached. The seated statue of the Buddha is nine feet in height and weighs 5.5 tons. In today's currency it is estimated to be worth 250 million U.S. dollars. The history of the statue reminded me that often the true worth of something (or someone) is not immediately evident. We cover ourselves with various disguises so that what we truly are is not revealed. From a spiritual standpoint, one could say that our mortal bodies hide the inestimable worth of the immortal soul.

We crossed the Chao Phraya River to see the Temple of Dawn in Thonburi. David took a photo of me standing in front of one of the gates guarded

David Mullis at Wat Arun, the Temple of Dawn, Bangkok, Thailand, July 1971. On this R & R trip, Mullis, Tom O'Brien, and I hired a driver named Mr. Charley to take us on a tour of Bangkok in his 1957 Pontiac. Mullis's friends in the detachment gave him the nickname "Mule." In later years he became a chaplain in the Navy (photograph by the author, retouched by John Phipps).

by statues of immense demon sentinels. We walked around the stupas of the temple admiring the bits of colored glass and broken porcelain that had been stuck into the stone. Then we boarded our boat again and passed by the place where the royal barges were stored and maintained. We continued on one of the klongs to the floating market. There were many boats filled with various kinds of fruits and vegetables in this area. Some were rowed by women wearing lampshade hats. One woman pulled up next to us in her boat, and we bought bananas as she held to our gunwale with one hand and gave us the fruit and took our payment with her other hand. Along the klongs people went about their daily lives, washing clothes, brushing their teeth, and just sitting on the docks and steps of the houses, watching the passing scene. I took a photo of children waving at us while sitting on steps that led down to the water. Out on the river again, we were amazed by the longtail boats with a propeller shaft that extended several feet from the stern. These boats went very fast, leaving a rooster tail.

Then Mr. Charley drove us out to TIM Land. Until recently, I had spelled the name of this park as "Timland," not realizing that the first three letters stood for "Thailand in Miniature." This park fulfilled its name by giving us a glimpse of many aspects of Thai culture, including elephants carrying and rolling logs into the river, Thai kick boxing, and cockfighting. I noticed that the birds in the cockfighting demonstration wore long metal gaffs on their legs. Fortunately, the demonstration did not last long, and I remembered that cockfighting, although at times practiced in the South, is an illegal activity. One of the most beautiful sights was young Thai women in colorful folk costumes doing the nail dance. Their fingers were capped with pointed pieces of metal that accentuated their graceful hand movements. I have learned only recently that TIM Land closed down sometime during the early 1970s, so Mr. Charley took us to an interesting and unique showcase of Thai culture that day.

Throughout the day we asked Mr. Charley about various sites and restaurants. He rated each one by the number system current in the Far East. For example, we asked if Nick's Number One, a well-known Hungarian restaurant, was truly a good place to eat, and he assured us, "Number one, number one!" On a different bennie trip to Bangkok, I had a chance to confirm Mr. Charley's rating of this restaurant. Spurlock, an "R" beat in the det, agreed to go with me to Nick's Number One. I knew that he would be interesting to talk with since he had a bent for philosophy. In the Philippines I had noticed one evening at the enlisted men's club that he was reading Nietzsche's *Thus Spake Zarathustra*. When we entered Nick's Number One, the hostess greeted us, and a waiter showed us to an outdoor table beneath an arbor at the back of the establishment. Spurlock and I ordered shish kabob, made with Kobe beef, which was served flambé on wooden skewers. To go with the meal, we ordered a bottle of Hungarian Bull's Blood wine, a vintage featured by the restaurant.

To top off the day, Mr. Charley drove us to a Mexican restaurant for supper. He parallel parked near the front door, and I saw that there were two Mexican restaurants side by side, and in front of each one was a dwarf dressed in chaps and a wide sombrero. As we stepped out of the car, each dwarf tried to persuade us to enter his restaurant. When we chose the one on our right, the dwarf for that establishment thanked us profusely, saying, "Gracias!" over and over. I do not recall what we ordered, but it was served in Thai style with warm, damp washcloths rolled and placed by our plates for washing our hands and removing grease from our fingers as we ate. When we left, our dwarf walked into the middle of the street, blew a police whistle, and held up his hands, stopping traffic from both directions as Mr. Charley pulled out of the parking space. I thought, "Only in Bangkok could there be such a strange and interesting mixture of cultures." Whether both restaurants were truly in competition or under the same management I did not learn. We realized, though, that Mr. Charley likely received a kick-back for taking his charges to the restaurant. It did not matter; he gave us a wonderful tour of Bangkok.

Visit to the Marble Buddha Temple in Bangkok

I believe that I went on three bennie trips to Bangkok. On one of them I hailed a taxi to go to the Marble Buddha Temple, but the driver spoke no English. I took out a Thai bhat note and showed him the picture of the temple on it. He nodded that he understood and took me to the entrance. The main doors in front were closed, so I walked around to a side entrance. I paused at the open door and listened to the chanted prayers coming from inside. Young monks, bare shouldered in their saffron robes, were kneeling in front of the altar. Their sandals lined the steps leading into the temple. The leader of the service, a middle-aged monk, kneeled on a platform before the huge statue of the Buddha, and the other monks were grouped before him on the carpet with their hands joined in a prayerful attitude. Incense sticks burned on the altar, and dried chrysanthemums and a black and white portrait of the king were on the table in front of the statue. I later learned that the monastery attached to the temple still preserved the king's chamber just as it was when he had been a young monk there. A bronze statue of Singha, a mythological lion in Hindu and Thai culture, stood upon the steps of the building where his room was located. Singha, of course, is also the name of a popular beer in Thailand.

While the monks continued to chant, I walked around the cloister and looked at the numerous statues of the Buddha in various situations lined along the wall. The statues depicted the Buddha praying, meditating, and teaching, with his hands and fingers positioned to signify the activity. The statues repeated the same themes over and over around the cloistered courtyard. An old man moved across the paving stones, sweeping sand and leaves before him. Droves of pigeons fled in front of him, wheeling upwards in flight, landing, and then rising again before the advancing broom.

The roar of the city traffic had become louder, and weak sunlight broke through the clouds and illumined the mist blanketing the temple grounds. I walked beside a canal lined with palm trees. Cigarette butts, candy wrappers, and pop-corn floated in the black water beneath the foot-bridges. A young monk in his saffron robe passed by with a furtive look on his face. He held one arm straight down, and in his fingers, I saw a lighted cigarette. He smiled and continued on his way. The sun suddenly brightened and made the tiered roof of the temple glow a brilliant orange.

Trip to Korat

One day during the rainy season when I did not have flight duty, I joined several other men on a trip to Korat. This was a short shopping trip, only for the afternoon. At first, I thought it was not worthwhile to go; then I recalled deters referring to Korat as "Ko-rot-rot-rot, Korat" and saying that it

Tim Barczak and Herb Shippey in front of the work building for VQ-1, Da Nang Air Base, 1971. This photograph was taken at the beginning of a brief R & R trip, possibly the time we flew to Korat, Thailand, for the afternoon. While stationed at Da Nang, I always wore my blue work cap (photograph by Mike Farmer).

was a good place to buy things, so I reconsidered and decided to go. The CTAs for the det quickly prepared orders allowing for "temporary additional duty" and exchanged our military pay certificates (funny money) for dollars. Then we boarded the P-3 for the flight. Our route lay over Laos, but because of bad weather, the pilot had to fly further north than anticipated. He came on the intercom and asked us to sit at our positions as if we were on a mission because this altered route took us over potentially dangerous territory. We were flying over an area controlled by the Pathet Lao, and he was concerned lest SAM sites might have been set up. I gathered that he also feared the possibility of an attack by a MiG since the North Vietnamese also operated in Laos.

When we landed, we took taxis into town. That rainy afternoon I walked around looking at the Buddhist temples, and I bought silk fabric for my mother, aunts, and grandmother, as well as a puzzle ring, a must item for anyone going to Korat. The puzzle ring consisted of four interlocked bands that fit together to create a unified ring. It took me a while to learn how to reassemble the ring after I took it apart, but I succeeded and often enjoyed working it while in Vietnam. I kept the ring for several years after I returned home until it finally broke. That afternoon I enjoyed a meal of Kobe beef with Bill Dillon and other members of the det at a local restaurant. Dillon explained that this beef came from cows that were given beer, along with their feed, and kept in pens and regularly massaged. The steaks were tender and succulent. Later that afternoon we all assembled in a hotel room that we had rented and piled our purchases onto the bed while eating snacks and drinking beer or cokes. In addition to puzzle rings, some of the guys had bought rings with tiger eye or blue sapphire settings. While we talked, I looked out the window at a traditional wooden Thai house back of the hotel and watched the rain drops steadily sprinkling the mud puddles in the yard. I became a bit homesick, thinking of lazy rainy afternoons back home. Then it was time to return to the airfield for the flight back to Da Nang. Even though flight duty was dangerous, we had the benefit of being with a unit that had its own planes, so there were some occasional perks such as bennie trips.

Bennie Trip to Manila

One of the memorable bennie trips I took was to Manila. En route across the South China Sea on the P-3, I talked to a member of the detachment sitting beside me. He was a detter with whom I had rarely talked. He had been to Manila several times before, so I thought he would be a good source of information about things to do and see. I asked him about the shopping in central Manila, but he said, "I don't know." Next, I asked him about interesting historical sites—I had heard about the bombed-out remains of the old city—but he replied, "I don't know." To every question, he gave the same answer, so I finally asked, "You have been to Manila before, haven't you?" He answered, "yes," but said he always just stayed in his hotel room. Then I understood. For many men in the detachment who had been away from women for several months, sightseeing was not a priority. My fellow detter wanted nothing more than to remain in his room with his female companion the entire time, calling room service to bring meals. Other than what he saw en route to and from his hotel, he had no knowledge of Manila. This was his reprieve from the war. I marveled that this quiet, undemonstrative guy had a flip side to his life. It was like learning that the local male librarian is a regular Don Juan.

Whenever I checked into a hotel during a bennie trip to Bangkok, it was not unusual to hear a knock on my door shortly after I had laid my bag on the bed. Then a somewhat stout, oleaginous man would come into the room, smiling and rubbing his hands together, asking if there was anything he could do to make my stay more comfortable, suggesting that perhaps he could arrange some company for the evening. This kind of fellow was typical of pimps that plied their business at the hotels where American servicemen stayed while on liberty. I encountered his kind more than once on bennie trips, and they did not seem to understand my polite refusals of their offers. They would persist, until it finally became clear that I was not going to do business with them. Then they would back obsequiously out of the room, smiling all the while, and leave their card on the chest of drawers—in case I changed my mind.

On one bennie trip to Bangkok, I encountered a different kind of pimp. This one was a thin young man who drove a taxi. As I emerged from the front entrance of the Florida Hotel to hail a taxi, he stepped forward, but instead of asking me where I wanted to go, he inquired if he might find me a girl for the night. When I politely declined, he offered to procure me a man for the evening. I gruffly refused this offer, but he kept trying to persuade me that he could arrange for a pleasant time. After realizing I was not going to accept his suggestions, he switched tactics and offered to buy me some coffee in the hotel coffee shop because he said he had never met anyone quite like me and wanted to learn more about me. I knew what he was doing but reasoned that this was a chance to learn something about a colorful character, so I accepted his offer. We entered the coffee shop, and I was astounded. There sitting at nearly all of the tables were perhaps thirty young Thai women, all waiting to be hired for the night. I had never seen so many prostitutes assembled in one place. My taxi driver showed me to a table at the rear of the shop and ordered coffee for the two of us. I recall little of what we discussed, but it was interesting to talk with him. I told him about my home in Georgia, and I think that I probably said I was a Christian to explain why I would not accept the kinds of arrangements he offered. He then told me some things about himself, most of which I tended to doubt. He confided that he had attended Cambridge University in England. I smiled politely. Throughout our conversation, he occasionally interrupted the discussion to say that he would still be glad to arrange some company for me, and I continued courteously to decline. Eventually, we finished our coffee and made our way among the tables of waiting girls, and he took me in his taxi to the place I wanted to go. I do not remember where this was, probably to a nice restaurant.

So as we approached Sangley Point, an American Navy Base across the bay from Manila, I understood why my companion knew almost nothing about the city. After deplaning, we made our way to the dock and took a launch across the bay. Ironically, this was one of the few times while in the Navy that I was actually on the water. We docked near the American Embassy, which was on Roxas Boulevard. From there we had only a short walk to our hotel. But first we went to a nearby bank to change dollars into pesos. By the time I had unpacked and washed up in my room, it was almost dark. I went downstairs and started out the front door when a Manila policeman stopped me. He said, "Please, sir, it is dangerous for you to be out on the street by yourself after dark. Let me call you a taxi or return inside the hotel." I had intended to walk down to Rizal Park to see the monument to Jose Rizal, the national hero of the Philippines, famous as a poet, novelist, journalist, and revolutionary who had helped bring an end to Spanish rule, but the policeman's warning cancelled that plan. I decided to remain in the hotel, and I was glad that I did because it turned out to be a nice evening. I went to the hotel dining room and ordered a delicious meal that included a tender steak, green beans, a baked potato, and coffee. While I ate, an attractive young Filipino woman in an evening gown came onto the stage at one end of the room and sang the most beautiful songs I think I have ever heard by a female vocalist. She was truly gifted, and her singing, quiet beauty, and graceful composure captivated me. One of the songs in her repertoire was "Yesterday I heard the Rain," a song that I have ever since associated with her. When she took a break, a group of Americans sitting together at a table invited her to come talk with them. The group included both men and women who worked at the American embassy. The men were dressed in barongs. It was obvious that they were regulars at the hotel dining room and that they came chiefly to hear the young woman sing. They talked kindly to her and expressed how much they enjoyed her singing. I returned to my room satisfied with the evening's entertainment.

The next morning, I went out to tour the city, but immediately upon exiting the hotel, I was met by a group of young boys begging. They surrounded me and held out their hands to receive money, while repeatedly saying, "Me-me-me-me-me!" They were trying to high-pressure me to give them money, and that displeased me. I tried to walk away, but they followed, cupping their hands at my elbows. I then reversed directions to try to shake them off, but they turned with me. It was an embarrassing predicament. I felt these street urchins were merely trying to take advantage of me and did not want to give them anything, but neither did I want them to tag along with me everywhere I went. Finally, exasperated, I handed out some pesos to them, and satisfied, they went away.

I walked on most of my tour that morning. I was reluctant to take a taxi since I had heard too many stories about American sailors who had been rolled in Manila taxis. Admittedly, some of these incidents involved a sailor who was drunk and set himself up to be a victim. According to other stories, though, a sailor would get into a taxi and tell the driver where to go. The taxi would travel a short distance, and then the driver would stop. Two thugs would get into the back seat on either side of the luckless sailor and hold him hostage until they could take him somewhere secluded, rob him, beat him up, and leave him unconscious on the street.

I enjoyed my stroll through Rizal Park, stopping at the Rizal monument, and then walked to the part of the city that had been bombed by the Japanese during World War II. This section of the city included several blocks of ruined buildings, most of them just battered walls flanking the street with nothing but rubble and grass behind them. I visited the Manila Cathedral and read the plaque at the entrance that gave its history. The first church on the site was built in 1502, and the present cathedral was the sixth building. Most of the earlier structures had been flattened by earthquakes, but the church before me was a reconstruction of the building destroyed during the Battle of Manila. I went inside, wandered around, and then continued my walk through the Intramuros sector. I did not get as far as Fort Santiago and some of the other old churches since I did not have much

PR-31, Sangley Point in the Philippines (1971), with the ground crew washing the plane. I took the photograph on an R & R trip to Manila. To reach the city, those of us on the flight crossed Manila Bay in a Navy launch. Ironically, this was one of the few times I was on the water during my time in the Navy, although I often flew over the water (photograph by the author).

more time for sightseeing. Finally, I hailed a taxi and took my chances so that I could get back to the dock on time to take the launch across the bay to Sangley Point.

Gaskins, a CTO in the detachment, was the only other person on the dock when I arrived. He was tall, lanky, and easy-going. I noticed that he had a number of red marks all around his neck, and I asked, "Good night last night?" He replied, "The mosquitoes were really bad." Then he looked at me in a knowing way, and we both laughed. He was leaning backwards against the dock railing with his arms supporting him on either side. His sleeves were pushed up, and I noticed he had a tattoo on one of his forearms. It was the word "Vietnam," misspelled "V-e-i-t-n-a-m," and the two green dragons embracing this orthographic travesty appeared to be weeping. In some ways this tattoo seemed an appropriate symbol of the whole American intervention in Vietnam. Soon the other men arrived, and we boarded the launch to return to Sangley Point.

On one of the bennie trips to Thailand, I was reading Thomas Wolfe's *You Can't Go Home Again*. As I sat in the P-3 on the flight back to Da Nang, I pondered the title and hoped that it did not apply to me or the other men in Det Bravo. But then I realized that what the title stated was, in a sense, true. We could not return to the homes we had left because they had changed, and we had also changed because of our experiences in the war. The pre–Socratic Greek philosopher Heraclitus wrote that one cannot step twice into the same river. When we returned home, things would be quite different. We wondered how we would adjust.

CHAPTER 18

SERE School

During the summer of 1971, the Navy sent me to SERE school in Southern California. This gave me an opportunity to return to the states and have several days of leave at home midway through my tour in Vietnam. *SERE* stands for "Survival, Evasion, Resistance, and Escape." The program was established to train military personnel how to survive if their plane went down in a remote area and how to cope with being taken as a prisoner of war. Completing the program also allowed me to get my air crewman wings, which I proudly wore on my dress uniform.

I flew August 7 in a C-130 Hercules from Da Nang to Tan Son Nhut Air Base in Saigon to begin my journey. The plane touched down with a loud thump and rumbling noise. The clunky landing made me think of the C-130 as a kind of flying dump truck. My next flight did not leave until the following morning, so I spent the night in the Tan Son Nhut terminal, sitting and lying down on the seats to make myself as comfortable as possible. Hundreds of geckos covered the ceiling and the upper parts of the walls. I went to the restroom but found it impossible to use the toilets, which were encrusted with dried filth that had not been cleaned in weeks if not months. I urinated into a lengthy trough into which water dripped from punctures in a long pipe. The walls of the restroom were completely covered with graffiti as high as a man could reach from thousands of troops who had passed through. Late that night I walked to the front entrance of the terminal and saw a young girl, maybe ten or eleven, and her brother, perhaps seven or eight, selling Ba Mươi Ba beer from a portable stand that they had set up. It was sad to see children reduced to this necessity as a result of the war. They should have been at home safe in a comfortable bed.

When I went out to board the plane the next morning, a guard in camos, ran a wand up and down my torso and legs to check for weapons. The plane flew to Okinawa and landed at Kadena Air Base, where everyone got off and walked around the terminal for a while. After returning on board and waiting to taxi, I saw a long black aircraft on the other side of the field and immediately recognized it as an SR-71 Blackbird. I raised my camera and took a photograph through the window. I felt a bit guilty about doing this, but at that distance I could make out few details. I knew about SR-71 reconnaissance flights from maps and pre-flight briefings at Da Nang. At that time the Blackbird was a classified aircraft, although today it can be seen in various air museums around the country. I had heard that it flew so high and fast the North Vietnamese could not shoot it down with SAMs or MiG-21s.

After we landed at Travis Air Force Base near San Francisco, I took a bus into the city and then boarded a Southwest Airlines flight to San Diego. I was quartered at the Coronado Island naval base. Since I had arrived a day early, I had time to do a little sight-seeing, so I went to Balboa Park and visited the San Diego Zoo. In particular, I remember the aviary. It was interesting to be inside the enclosure with exotic birds from all parts of the world. I toured an art museum in the park that housed the paintings of Jackson Pollock and, before leaving the park, called my parents collect from a pay phone to let them know I was in the states. That evening I strolled along the beach past the landmark Coronado Hotel. As I walked around, I kept recalling the recent rocket attacks at Da Nang. It was good to know that I could sleep peacefully in the barracks on the Coronado base. During the night, though, someone in the room above dropped a shoe, and I popped up ready to run to the bunker before remembering where I was. I lay awake for a while listening for the other shoe but never heard it drop.

I took some nice photographs at the zoo with the Asahi Pentax camera I had bought at the base exchange in San Miguel, but the shutter malfunctioned and locked. I took it to a shop in downtown San Diego, but they said it would cost $150 to repair the camera and would take several days. I decided to wait. When I returned to the Philippines, I went down to the Subic Bay exchange one afternoon, and a Filipino man who worked in an equipment repair shop said he could fix the camera. He told me to come back in an hour, so I went to the base library and read for a while. When I returned, the camera was ready, and he charged only five dollars. The camera worked fine for the next thirty years.

Most of the participants in SERE school were jet pilots. I was one of the few enlisted men. The first part of the training was classroom instruction. Some of the subjects covered included survival tactics for finding water, food, and shelter; what we should and should not say and do if we were captured; and strategies for surviving in a prisoner of war camp. If I remember correctly, we spent three days in class and then went outside for practical instruction. This involved training in survival strategies in the water, on the beach and land, and finally, in a prisoner of war camp.

During recruit training at Orlando, along with the rest of my company, I had already been taught some basic skills for survival in the water.

We learned that almost any part of the sailor's uniform could be used as a floatation device if we were forced to abandon ship or found ourselves in the water without a Mae West vest. For example, we could take off our trousers in the water, tie a knot at the end of each leg, zip the zipper, and then raise the trousers in the air, bringing them down suddenly into the water. Voilà, water wings. The sailor's white hat could be let down like a bowl to hold a bit of air. The shirt could be buttoned up tightly to the chin. By blowing into it, we could perhaps trap some air. We were also taught that, if no land was in sight or if we were far away from the shore, it was best not to try to swim because we would tire out and drown from overexertion. The best thing was to use clothing as flotation devices and drift with the current or simply to do the dead man's float, relaxing as much as possible, raising the head up every minute or two with just enough effort to catch a breath and then go back down to relax.

In SERE school we went to the pool at Coronado to learn additional survival skills in the water. We were taught how to leap from a height into the water safely. The first impulse of some macho guys might be to dive headfirst into the water, but this was not a wise technique if one had to leap from the side of a ship into the sea. Instead, it was safer to fold our arms across our chest, jump, and then cross the feet on the way down to hit the water as upright as possible without injuring ourselves. We practiced doing this from the high dive at the pool. Then we were taught how to swim in the water without being ruptured during an underwater explosion. Since sound carries better in water than in air, it was possible to be seriously injured with concussion waves passing up the rectum. To prevent this, our instructor said, we should cross our legs to close up the rectum as tight as possible and swim with our arms only if an explosion was likely. Then he showed us what to do if the surface of the water were covered with burning oil or gas. We had to swim underwater and, before coming up for air, use our hands to swish the surface above us to try to clear a space to permit the head to surface long enough for a quick breath of air. This process could be repeated until one cleared the burning surface.

The next day we went to the beach at the tip of Coronado Island to spend the night. From that point we were not given any food, although we were allowed water and black coffee. To eat, we had to find it or catch it. The instructors told us that, if we were cast away near the ocean, there was no need to go hungry or thirsty. They showed us how to use the various parts of a parachute. The cords could be cut up and tied into a net to cast into the water to drag for crabs or lobsters. Sections could be cut from the cloth, soaked in the water, filled with shrimp or crabs, and then suspended by a tripod over a fire. We each got a morsel or two cooked this way. They showed us how to look under rock ledges in the water for abalone. Before we left the classroom, they said we were in luck since the grunion were supposed to be running during the next few nights, but I never saw any of these small fish, which during mating season swarm the beaches of southern California.

One of the survival techniques we learned on the beach was how to build a makeshift solar water distiller. First, we dug a hole in the beach a little distance beyond the tide line. The hole was maybe a foot to foot and a half deep and about two feet in diameter. If it was located properly, the sides and bottom would be moist without caving in. Next, a cup or container of any sort was placed on the bottom of the hole in the center. Then a plastic bag or sheet, maybe even part of the chute, could be spread over the hole, placing sand around the edges to keep the cover from blowing away. Some pebbles, small seashells, or sand could be placed in the center of the cover, leaving it loose enough to slope downwards over the cup or container on the bottom. Then one can simply leave the still for a while, maybe digging another in the meantime. The heat of the sun causes the water to evaporate and accumulate on the underside of the cover, and the water then drips down the sloping sides into the cup. Admittedly, this is a slow process, but if one had enough covering materials and receptacles, coconut shells, for example, several stills could be dug on the beach to provide enough pure water to survive. I thought this was an ingenious technique.

DWEST (Deep Water Environmental Survival Training) was part of our training at Coronado. One day we were taken aboard a boat and transported to the entrance to San Diego harbor opposite Point Loma. The purpose of this part of our training was to teach us how to survive if we were forced to parachute out of a plane into the ocean. It is a sad fact that some men have died after safely bailing out of a plane over water. The reason for this is that, once the man is in the water, the wind may fill the chute and drag him, and he may become entangled in the chute. Also, the chute may function as a sea anchor, creating drag when he tries to swim. If he does not know how to release himself from the parachute, he could drown. In this training event, we had to put on a harness and then ascend to a tower at the stern of the boat. The tower was at a certain height so that a drop from it would approximate the force someone would experience hitting the water in a parachute. We stood in line waiting our turn to jump from the tower. Once we were on the tower platform, draglines were attached to our harness with a D-ring. After dropping into the water, we were supposed to let the boat drag us while we were on our stomach. Next, we were to flip over to experience the drag on our back and then to turn back onto our stomach before releasing our harness from the draglines. We wore a Mae West life preserver under the harness. I was a bit anxious as I climbed the tower to await my turn, but once in the water, I did as instructed, allowing myself to be pulled on my stomach, back, and stomach again before disconnecting the D-ring from the harness.

Once I was released, I swam over to a life raft, where other men had already gathered. They helped me aboard, and then we practiced shooting off various types of colored flares into the air. A helicopter came to rescue us and hovered at a slight distance from the raft. I am not sure what type of helicopter it was, but I think it was a Sea King. A crewman squatted by the door of the helicopter and dropped a horseshoe collar. From our training, we knew that we should let the collar hit the water before grabbing it because there would be static electricity that could deliver quite a shock. One by one, the men were hoisted aboard the helicopter. When it came my turn, I slid off the raft and swam to a spot beneath the helicopter. I allowed the collar to fall into the water before I put it over my head and under my arms, but I had not comfortably adjusted it before the crewman started the windlass to haul me up. As a result, the collar caught my neck and forced it back so that I thought I would either suffocate or have my neck broken. I wanted to yell to the crewman to let me readjust the collar, but he could not hear because of the noise of the helicopter. Fortunately, the pressure did not get any worse, and he hoisted me up. He reached out from the door and hauled me in. Then I sat on a bench with the other trainees while more men were lifted into the helicopter. At one point the helicopter engine changed in pitch, and we dropped a few feet before the engine resumed its normal sound. I was startled that we were about to crash into the bay. After everyone was safely aboard, the helicopter took us to the tarmac at Coronado Naval Air Station, where we disembarked. That was the only time I have flown in a helicopter. In Vietnam, because of our security clearance, men in our detachment were not supposed to fly in helicopters, only in fixed-wing multi-engine aircraft. I suppose the reason was that there was a greater likelihood that choppers would crash, and we might be captured and interrogated by the enemy.

On another day, we went by bus to Miramar Naval Air Station, just north of San Diego, for night vision and pressurized training. I do not remember much about the night vision part of the training, except that it involved seeing instrumentation by red light panels. While at Miramar, we were taken to a room with a pressure chamber. A few of us at a time entered the chamber, which was a large white tank with windows for observation by the trainers. We had oxygen masks that we were to put on when the air pressure dropped to simulate flying at a high altitude in a jet. I recall putting on the mask at that point and breathing somewhat nervously through it until the pressure returned to a higher level so that we could remove the mask. Fortunately, while flying in the A-3, one of the aircraft to which I was assigned, I never had to use an oxygen mask, although I had one attached to my flight helmet. The cabin of the A-3 was always pressurized shortly after takeoff, so we would have needed the mask only in an emergency or while bailing out at a high altitude. As mentioned near the beginning of this memoir, one time I tried, unsuccessfully, to put on the mask when I thought we were about to crash, but the pilot pulled the plane out of the steep dive, and the rest of the mission went smoothly.

After the instruction at Coronado, buses transported us to a training area near Warner Springs, California. From our encampment, I could see the Mount Palomar observatory on top of a mountain in the distance. I wished I could go up to the observatory to tour it because I had often read about it and the huge mirror in its large reflecting telescope when I became interested in astronomy in high school. But we had duties to perform, so I helped set up a tent made from a parachute and suspended from a tree limb. This was where I and several other men were to sleep that night while not standing watch.

All of us were hungry since we had now gone for two days without food or drink, other than water and black coffee. We were told that we could eat anything we could hunt or find, but the camp area had been so thoroughly scavenged by previous training groups that there was little available. One of the men cut up a prickly pear cactus lobe, and I ate a bit of it. I realized that, when you are hungry, all you can think about is food. I remembered the delicious meals my mother, grandmothers, and aunts had prepared. I watered at the mouth, thinking about my father's fried perch, hushpuppies, and cheese grits. Just before dark we received C rations since we were to start our prisoner of war experience the next day. I opened the canned beef and the other containers and thought this was one of the most delicious meals I had ever tasted. I licked the gravy and crumbs from my fingers. Someone rightly said that hunger is the best sauce.

While I was sitting by the fire during my time on watch, the moon rose over the hill behind the camp, and coyotes began to make a yip, yip, yip noise. This was the first time I had ever heard coyotes. I noticed movement in the dry grass near the fire and, upon investigating, discovered it was a rabbit. I picked up a rock to throw at it, thinking about carrying out our instructions for hunting. But the rabbit stopped and eyed me, and I decided I was not that hungry.

While we sat around the campfire, some of the men were discussing American history. One of the officers from New England referred to the Plymouth Plantation Colony as the earliest English settlement. I mentioned that the settlement at Jamestown, Virginia, had been established earlier, and he seemed surprised and not inclined to believe me. I in turn was surprised that he had so inaccurate a knowledge of colonial history.

The next morning, I accompanied a group of Air Force pilots to the top of a knoll near the camp. We were given a map and told to triangulate our position, according to the instructions we had been given in class at Coronado, and then mark it with an X on the map. The pilots busied themselves with the mathematics, debating the results among themselves, and I left them to their task, realizing they were far better at calculations than I was, math being my weakest subject. Instead of trying to do the math, I simply looked at the map and compared it to the landscape. I saw a dark green line of trees snaking across the dry countryside to our left and noticed a stream marked on the map in that direction. Next, I observed that the map showed a hill to one side of this stream, using a series of short lines to delineate greater elevation, and in front of the hill was a small rounded elevation. This I concluded was our position since we were standing on a knoll before a higher hill with a stream to our left. But I did not voice my opinion since I was the only enlisted man in the group and the officers were trying to use the methods we had been taught. They marked where they thought we were and showed their decision to the observing officer. It turned out that they were wrong and I was right. I realized then that careful observation and common sense may sometimes be more useful than involved calculations. I knew how to read maps because, ever since childhood, I had enjoyed studying them. I especially liked the maps that came folded inside issues of *National Geographic*. When I was seven or eight years old, some evenings I would open a road map on the kitchen floor, while my parents and I listened to the radio, and then take a toothpick and trace roads on the map, pretending I was driving a car along those routes marked in red and black.

The next day our prisoner of war training began in earnest. We were taken by truck to a broad open area covered with brush and scrub trees. In the distance we could see a flag waving from a pole. Our instructor told us that, if we managed to reach the flag without being captured, we would be rewarded with a sandwich and some milk. First, though, we had to get past the simulated enemy soldiers patrolling the field. These men wore dark blue uniforms that included a cap with a red star on the front. They carried rifles that fired blanks. Then we were told to begin evading the enemy.

After walking into the edge of the brush, I dropped on all fours and started crawling. I went a short distance and rested beneath some dense bushes and waited. It did not seem wise to go too fast. Not far away I heard the soldiers moving and shouting, "I see you, American pig! Stand up!" They fired shots into the air, but I did not fall for this trick. I stayed put. There were shouts and more shots and the sound of movement in the brush nearby. Then for a while everything was quiet. I stayed in place for several minutes, but then began to reflect that the purpose of this exercise was to try to avoid capture while at the same time striving to reach the goal. So I decided that I should move. This was a decision I soon regretted. I moved close to the ground in a crouched position and came to a two-track dirt lane through the field. To get across, I would be in the open. I stood up to cross the road, and immediately a soldier coming around a bend in the road yelled, "Halt, American pig!" I decided to run, and he fired his rifle into the air, shouting, "Halt! Halt!" I stopped, and he said, "That was foolish. I could easily have shot you." He marched me to a staging area where there were two trucks, along with some captured men sitting in rows on the ground. Near the edge of the clearing, there was a waterboard, slightly inclined so that the head of the man on it was lower than his feet. A tee shirt covered his face, and an enemy soldier was pouring water over his mouth as he sputtered and gurgled. Every time the man tried to breathe the cloth of the tee shirt was sucked inward. The soldier was shouting questions at him, pausing, and then pouring more water.

The officer in charge came up to me and said, "The first and last words out of your mouth will be 'Sir.' Do you understand?" I replied, "Yes, Sir." He grabbed me by my shirt front and threw me to the ground, screaming, "What did I just tell you?" I was a fast learner and answered, "Sir, you said that the first and last words out of my mouth would be 'Sir,' Sir." He leaned over and jerked me to my feet and yelled into my face, "If you do not obey every order instantly and exactly, it will be you on the waterboard!" He then removed my glasses and the wallet from my pocket, along with my ID, and made me climb into the back of one of the trucks, where other prisoners were already sitting. A guard placed a canvas hood over my head.

We bounced along a rough road to the prisoner of war camp. When we stepped down from the truck, guards removed our hoods and made us undress down to our skivvies. Then one of the guards proclaimed, "Your government mistreats our people and cowardly attacks our nation, but we are a nation of peace and abide by the Geneva Convention rules for prisoners of war. These rules say that we have to keep you clean and healthy, so the first thing we do is wash you." At that point some of the guards turned water hoses on us. Guards then replaced our hoods and led us to our cells. My guard marched me along a line of metal boxes and then stopped. "This is your cell. Get in!" Motioning to what appeared to be a lard can in the corner, he said, "The can is for your urination and defecation. You are to stay at attention on your knees and wear your hood at all times. When I bang on the box, you will shout your number." He then told me my number and slammed the door. The cell was a cube about waist high. A little light came through the cracks around the door. In the distance I could hear banging and shouting. From our training, I knew that I did not have to obey everything I was told to do in a prisoner of war camp, so I removed the hood and sat down as comfortably as I could. When I heard the guard coming, banging on other boxes, I replaced the hood and got back on my knees.

It was late afternoon when we arrived at the camp and, and soon it was dark. We had been instructed to attempt to escape, but I knew that, without my glasses, in a camp surrounded by a fence topped with concertina wire, doing that would be impossible. Now and then I heard the sound of yelling and machine gun fire from one of the guard towers and assumed that someone was trying to escape. I later learned that some of the men who went through SERE managed to escape two or three times.

After a while the guard brought me my clothes and glasses and told me to sign a form on the clipboard. I hesitated, but we had been instructed to do whatever we could to improve our comfort and chances for survival. As a result, I signed the form and was able to stay warm during the cool night. But it was a long night with little time for rest. Eventually, my guard ordered me out of the cell with my hood on and led me through the camp. I did not know where he was taking me. We crossed a wooden bridge over a ditch or a small stream before coming to a building, where he directed me up the steps. When my hood was removed, I was standing in a brightly lighted room before an interrogator sitting behind a desk. He wore a dark blue uniform with a red star on his cap. He began to question me about my unit and what I was doing in the area. To every question, I gave only my name, rank, and serial number. In the corner behind me was a tall, muscular guard with a scowl on his face. From time to time he smashed his fist into his hand and said, "Let me beat him!" The interrogator lighted a cigarette and calmly replied, "No, no. There is no need for violence. I think that Shippey here can be accommodating. Surely, Shippey, it is just a small matter to tell us about your unit and your mission. No harm can come from that. After all, you are hardly in a position to negotiate, and you have been abandoned to your fate in this camp." Again, I gave only my name, rank, and serial number. With that, the goon in the corner dashed across the floor, grabbed me by my collar, and repeatedly banged me against the wall, which had a plywood facing designed to make the banging seem more brutal than it was. After enduring the banging a few times, I dropped to the floor, as we had been instructed to do if we were subjected to beatings. The guard picked me up and stood me again before the interrogator. He stubbed out his cigarette with a sad face and said, "We do not wish to do you any harm, but regretfully, since you refuse to cooperate, you leave us no choice." Then his demeanor changed, and he said, "Take him to the black box!"

The guard led me outside to a shed with several black wooden boxes in rows. Each box was about the size of a child's coffin. Opening the lid, the guard directed me to get in with my legs crossed since that was the only way a grown man could fit into the box. I did as I was told, and he closed the lid. I tried to get as comfortable as possible in this confined space and discovered that I could raise myself slightly to relieve the pressure on my legs. Actually, I was glad to be in the box because for a while I was left alone. I was worried my legs might go to sleep, but this did not happen. Overall, I was reasonably comfortable because sitting cross-legged on the floor or the bed had always been a favorite way of relaxing for me. A man in one of the other boxes cried out, "My legs are hurting!" The guard gruffly replied, "I hope they drop off!" After maybe twenty or thirty minutes, the guard let me out of the box and, replacing the hood over my head, marched me back to my cell.

Throughout the rest of the night I was led to indoctrination and interrogation sessions to "correct" my capitalist views. In one of the classes, the instructor, a young man about my age, began talking about The Declaration of Independence, arguing that "you Americans" do not live according to the freedom and equality promised by this great document written by Benjamin Franklin. At that point I interrupted him and said, "Wait a minute. Franklin did not write the Declaration of Independence. It was drafted by Thomas Jefferson and then submitted to a committee before being presented to the Continental Congress." The instructor dropped his enemy persona and said, "Really?" For a few minutes before I moved on to the next session, we had an interesting discussion about American democracy.

At dawn the other prisoners and I were let out of our cages and marched to an assembly ground within the compound. The guards, brandishing their rifles, told us we had to work for our breakfast. They directed us to rake the ground of the assembly area with our fingers, and we proceeded to do this while they hovered over us, yelling, "Faster! Faster! No malingering!" It hurt to rake the rocky ground in this way, and I soon had dirty hands and sore fingertips. I was reminded of the times in my childhood when my African American neighbors in the country raked the dirt yard around their house with brooms made from branches of gallberry bushes tied together, creating neat swirling patterns. My mother had also told me that was how she and her family kept the yards neat when she was a child. I was now making swirling patterns in the dry, gray dirt with my fingers while the guard shouted, "No malingering!"

Finally, it was time for breakfast, and we prisoners marched past a huge pot over an open fire, where we were served watery oatmeal. The commandant kept yelling about how we deserved nothing for our bad behavior and the depredations we had made on their country, but he again said that they, unlike our military, were willing to follow the rules for prisoners of war under the Geneva Convention. We were oblivious to what he said as we quickly finished the gruel we had been served.

Then it was time for a war crimes court. One of the prisoners was led to the witness box of this outdoor courtroom, where one of the camp's minions read out a list of abuses committed by the American military and wrongs perpetrated by the prisoner. The prisoner yelled out to object and made a move to escape, but the guards quickly surrounded him, firing shots into the air. I assumed that this slight rebellion had been staged. The trial continued for about an hour with more accusations. Periodically, though, a siren blared, and we were ordered to take cover because of an air raid by American planes. There was a sandbagged bunker, but only a few men could fit in it. The rest of us prisoners simply crouched on the ground until an all-clear siren sounded. The commandant then harangued us further about atrocities committed by the Americans.

At mid-morning we prisoners were lined up in rows before the camp's flagpole. A man was lying on a waterboard behind the pole, and a guard was pouring water over the tee shirt on his face. The commandant said that because of our uncooperative behavior this man had been singled out. A guard raised the flag for their country on the flagpole, and I saw that it resembled the flag of North Vietnam. Then the commandant said, "In our country we show respect to the flag by bowing to it," and he demonstrated a deep bow. He directed us to turn around and told us that, when we turned back around, we should at his command bow to the flag. Most of us did as he directed, bowing to the flag, but a few men refused to bow. The commandant was not pleased. He held a canteen aloft and pointing to the man on the waterboard, shouted, "If you fail to obey my orders instantly and completely and do not show proper respect to our flag, I am betting that I have more water in this canteen than this man has breath in his body!" The man on the waterboard continued to gurgle. The commandant then directed us again to turn around, and at his command, we did another about face and bowed before the flag. Unsurprisingly, he was again not pleased and yelled for us to turn away from the flag again. This time when we turned back around at his command, the American flag was snapping in the breeze against the blue California sky, and all of us instantly popped to attention and saluted. We held the salute while a scratchy recording of "The Star-Spangled Banner" played over the camp's loudspeakers. The American flag had never been more beautiful to me than it was at that moment.

The commandant dropped his persona and, addressing us as "gentlemen," congratulated us on completing SERE school. We then walked to buses that were waiting to take us back to Coronado. As I sat in the air-conditioned bus, enjoying the comfort of the cushioned seat, I was relieved to have passed successfully through the ordeal of SERE school. Completing this training would allow me to wear the air crewman's wings on my dress uniform. I stared out the window at the dry Southern California landscape, contrasting it with the lush vegetation of South Georgia. I then realized that, after all I had been through, my hemorrhoids were acting up, and I quite literally had a pain in the rear.

CHAPTER 19

Return to the Philippines

After returning to the Philippines from SERE school, I could not go back to Da Nang immediately since the officers in charge of the Fleet Support Detachment, and maybe higher up, were debating whether to continue operations out of Da Nang or instead to fly missions off carriers in the Gulf of Tonkin. This last possibility made me uneasy. I definitely preferred being able to fly from the airbase. I spent about a month and a half at San Miguel and enjoyed just being there for a while.

Though I had arrived in the Philippines less than a year earlier, the land and its people had become special to me. The stretch of coast north of Subic Bay in Zambales Province had become a home away from home, a beautiful and tranquil place, especially in comparison to Vietnam. Da Nang was barren of trees and cluttered with rusting CONEX units, discarded tires, tangles of concertina wire, oil-soaked lots behind shops, and bunkers spilling sand from the aging fabric of the bags that composed them. Da Nang was a war machine with the constant roar of jets taking off and landing. San Miguel was dark-haired women, hibiscus flowers blowing in the noon wind, quiet nights disturbed only by roosters crowing against the star-sprinkled sky, green surf crashing onto a steep beach, tidal creeks flowing with clear water, fishermen beside their banca boats mending their nets, and splendid sunsets over the sea viewed from the nipa hut. The waves coming to shore became foam that rushed up the gray volcanic sand of the beach like a bolt of white silk carelessly tossed and then withdrawn in shimmering ripples. At sunset clouds over the West Philippine Sea caught the afterglow, casting crepuscular rays over the dark mountains behind the beach.

One morning after my return, I went out early simply to walk, marveling at the sight of women walking to work on the base, homes set in neat yards, and palm trees with their fronds twisting in the fresh sea breeze like Thai women moving their arms in a graceful nail dance. My eyes were thirsty for tranquil domestic scenes. The jeepneys sporting their gaudy plastic streamers and chrome trim were beautiful to me. I was pleased even with the sight of a barefoot elderly woman driving her cows to pasture along the beach with a pointed stick, jabbing and striking their haunches by turns. These scenes filled me with a calm sense of mystery that soothed my spirit and fortified me for the inevitable return to Da Nang when the time came.

Climbing a Mountain

Being a flatlander from southern Georgia, I have always been amazed by mountains, so the Zambales Mountains that extend along the west coast of Luzon captured my imagination. Two prominent peaks in this range near San Miguel are Mount Maubanban and Mount Pundaquit. I could not take my eyes off them by day or night whenever I was outside. By night they loomed as huge masses ready to engulf the base and the nearby town of San Antonio, but during the day they shrank back to their true dimensions. Much of the time clouds hovered around the summit of Mount Maubanban or wisps of mist rose from the ravines just below the peak. In the late evening sunlight, the ravines on either side of the ridges extending down from the summit stood out stark and blue, and all the singularities and cragginess of the mountain were revealed. At noon on a sunny day the grass-covered slopes glowed with emerald richness, and during the rainy season the waterfall halfway up was visible as a tiny, white line quivering ever so slightly against the background of the dark-green foliage.

I think that it was during September of 1971 when I went with some friends from the det on a climb to the waterfall on Mount Maubanban. I accompanied Dave and Paul to San Antonio, where we met Ron, who was living with his girlfriend, Dora, at her house.* While we waited in the yard for Ron to get ready, I noticed that coins were pressed into the concrete steps leading up to the entrance. This I assumed was for good luck. Dora also brought along for the outing another young woman, Trina, and her little girl, Reyna, a tiny fairy-like child with huge eyes. I do not remember whether Trina was Dora's sister or friend. We took a jeepney through San Antonio along dirt streets bordered on either side by cement block walls with frayed leaves of banana trees drooping over them. Chickens scratching in the street jumped out of our way as we splashed through mud puddles. The jeepney driver deposited us at a grassy area near the bank of a tidal river we would have to cross to reach the base of the mountain.

Fortunately, all of us were wearing shorts, except for Ron, who had

---

*I do not remember everyone who went on the climb this day, so I have used fictitious names.

on blue jeans, so fording the river did not cause us to hesitate. During the crossing Ron carried Reyna piggyback, and Dave held his camera above his head. The stream was maybe fifty feet wide, and the current was strong. The water came up to our waists and chests and at times threatened to knock us off our feet. After coming out of the river, we crossed a mud flat and then followed a fence to where a farmer was hacking at bamboo poles with a machete. Dora asked if we could cross his land to reach the mountain, and without replying, he pointed to the path. I sensed that he was not entirely pleased with our presence.

The soil near the base of Mount Maubanban was red clay, wet and slippery. Low clumps of trees and bushes were scattered here and there. We ascended by following the stream that led from the waterfall. It tumbled down toward us through a green tunnel of trees in rapids and small waterfalls, swirling around in clear, shallow pools in some places. We waded for a while in one of the pools, and then I noticed Reyna, who sat on a boulder near the edge of the stream where her mother had placed her. She was more than ever like a fairy child or the offspring of a naiad sitting upon the rock with her tiny legs folded beneath her and her head tilted back with her short, black hair falling onto her shoulders. In that setting she was a perfect subject for a painting or a photograph. A great painter might have given much to have her pose for him, sitting so charmingly upon her rock. I wished I had brought my camera. Dave, however, had his and took her photograph.

Dora, Trina, and Reyna remained near this spot while my friends and I continued our ascent to the waterfall. Dora and Trina decided that the climb was too steep and dangerous for the child. We slowly worked our way upwards, catching hold of tufts of grass and trunks of saplings, wading through waist-high grass, sometimes tripping over large rocks hidden in the undergrowth. I remembered there are cobra snakes in the Philippines and was afraid of coming upon one.

Finally, we reached the clear pool at the foot of the waterfall. The water descended a fifty-foot natural chute of rock, falling in a white spray about three yards wide. We waded into the pool and worked slowly upwards a little way along the slippery rocks bordering the spray and then sat down in the water and slid down the smooth rock into the pool below. We also simply sat at the base of the fall, letting the water descend upon our backs. After enjoying sliding a few times, we began working our way downward along the stream, often slipping on the wet rocks. For part of the distance, I had to slide along the boulders while sitting down since there was danger in falling over a precipice of ten or fifteen feet with the water leaping and swirling over it.

We rejoined the women and Reyna and descended to the pasture at the base of the mountain. There were some guava trees there, and we climbed onto the lower branches to pick some of the fruit. I had never tried guava before and realized, upon biting into it, that it was very seedy. We all laughed and spat the seeds onto the ground. Finally, before re-crossing the river, we sat in a row on a log for a photograph. I noticed a pile of carabao dung on the ground in front of the log as Dave prepared to snap the photo. After crossing the river again, we waited for a long time before motorized tri-wheelers came along the road to take us back to the village. A few days after our adventure on the mountain, the commander of the communications station ordered that no one should go up to the waterfall on Mount Maubanban since the stream was the source of the water supply for San Antonio. I was somewhat embarrassed but realized that we were probably not the only group who had made the climb.

Epiphany

One night after returning to San Miguel from SERE school, I was in the upstairs lounge of the barracks reading William Faulkner's novel *The Hamlet*. I was thinking about the South and the part it has played in the history and culture of the nation when a guy I knew came in and sat down. I think he was one of the men stationed aboard ship in the Gulf of Tonkin rather than at Da Nang. We began talking about geographical regions of the United States, and I ventured that New England and the South were the two poles that had shaped the American character. Being from Illinois, he pointed out that the Midwest had also played a prominent role. Later that evening, reflecting on what he had said, I saw that he was right and that I was being too provincial in my thinking. As I consider that conversation now, I realize that we both needed to expand our horizons to understand that the West, especially the Southwest with its Spanish-Mexican settlements dating from the sixteenth century, also had a major part in shaping the American character and that we should not forget the enduring role of Native Americans and the multitudes of people who came from countries all over the world. All had made important contributions to American culture, and as members of the nation's military, whether they agreed with the Vietnam War or not, we were representing all of them. Then my thinking expanded to include the Vietnamese people as well, those in both the South and the North, for they had become inextricably linked to America and its history. I had no animosity for the North Vietnamese or the Viet Cong, even though we were waging a war against them and they had killed thousands of our men. Rather, I had compassion for the Vietnamese people because of all they had suffered during the war and its aftermath, and I hoped that they did not hate us because of all the damage we had inflicted.

While working to complete this memoir, I woke up one night in the wee hours and could not immediately go back to sleep. I kept thinking about Da Nang and my travels in Thailand, the Philippines, and America, remembering how much I had learned while in the Navy. Lying there staring at the ceiling, I pictured the Earth as it rotates in space with the terminator line, marking sunrise on one side of the globe and sunset on the other. I envisioned the Earth turning towards the sunrise as the terminator line passed across the Atlantic, and then the East Coast, the Midwest, the Rocky Mountains, and the Pacific coast, moving across the Hawaiian Islands, as night drew back and day came to the other side of the globe in East Asia, touching Mount Maubanban in the Philippines, and Monkey Mountain in Da Nang, and then moved on, bringing morning to the pagodas of Bangkok, the ghats of Varanasi in India, the Steppes of Russia, the minarets of the Blue Mosque in Istanbul, the spires of Notre Dame de Chartres in France, and Mount Snowdon in Wales, passing over land and sea, embracing the world. I also thought of the terminator line that simultaneously brings sunset and night and hoped that the gradual envelopment of the globe in darkness was not a metaphor for the future, which is ambivalent, for the sun is always rising and setting on some part of the Earth. I recalled the photograph taken by the astronauts who landed on the moon, showing the Earth, like a precious lapis lazuli jewel, blue and swirled with white, floating against the black velvet background of space above the pallid lunar surface. I realized that, in spite of our many conflicts and differences, we are all one people on this orb and that our compassion, understanding, and acceptance of one another must move beyond our small bit of Earth to embrace the whole of it. Being in the Navy and coming into contact with men from different parts of the nation, as well as people from other nations, helped me on my journey to this kind of understanding. I saw my region in the southern United States as a part of the wonderful whole. Then I imagined myself stepping outside into the yard to look at the night sky, as I had often done, observing the stars in all of their splendor, arranged in constellations—Ursa Major, Cassiopeia, Taurus, Orion, and Canis Major—and the Milky Way, stretching diagonally across the sky like a pale road leading outward past the Magellanic Clouds, the local group, black holes, quasars, and billions of other galaxies, moving steadily outward, until I could see the entire universe like an intricate web of lights strung across the void, each infinitesimal spark a galaxy holding billions of stars. I realized how petty our wars and conflicts seem against the vast panorama of creation and stood in awe of its magnificence and the One who created it and sustains it moment by moment. Then I came back to reality and realized that I needed to go back to sleep because I had to go to work the next day. An epiphany, after all, must be followed by a return to everyday reality. Likewise, the beauty and tranquility of the Philippines had to be followed by my return to the grimness of the war in Vietnam.

Afternoons on the Beach

One afternoon while walking along the beach at San Miguel, I met a boy, maybe eleven or twelve years old, wearing shorts, a tank top, and a ball cap. He asked me for some money, and I replied by asking him his name. "El Mundo," he said. Remembering the street urchins I had encountered in Manila, I smiled and said, "I know that is not your name. It means 'the world.'" I continued talking with him for a few minutes, answering his questions, while he climbed on top of an overturned banca boat. Ever so often he again asked for money, and I put him off by continuing to talk. After a while he grew tired of the conversation and walked south along the beach in the direction of his village. Thinking about him now, almost fifty years later, I realize that, in a sense, El Mundo was an appropriate name for him since he represented so many kids in the world living in third-world countries. To him, even an enlisted man in the Navy must have seemed rich. That thought brought to mind what the commanding officer of the station had said to us when we arrived about how, to the local people, San Miguel was like a paradise set down in their midst.

I walked along the beach on a warm September afternoon. Rain squalls were moving in the distance over the West Philippine Sea. Dark gray lines slanted obliquely towards the green surface of the sea where rain was falling. A cloud moved into the coast south of me and passed before the mountains, lashing the palm trees. The rain advanced, and the mountains vanished behind an opaque wall of white. Sea birds flapped sideways against the wind, heading out over the waves. The rain reached where I was walking and slashed the water in the tidal pools and pelted the volcanic sand of the beach. The rain made a sucking sound all around me as the coarse sand absorbed it. I was soaked but did not mind. As I returned along the beach, I was again amazed at how beautiful the Philippines could be and thought of the communications station and its surroundings as a serene spot, a refuge for a while from what was happening on the other side of the South China sea.

CHAPTER 20

Da Nang Again

As mentioned earlier, returning to Da Nang after SERE school and being in the PI for almost two months was a relief. It may seem odd that I should have thought of returning in that way, but to some extent it was like coming home. I think this feeling had to do with the fact that the men of the detachment, in spite of all their differences, formed a kind of family. There was always someone to talk with, someone who understood, at least in part, what you were experiencing. We had shared the flights, the rocket attacks, the crazy times, and the uncertainty that comes from hazardous duty. Years later I read Sebastian Junger's book *Tribe*, in which he presents the idea that men in war or other types of dangerous duty form a tribal bond. Their compeers become a support group. They endure danger together, they hurt together, they weep together, and they laugh and have fun together. He claims that, when they separate from the unit and return home, they may no longer have this kind of support and feel alone, not knowing how to rejoin their former life. He argues that this, in addition to the trauma of battle, may be a cause of PTSD. Tim O'Brien presents this kind of scenario in *The Things They Carried*. Norman Bowker returns from the Vietnam War to his hometown in Iowa and discovers that his girlfriend has married, his father is not easy to relate to, and his friends have moved on with their lives. He drives round and round the lake in the town, quite literally going in circles, not knowing what to do with himself. Eventually, he commits suicide by hanging himself at the local YMCA. His Army unit in Vietnam had been his support group, in a sense his family. Whatever the reason was, I was relieved to be back in Da Nang, even though some of the most dangerous times that I experienced were still ahead of me.

Adventures in Flying

Although I still flew some on the EC-121 and the EP-3B after my return, much of my flight time was on the EA-3B. These were always

Aerial view of the north end of Da Nang Air Base. The base had two runways, both approximately two miles in length. Det Bravo was on the west side of the base, the far side in the photograph. Freedom Hill is immediately behind the midpoint of the base. The Annamite Range is in the distance (photograph by Bill Dillon).

exciting missions. Sitting back of the pilot in the cockpit, although facing the tail of the plane, I had a panoramic view. We sometimes flew over the Gulf of Tonkin during the day, but more often our track was over Laos at night. The scopes of my radio receivers glowed green in the darkness, and I kept a sharp look-out for spikes indicating air activity. Sometimes, though, I looked up to see the moon or the stars. One night I noticed Orion off our port wing as we flew south on our track, and I remembered looking at this constellation from the front yard of my home. Being over possibly hostile territory at the time did not seem quite so intimidating since the constellation connected me with home. At times on one of my receivers, I had a MiG-21 up, flying towards us on a heading of 270 degrees, and I did not know if we or some other aircraft was the target towards which the pilot was being guided. I and the others who flew on these missions were living life on the edge, and for me it was difficult to come down from the high produced by the excitement and danger of those events.

By the time I left Da Nang I had 1,298.8 combat flight hours. This did not represent the actual number of hours I had accumulated since, each time I flew on Black Track in the A-3, twenty-five hours were added to my flight time, even though these missions took only four to four and a half hours of real time. At any rate, for ten months of duty that was a fairly large amount of flying. It is amazing to me that I accumulated this much flight time since I had always been somewhat afraid of flying and vowed upon entering the Navy that I did not ever want to have flight duty. In retrospect I am glad that I had that opportunity to fly with the Spooks. Those hours of being air borne in the EC-121, the P-3, and especially the A-3 were some of the most exciting, dangerous, scary, stress-filled, demanding, beautiful, and wonder-filled times of my life. So here I want simply to convey some impressions of what it was like to fly.

Pre-Flight Duties

Before an A-3 flight Tim Yerdon and I sometimes had the duty of going to the mess hall to get canisters of water and coffee for the crew. We also picked up cinnamon rolls with a yucky-looking green icing. I suppose these provisions were for all of the crew and not just the officers, but I do not recall partaking of them while flying on the A-3. I was too busy monitoring the air traffic of the North Vietnamese Air Force to have time for refreshments. Besides, there was no place at my position to set a cup of coffee or a cinnamon roll. Yerdon sat in the fuselage with the rest of the crew and monitored SAM radio communications. Before flights I sometimes saw him carrying an encryption device that looked like a huge flash drive with a handle attached on one end and on the other an opening in which were several rods set at various lengths. This crypto gear provided a secure voice circuit for the plane to communicate with Red Crown and other ships in the Gulf of Tonkin.

Prior to a flight we looked at a huge map that hung on the wall in the workspaces. This map showed the tracks of any drones that were scheduled to do a fly-over of North Vietnam that day. It also gave the track for any SR-71 Blackbird that was going to fly reconnaissance over the country. During the war this was a highly secret aircraft, but today it is on display at various air museums around the country. These supersonic jets flew so high and fast that the North Vietnamese could not shoot them down with MiGs, anti-aircraft artillery, or SAMs. I was told that after a mission the skin of the fuselage was so hot from air friction that it could not be touched for quite a while. This was an impressive aircraft. As mentioned earlier, while on my way to SERE school, I saw one of these planes from a distance preparing for takeoff at Kadena Airfield in Okinawa when my plane stopped there.

I recall going to one or two pre-flight briefings with VQ-1, but the usual routine for TacAir Spooks was simply to go to our own workspaces and gather our reel-to-reel tapes, legal pads, and pens. If I was flying in the A-3, I grabbed my helmet and put on a torso harness, which could be attached to the parachute at my position. Aboard the EC-121 and P-3, we sat at our assigned ditching stations for takeoff and were also supposed to put on flight gloves in case the plane crashed and we had to place our hands onto hot metal in escaping, assuming that we survived the crash. After we were in the air, we went to our various positions and got ready to begin monitoring. I threaded the reel-to-reel tapes onto the two tape recorders mounted over my two radio receivers. Then I put on my headphones and began listening for air activity as we approached our track. Sometimes early in the morning I could hear ground control at Hanoi Bac Mai warming up for the day's training. The controller would adjust his radio with squeaks and squawks

Mike Barnowski and David Gilbert standing beside an EA-3B, Da Nang, 1972. They have on the helmet and torso harness worn by the crew of an A-3. The harness could be attached to a parachute at the crew member's position. As a TacAir op, Barnowski sat in the cockpit immediately behind the pilot, and Gilbert, as a SAM op, had a position in the fuselage (photograph by David Gilbert).

and then say several times, "*Một, một, một, một, một. Một, hai, ba, bốn, năm; một, hai, ba, bốn, năm*" ("One, one, one, one, one. One, two, three, four, five; one, two, three, four, five"). Then eventually, I would hear the command to take off, and the formation flying or practice ground control intercept training for the day would begin. I settled into my routine and kept the evaluation officer informed about what was happening.

A Strange Day

One morning when I climbed into my position in the A-3, we had a different pilot, a Navy captain who had flown down from VQ-1 in

Japan to get his flight pay and hazardous duty pay. A young lieutenant was in the navigator's seat, and I realized he was accompanying the captain since I had not seen him before. The captain was busy with the pre-flight check and kept asking the lieutenant questions: "What does this do? What is this gauge? Now what is this for?" I gathered that the lieutenant was also a pilot familiar with the A-3 because he continued giving explanations. The captain appeared to be in his late fifties or early sixties, and the longer I sat there listening to his questions, the more nervous I became. I wondered, "Does he really know how to fly this plane?" Finally, the check was complete, and we taxied out to the runway and took off.

That morning we flew over the Gulf of Tonkin, and for a while everything was normal. Then in the middle of the flight, I heard the captain stirring in his seat, and after a while, the lieutenant turned to me and asked, "Can you hand the captain the pilot's relief tube?" I did not understand what he was referring to and naively asked, "What is that?" The lieutenant replied, "The tube in which the pilot pisses. It's a long hose with a funnel attached." It had never occurred to me that anyone could take a leak while flying in the A-3. I assumed that we simply had to hold it. The lieutenant explained that the captain could not find the tube where he was sitting and it might have fallen down alongside my seat. I ran my hand down the side of my seat next to the bulkhead but could not feel the tube. At this point, the captain put the plane on autopilot, got up from his position, and came back to where I was sitting. He leaned across me, groping for the relief tube for two or three minutes, but he too could not find it. He then went to the relief tube in the back of the plane, and I prayed that he would not fall and knock himself unconscious as we barreled along through the sky with no one piloting the plane since the A-3 does not have dual controls. Looking much relieved, he returned to his position, and the flight returned to normal. Near the end of the flight, however, I heard him radioing the USS *Enterprise*, asking if we could land on the carrier, which was on station in the Gulf. He wanted to practice his carrier landings. At this point I was praying again since I had never been trained for carrier flights and realized that a plane landing on a flight deck went from approximately 150 knots to zero in one second when the tail hook caught the wire. I had visions of the jet missing the wire and going off the end of the fight deck into the sea with thousands of tons of aircraft carrier bearing down on us. Fortunately, the *Enterprise* was too busy with its launch schedule to take us aboard, and I learned that the captain and his young aide flew out later in the afternoon so that he could practice his carrier landing and takeoff. All in all, that was a strange day.

Interesting Sights

One night on the A-3 we were coming off track over Laos, where the weather had been clear, but as we descended towards Da Nang, we came down through a thick cloud cover. I could see the running lights flashing and illumining the clouds around us. Then I noticed something strange. A blue light appeared along the leading edge of the port wing and around the top of the engine cowling. I was puzzled by this phenomenon, and then I realized that it was St. Elmo's fire. I had read about it in Herman Melville's *Moby Dick*, and it had also been depicted in the movie version of the novel. The blue light continued to glow for a minute or two and then disappeared just before we broke through the clouds and saw the runway lights of Da Nang in the distance.

One afternoon I was sitting by the porthole in the rear of the P-3 as we were coming off track. We were flying about fifty feet over a relatively smooth cloud cover with sunlight brightly reflecting off it. I imagined that we were moving above an extensive field of snow with here and there a slight protuberance. The shadow of the plane flickered as it passed over irregularities on the cloud surface, and then I saw that the shadow was enclosed by a rainbow halo. On another occasion I happened to glance out the porthole of the P-3 and saw for an instant the brown bat-like sail of a junk on the sea below us as we returned to Da Nang. Again, on the P-3 late one afternoon, I looked through the porthole towards the west and was surprised to see the coast of North Vietnam maybe thirty or forty miles away. The sun was about to set, and it illumined the bays and inlets of the coast, as well as a river, which reflected the golden light a good distance into the interior of the country. That was my only sight of North Vietnam. While on track aboard the P-3 one cloudy day, it was almost dark when someone mentioned that he could see China. I went to the porthole and saw far away a dark line extending across the gray surface of the sea. This was the coast of Hainan Island in the northeastern part of the Gulf of Tonkin. In 1971 Mao Zedong was still alive, and it did not seem likely that any American would be able to visit China. Of course, that changed about a year later when President Nixon went to China and was greeted at the airport in Beijing by Prime Minister Zhou Enlai.

Air Strike

Anyone might think it strange that, with all the bombing and fighting going on in Vietnam, we did not see more of this kind of action. One time, though, I saw an air strike from the TacAir position on the A-3. We had diverted to Thailand after a mission because of bad weather at Da Nang, and we were returning from an overnight stay at either Udorn or Ubon. We were over the jungle in Laos, and I was looking from the cockpit at a place where a river looped below us. Against the dark foliage, I saw something white that kept getting larger. I could not make out what it was and was becoming leery of it. Then a silver speck suddenly swooped over the spot, and there was a flash with a circular shock wave. I realized that the white spot was a smoke marker and that I had just witnessed an air strike. The event seemed distant and unreal, but some men down there likely died.

On that same flight back to Da Nang, we saw two B-52s several thousand feet above us going north. They appeared white against the blue background of the sky. Our pilot mentioned that we needed to be careful that we were not beneath them when they released their bombs, a danger that had not occurred to me.

Tense Moments

One day we were getting ready to go on track over the Gulf of Tonkin in the A-3, and we were already beyond the point that marked the demarcation between North and South Vietnam. Facing the rear of the plane, I saw another aircraft behind and a little above us. Knowing the preferred shoot-down position of a MiG, I became a bit nervous. I realized this was probably a Navy jet that had just taken off from Da Nang and was on its way to a carrier in the Gulf, but I notified the pilot through the intercom that another aircraft was behind us. After a while, the pilot asked me if the plane was still on our tail, and I confirmed that it was indeed still there. The pilot did not take any evasive measures, and in a few minutes the plane took a different course. Coming off track on the A-3 on another day, the pilot mentioned that our IFF (Identification Friend or Foe) transponder was not working. This meant that ground control at Da Nang could not determine by the IFF system if our aircraft was hostile or friendly. We spent several tense minutes returning to the field, and I wondered if we were shortly going to have the company of an F-4; however, the pilot must have maintained radio contact with the control tower because we were able to land without an incident.

Buzzing the USS Ranger

One afternoon as we were coming off track in the A-3, our pilot wanted to do a flyby of the USS *Ranger*, one of the aircraft carriers on station in the

Gulf of Tonkin. I suppose he radioed the carrier to let them know we were approaching. He descended to a low altitude and spotted the wake of the ship, and for several minutes we followed it. I could clearly see where the carrier had passed and was surprised that the wake lasted so long. Eventually, we came up to the *Ranger* and flew by on its port side as the men on the flight deck waved at us. We were so close that a man with a strong arm and a good aim might have thrown a baseball and hit us. Another carrier I saw in the Gulf of Tonkin was the *Enterprise*, thirty-thousand feet below us as it was making a turn to port accompanied by its escorts. Gazing down on the carrier, I saw another jet pass below us at an angle to our path, and the perspective from our movement made it appear to be flying sideways. I also saw the *Enterprise* anchored at a distance in the entrance to Subic Bay. While assigned to Coronado Island during SERE training, I saw three carriers docked in San Diego harbor, one of which, if I remember correctly, was the USS *Constellation*. In November 2017 the Spooks had their third reunion at Patriot's Point in Charleston, South Carolina, and held a two-bell ceremony on the flight deck of the USS *Yorktown* to honor men of the detachment who had died. This was the first reunion I had a chance to attend. My son Daniel and I were moved by the ceremony and enjoyed touring this World War II carrier. While flying out of Da Nang, I was glad that I never had to land on and take off from an aircraft carrier, but in looking back, I think that would have been an interesting experience. Other men in our detachment, as the war was winding down, sometimes had to remain airborne over the Gulf of Tonkin for as long as fourteen hours. At the time they were based at Cubi Point in the Philippines, but returning there to refuel required too long. As a result, they recovered aboard a carrier on station and took off again several times and sometimes also refueled in air. Gary Nelson provides an account of this in Bob Morrison's history of the detachment.

Aerial Ballet

On another afternoon I was aboard the A-3 en route to Bangkok. We had already crossed the Mekong River and were moving steadily across the flat terrain of Thailand. Thirty-thousand feet below I could see red clay between green fields. Billowy clouds moved slowly to our rear, and I could see their shadows imprinting the ground. The A-3 yawed gently in a regular motion from the setting of the automatic pilot. That motion and the low roar of the engines made me sleepy. Suddenly, there was a silver flash through the cockpit. Far below the metal roof of a barn had caught the afternoon sunlight. I relaxed and closed my eyes to rest.

The engines changed pitch, the A-3 banked, and I saw a huge cloud mass sailing upward past the cockpit. The jet banked sharply and wove its way down between the clouds, inclining first to starboard and then to port, gradually descending. Below were low hills and forest with here and there columns of smoke rising from farms where land was being cleared. The plane made a long bank, returning back upon the huge cloud mass and then veering in the opposite direction on another extended circle. Then I realized what was happening. The pilot was expending fuel before making the approach to Don Mueang Airport. For thirty to forty minutes we weaved our way through the clouds, sometimes passing through their tips in opaque grayness, circling above the hills northeast of Bangkok in a kind of aerial ballet. The fields were a rich yellow-green that absorbed the late afternoon sunlight and turned it into glowing colors that would shame even the most resplendent macaw. Clumps of palm trees scattered about the countryside marked farmhouses, and I could see the windshields of cars and trucks reflecting the sunlight as they moved along the roads bordering the canals that crisscrossed the landscape.

The jet descended, and I could discern workers, their trousers rolled

PR-1 at Don Mueang Airport, Bangkok, taking on fuel for the return to Da Nang after a bennie trip, late 1971 or early 1972. A C-47 is in the background on the right. This was my last trip to Bangkok during my time in Vietnam. In 2010 my wife, Sue, son Philip, and I visited Bangkok but landed at Suvarnabhumi Airport, which replaced Don Mueang as the international airport (photograph by the author).

up, bending over their work in the rice paddies. I could see water buffalo swishing their tails, thrusting their heads upward as they drew heavy plows. Then I could see white lotus blossoms on the black canal water as we made our final approach to the airfield. The jet and its shadow rushed to meet each other, uniting once more into an earthbound reality as the jet bumped and pressed nose-down onto the runway with the engines roaring. I felt the drag chute blossom behind us. We taxied to a spot a short distance beyond a C-141 Starlifter, drooping its wings above the white-hot concrete. It was good to climb down from the A-3, remove my helmet, and savor the momentary peace and quietness of the airfield before we made our way into Bangkok. From the eaves of nearby buildings, I could hear sparrows chirping.

Christmas in Da Nang

It is always difficult for men and women in combat zones to be away from home at Christmastime. The year 1971 marked the second year I had been away from my family, so naturally I was homesick and kept thinking about all the wonderful Christmases I had enjoyed in earlier years. I knew I would miss Christmas Eve with my mother and father, a time when we read the story of the birth of Jesus from Luke 2 and then afterwards opened presents. I would also miss the Christmas dinner with a roasted turkey or honey-eyed ham sliced in a spiral cut, along with the red velvet cake and Japanese fruitcake that my mother baked for dessert. Most of all, though, I would miss just being with my mother and father and all of my extended family. So that second Christmas in Southeast Asia was difficult. We did, however, take time to celebrate the holiday, and Christmas in Da Nang was different, to say the least.

As the holiday approached, Bob Hope brought his Christmas show to Da Nang. This had been his annual gift to American troops overseas since World War II. I did not attend the show since I had duty that day, but I heard radio communication from his jet as it approached the airfield at Da Nang. I was on track aboard the P-3 that evening and tuned down to a strong signal that appeared on my scope. Da Nang air traffic control was talking with women who were stars in the show. They had apparently gone to the cockpit of their jet to talk to and joke with the air traffic controllers as they prepared to land. Some of the men from the detachment were able to attend the show and took photos. I appreciated what Bob Hope and the performers did for the troops, and the show was apparently a great success, in spite of the rainy weather.

On Christmas Eve as darkness settled over the base, I walked from our

Bob Hope Christmas Show, Da Nang, 1971. Some of the Spooks attended the show, but I did not go since I had duty that day. The previous night, when we were about to come off track from a mission on the P-3, my radio receivers picked up chatter between women in the show and ground control at Da Nang as Bob Hope's plane was preparing to land (photograph by Tim Yerdon).

work building to the barracks. A helicopter wrapped in colorful Christmas lights passed overhead, playing "Jingle Bells" from a loudspeaker. It continued to cross back and forth over the base and surrounding installations, blaring out Christmas carols. The highlight of that Christmas, though, was a bash in the Spook mess upstairs in the barracks. The centerpiece for the occasion was a whole roasted pig on a board in the middle of the pool table. A billiard ball, in lieu of an apple, was placed in its mouth. Surrounding the pig was a Lucullan feast, featuring numerous dishes, including a cheese ball, crackers, mixed nuts, chips, cookies, fruit, candy, cokes, beer, and Cold Duck. Around the table Christmas ornaments hung by threads from the ceiling. After we had all partaken of the food, the Cold Duck bottles were opened. The guys enjoyed shaking the bottles so that the corks popped and went flying across the room with foam spilling out of the bottles onto the floor. The men took special joy in aiming the corks at the Christmas balls. When one was struck and shattered, everyone yelled with delight and slapped the shooter on the back. As the evening proceeded, only the hooks for the ornaments hung from the threads, and broken pieces of colored balls lay in all the serving plates and bowls on the table, blending in with the nuts, cheese cubes, and crackers. Fragments from the ornaments littered the floor, causing everyone to slip and slide as the bacchanal continued. Empty bottles of beer and cokes lay randomly scattered over the floor, along with broken potato chips, and smashed pieces of cheese. As each bottle of Cold Duck was emptied, it was placed on the platform where the poker table was located. In the wee hours of the morning, there was a line of bottles like stage lights along the edge of the platform. During the evening many of the guys paid their respects to Marduk, a name given by Rudy Cole to the concrete top of a shrapnel metal drum just beyond the rail of the stairs leading up to the mess. This was a spot for puking. From long usage as a place for these oblations, the concrete surface was covered with a green fuzz and other vile things. When Christmas morning came, the Spook mess was quiet; all the revelry of the evening was spent. When the door opened, the light shone in, illuminating the detritus of the celebration. A different kind of Christmas, indeed, certainly not a silent night. But the Bob Hope show and the detachment Christmas bash provided the men at Da Nang a brief respite from the war. These events were a catharsis for all of the pent-up emotions and stress resulting from hazardous duty.

Sacred Heart Orphanage

Occasionally, men from Det Bravo visited the Sacred Heart Orphanage at China Beach. Roman Catholic nuns staffed the orphanage and appreciated any supplies or gifts that men from the various military units in Da Nang gave to help the children. I went on only one of the det trips to the orphanage, but some of the guys visited several times and enjoyed being with the boys and girls. Randy Bennett was one of these men, and as mentioned earlier, there is a photo of him smiling and holding a little girl wearing a blue sweater. I remember that on the visit I made, one of our chiefs was a bit miffed when he lost a wristwatch at the orphanage, but I thought that was a small price to pay for any good that we could do for the benefit of the children.

Night

In the humid darkness of the Vietnamese night, a helicopter chops its way across the base towards Freedom Hill. I sit quietly by a solitary lamp, reading André Malraux's *Antimemoirs*, how he writes about the American fleet riding the sea off Da Nang. A mosquito sounds its triumph in my ear, and I swat in vain. I hear the click of Spook's claws; then she settles for the night into the cardboard box inside my cubicle. Upstairs in the Spook mess, music by Santana is playing. I insert my Joni Mitchell cassette into the player and listen to her singing "Blue," "River," and "The Last Time I Saw Richard."

The music makes me sad and nostalgic. Lying in my bunk before going to sleep, I wonder if the barracks might get a direct hit from a rocket. I decide not to worry about that and think instead about home, where it is almost noon. Late at night there is time to think about home. I remember walking down Gordon Avenue out into the country with my bird dog Dan and any of the neighbors' dogs that wanted to go with us rather than lie under the carport of their houses and be bored. We had some adventures. Sometimes we walked up a covey of quail in a field next to the road. Sometimes I heard them moving before the dog pointed, and I would say, "Close in here now! Close!" It was beautiful to see him hold a point. Then suddenly, the covey would start up, making my heart skip a beat. Dan would rear back, watching them dart for the woods. Then we would make our way through the swamp across drainage ditches. One time the dog fell off the log we used to cross the ditch. In his efforts to get back onto the log, he kept twirling around it and dropping back into the water. I laughed until I almost cried and finally went to his rescue. Sometimes he and I sat on the back-porch steps at night and listened to the other dogs barking down the street. In the distance we might hear a train whistle, and then everything was quiet. I looked at the stars and wondered about the names of the constellations. I wondered what the future might hold. The dog reached over and nibbled along my arm with his front teeth the way he might try to get at fleas on his side. This was a mark of his affection, and I rubbed his ears and said, "Youse old hound!" Those were good days. How I missed just sitting on the back steps and listening to the sounds of the night. A brief burst of M16 fire in the distance brings me back to the present reality and the realization that I must fly again in the morning on the P-3.

Packages from Home

Shortly after I arrived in Da Nang, I received some Valentine chocolates in a heart-shaped box. The center of this box, sent by my mother, had been smashed in transit, but I ate the candy anyway and enjoyed it because it was a link with home. In thinking about the candy nowadays, I recall a scene from the movie *The Battle of the Bulge* in which the German tank commander, played by Robert Shaw, called his officers to a meeting. He held up a chocolate cake and mentioned that it had been captured that morning from an American Army private. He asked the officers if they knew what that meant. There was a long silence, and then the commander said that it meant they had lost the war because the Americans had enough fuel to fly chocolate cake across the Atlantic Ocean while there was not enough petrol for their Panzers to continue fighting the battle. During the Vietnam War the infrastructure of the American military was impressive. It had the means to fly packages across the Pacific to enlisted men in Vietnam so that I could enjoy smashed Valentine chocolates from my mother, my roommate Rusty could receive Edelweiss cheese from his wife, and LeBrun could announce, eyes aglow, "They've got fig newtons in the mess hall!" It was not for lack of infrastructure that America did not win the war.

Strange Sights and Unusual Happenings

One pleasant, sunny afternoon, I was relaxing in my room in the barracks. I lay back on my bed and suddenly felt the bed and the floor shaking. The shaking lasted for a few seconds and then stopped. I stood up and wondered, "Earthquake?" Then I went outside, but nothing unusual seemed to be happening. It was a calm, beautiful afternoon; there was no sound of explosions or fighting. In the distance I could clearly see the misty mountains behind Freedom Hill. Then it occurred to me what I had just experienced. The trembling of the earth was caused by B-52s dropping their bombs maybe twenty or thirty miles to the west. I was amazed at the power of the bombing that could shake the ground like a mild earthquake from such a distance.

One foggy morning I was walking from our work building to the barracks. I was passing the VQ-1 hangar when I saw something strange coming towards me in the fog. At first, I could not make out what it was; then from the mist there emerged a guy riding on a tall unicycle. Just before he reached me, he turned into the hangar, and I realized he was one of the mechanics going to work. This was just one of the strange, random things that I saw from time to time, but In Vietnam I had come to expect the unusual.

As mentioned earlier, a few Marine guys were assigned to work with us in the detachment. One morning we woke up to find the words "Tiger Security" painted in huge yellow letters on different things in our compound. The Marines had obviously had a wild night. "Tiger Security" was painted on the water tank, on the walls of the heads, and on the water buffalo tank next to one of the heads, as well as other places. These Marines worked and played well with the Navy detters. Occasionally, though, they had to remind us that Marines were different. A few times they went on raiding parties to other areas around the base. They brought back plywood, corrugated tin pieces, cinder blocks, and other items they wanted for some pet project. They took pride in being able to get into and out of another unit's area without being caught. Sometimes, though, they had to beat a hasty retreat in the detachment truck. I recall that one of the Marines had abrasions and scratches on various parts of his body from falling off the back of the truck on one of these escapades.

Near the end of my tour in Vietnam, Spook, one of the two det dogs, became attached to me and sometimes slept in a cardboard box in my room. I affectionately called her "Spooky." One afternoon I noticed that she was jerking spasmodically as she walked as if he she were having a seizure. I was concerned that she might die. The duty driver and I took Spook to the veterinarian on the Air Force side of the base. I held Spook in my lap while we rode, and the muscles in her body continued to jerk and made popping noises. When we arrived, the vet looked at Spook and asked if she had recently had puppies. We replied that she had. He diagnosed her as having a calcium deficiency and took up a syringe to inject her. He said, "This is a miracle cure. She should be better in a few minutes," and that is what happened. In a little while the seizures stopped, and Spook began hassling in a normal, relaxed way. We returned to the barracks much relieved.

One of Spook's litter was named "Killer," though I called this cute roly-poly puppy "Killer Diller." I enjoyed holding Killer and talking to him. Unfortunately, he disappeared shortly before Christmas, and I suspected that he went to someone's dinner table.

A reminiscence in the detachment history by Bob Morrison relates what eventually happened to the det dogs. When the detachment was preparing to close down at the beginning of 1973, no one wanted to leave the dogs behind. Beggar died in 1972, apparently the victim of poisoning, but Spook and Brutus, one of her litter, were still with the det. According to Duane Mann, Mike Barnowski and John Phipps built wooden crates for the dogs, and valium to drug the dogs was obtained from the hospital corpsmen next door. Then Spook and Brutus were shipped in the crates, labeled "Drug Dogs," to the Philippines, where they lived with Duane in the village of San Antonio, near the naval communications station. When his tour was up, the dogs remained in the P. I.

One morning when I did not have flight duty, Clay West, a CTM1, needed to go up to the communication station on Monkey Mountain and offered to let me ride with him. I gladly accepted because I had many times looked at the huge satellite dishes halfway up the mountain on the other side of the base and wished that I could go there. West was a good man,

Herb Shippey with Spook, one of the detachment mascots. "Spooky," as I called her, had several litters of puppies during the det's time in Da Nang. Beggar, another mascot, was one of her offspring while I was there. Spook sometimes slept in a cardboard box in my cubicle in the barracks. She and Beggar often ran with us to the bunker during a rocket attack. This photograph was taken December 26, 1971, my twenty-seventh birthday (photograph by the author, retouched by Aron Cook).

quiet and efficient in everything he did, and I enjoyed the ride and talking some with him. When Typhoon Hester hit Da Nang, he was one of the men on the roof of our barracks placing sandbags to prevent the tin from being stripped off. We left the airfield and crossed the bridge over the river. Then we passed through Tien Sha on the road leading up to the mountain. A flat-bed truck zoomed around us. It had no cab, just the seat, the dashboard, and a steering wheel. An Army guy wearing a sleeveless undershirt was driving the truck and clinging to the back of his neck was a tiny yellow monkey with its tail streaming in the wind. Then we started on the winding road that led up the mountain to the communication station. The mountain was covered with trees, but occasionally, there was a gap through which I could see Da Nang Bay spread out below us and the jagged mountains on the north side of the bay. The scene was majestically beautiful, and I realized what a wonderful place Da Nang would be to visit if there were no war. I remained in the truck while West went inside to deliver whatever he had brought in a small cardboard box. On the return trip we stopped briefly at the military hospital in Tien Sha and went inside. I do not recall why West wanted to stop there. All that I remember is seeing a long open ward with many wounded and sick men lying in the beds and nurses moving quietly among them.

On two occasions while I was at Da Nang, some of us not on flight duty for the day had a chance to spend a morning at China Beach. The shore curved slightly with Monkey Mountain on the north end of the beach. From the southern end, we could see Marble Mountain misty blue in the distance. On the first occasion, the surf was not very high, but we enjoyed body surfing before stopping for lunch at a picnic table. On the second visit, a typhoon had just passed, and the surf was dirty with branches and limbs washing onto the beach. We did not try to swim that day; we just walked along the sand, marveling at the amount of trash in the water.

The power of F-4 Phantom jets continued to amaze me. One afternoon I saw one turn upwards over the airfield and do a zoom climb almost straight up. I stood and watched the jet ascend until it was just a dot and then disappeared into the blue sky. The roar of the Phantoms at takeoff drowned out all other sounds, and many times I stood and watched them at night as they headed north on a bombing run. I also saw them returning from bombing missions during the daytime. When we taxied out towards the end of the runway on the A-3, we had to wait our turn for takeoff. F-4s descended in front of us, deceptively quiet at first with just a slight whistling noise. Then we got the full blast of sound as they passed and touched down on the runway with the yellow, slitted drag chute popping open. At times I found it hard to believe that I was there witnessing all of this and being involved in it—Shippey, the guy who was afraid of flying.

It was during these last few months in Da Nang that some of the shoot-downs and attempted shoot-downs that we monitored occurred. This was when all-hell-breaks-loose day happened. I and the other men assigned to daily flights continued to do our jobs to the best of our abilities. Most of the time when I was on mission, I was too busy listening to activities and keeping a record of them to have much time to think about being afraid of flying.

CHAPTER 21

Final Days
in the Philippines

Near the end of my time in Vietnam, we returned from reconnaissance flights over the Gulf of Tonkin to Cubi Point rather than to the base at Da Nang. Cubi Point was a naval air base at Subic Bay. I do not remember most of those trips, but one of them stands out in my mind because I wrote about it in my journal some years later. What I chiefly recall is that going back to the Philippines after being away for a while was like returning home. Da Nang was a war machine; the Philippines, by contrast, was a place of beauty and peace. Upon landing at Cubi Point and then taking the Navy bus up the coast of Zambales Province to San Miguel, I felt an immense sense of relief. The stress of being always on the alert dissolved, and I could simply enjoy being myself in a pleasant, peaceful environment.

On one trip our bus moved along the winding road through the Philippine night, following the curving shoreline of Subic Bay. For a while I could see the silhouette of the Five Peaks against the night sky. They lay to the north of the entrance to the harbor. Then we were past the bay and its surrounding mountains, moving through level land with rice paddies on either side. It was perhaps one of the rice harvesting seasons, for all across the landscape small fires dotted the countryside where farmers were spending the night in their fields. The tropical night had a slight edge of chill borne in by the sea breeze. We passed by camps close to the road where men squatted around campfires warming their hands. The red glow from the flames flickered on their faces and outspread fingers, and sparks spiraled upwards from the burning straw. Palm trees with drooping fronds stood darkly along the margins of the rice paddies.

We passed by a thatched house on stilts. A dim light glowed from one of its windows. In the rice paddy beside it I saw the reflection of a star. Across the patchwork of countless rice paddies, a pre-dawn mist was forming. On our left the peaks of Mount Maubanban and Mount Pundaquit rose black and immense against a backdrop of stars. We passed through sleepy barrios disturbed only by the barking of dogs. Bits of broken glass in the road reflected the glow of the bus headlights. Some of the houses were protected by walls with shards of glass set along the top as a chevaux-de-frise. Cool, refreshing air rushed in through the open window next to me. I relished the calm and mystery of the night, the enchanted spell that lay over the marshy creeks the bus crossed, rattling over the planks of old bridges that resounded like pistol shots in the stillness. The mystery and beauty of the night filled me with a sense of awe and reverence, and I wanted to ride like this forever, forgetting about the war across the South China Sea. But somewhere in the darkness I heard a rooster crow, and the bus turned onto the approach to the base. Then I saw the two white-helmeted Marines at the guardhouse unbarring the gate for us to enter. I would have to be up for morning muster by seven o'clock.

In late February 1972, my time in Da Nang had ended, and I was in the Philippines. A few days before I left Clark Air Base to return to the states, I had an opportunity to take a trip from San Miguel to Baguio City and the Air Force's John Hay R & R base in the mountains of Luzon. Three young officers had reserved a van, and somehow—I do not remember the details—I was allowed to accompany them. One officer drove, the other two sat in the rear, and I was in the front passenger seat. To pass the time, the officers played trivia, taking turns posing questions about history, literature, and various other topics. When I answered some of the questions, they seemed surprised that an enlisted man knew the answers, but they were kind and seemed to enjoy talking with me. I recall that one of them mentioned his mother was studying Sanskrit, a somewhat strange choice among languages to learn, I thought, but perhaps no stranger than those I had studied, including Latin, Anglo-Saxon, Middle English, French, German, and Vietnamese. In later years I added Mandarin Chinese and dipped into Hebrew and New Testament Greek. On one occasion when a student asked me how many languages I knew, I named all of those I had studied but said the only one in which I had a modicum of proficiency was a South Georgia dialect of English. Sanskrit, though, would have been a good language to study if one planned to read in the Vedas, the *Ramayana*, or the *Bhagavad Gita*. I reasoned that perhaps this officer's mother had an interest in Hinduism. Certainly, during the Vietnam War there was a lot of interest in Indian gurus who visited America, especially among hippies.

When we reached the mountains, we wound around hairpin curves on the ascent to Baguio. At one point I looked down and saw scores of rice patties at descending levels with the sky reflected in each of them. I thought of the rice terraces of Banaue, a place I wanted to see while in the Philippines but never had an opportunity to visit. When we arrived at the R

& R base, the officers went their way, and I went to a cabin that I had all to myself. I ate supper at the base dining hall and ordered shrimp tempura and coffee. Before dinner arrived, I ordered a Gibson, a drink I had never tried. I was intrigued by the fact that it included a pearl onion rather than an olive. Although I do not drink alcohol today, in the Navy I tried different types of drinks, including a Manhattan, salty dogs, a grasshopper, Burgundy, champagne, sake, sauvignon, claret, sparkling Rosé, and port.

After the meal I strolled along the stone wall that lined the edge of the mountain on which the base stood and looked across the valley to the mountains on the other side. As stated earlier, mountains have always been a wonder to me since I grew up in the coastal plain of Southern Georgia, where even a moderately high hill is rare. Baguio City is nestled among mountains 5,000 plus feet high. The air was definitely cooler than it was on the coast of the West Philippine Sea. Here and there I could see brush fires burning where farmers were clearing their fields. Smoke tinged the air. It was cool enough for a fire to be comfortable, so that night I sat by the fireplace staring into the flames and drank some Liebfraumilch and munched on oatmeal cookies that I had purchased late that afternoon at the base exchange. I thought about many things, but it was good just to be there, not worrying about having to fly on a mission or rockets hitting during the night.

The next day I ate lunch al fresco on the porch of the golf course clubhouse and marveled that on that part of the base there were huge pine trees similar to those in Georgia. That afternoon I went into town and visited the open-air market and the park in front of the cathedral. In a park near the cathedral soldiers in olive greens were lined up going through maneuvers. Women walked across the park in front of them, carrying buckets of water on their heads. Some of the women used a ring of twisted grass as a cushion for the water bucket. I went to shops that sold wood carvings and bought a tiered Lazy Susan made of narra wood and a punchbowl and cups of monkeypod wood for my mother, along with a carved cigarette box for my father. I also purchased small statues representing the Igorot people who lived in the area, one of a man with a dog and another of a bare-breasted woman. In later years I sometimes prudishly hid this latter statue when company came to our house in Albany. Now that my parents have passed away, I have all of these items, and on special occasions my family and I have used the Lazy Susan.

While in Baguio, I enjoyed the pleasant weather and admired the beautiful poinsettias along the streets, but I did not visit a Catholic school famous for fine silver filigree jewelry made by the students. I did, however, stroll through the extensive open-air market, marveling at the array of goods for sale. Here I saw Igorot people who had come into town from the countryside to shop. The following morning, I took a base taxi to meet the officers for the return trip to San Miguel and gave the unfinished bottle of Liebfraumilch to the driver.

CHAPTER 22

Return to the World

I left Clark Air Base in the Philippines around 8:00 a.m. on March 4, 1972, and landed at Travis Air Force Base, California, at 7:30 a.m. on March 4. According to the clock and the calendar, I arrived before I left because of crossing the International Date Line from west to east. I was reminded of the limerick about a "young lady named Bright / Whose speed was faster than light," how she "set out one day / In a relative way / And returned on the previous night." The flight across the Pacific was uneventful, except for a bit of turbulence over the Aleutians that caused the plane suddenly to drop several feet and made everyone gasp. At one point I looked out the window and saw a small island that was simply a mountain capped with snow, protruding from the Bering Sea.

Al Pearson, a friend from San Miguel, sat beside me on the return flight. We made plans to get together for a meal that evening in San Francisco, but he said that, depending on his flight connections, he might not be able to come. He suggested that we meet in the lobby of the Mark Hopkins Hotel at 3:00 p.m. If he did not arrive after an hour, then I would know that he was unable to make it. Accordingly, I took a taxi to the Mark Hopkins and waited for an hour. He did not show, so I walked to the YMCA, where I had stayed when I first visited San Francisco en route to Vietnam. The Mark Hopkins was out of my price range, but I enjoyed sitting in an elegant chair in the lobby and watching the affluent guests pass by. I never saw Al again.

On the way to the Y, I walked down Grant Avenue through Chinatown and met an elderly woman wearing a long coat and a knit cap. As she approached, she held up three fingers and asked for three pennies. I was so surprised by the request that I did not offer anything, and she continued on her way. Early the next morning, I took a taxi to the train terminal in Oakland, and as we passed down Market Street, I saw the same woman walking along the sidewalk. She was apparently a homeless person not in her right mind. My heart went out to her, and I have thought about her several times over the years. She reminded me of similar homeless people I had

184

met when I served as a student missionary at a rescue mission in Oklahoma City during the summer of 1964.

I wanted to wrap up my overseas tour with a railroad trip on an Amtrak train from Oakland to Los Angeles, and I thoroughly enjoyed the ride. We traveled through several tunnels in the mountains of the Coastal Range and at one point moved along the coast so that I could look out over the Pacific. Some of the time, though, the train passed behind warehouses, rusted-out buildings, and junkyards. It was a beautiful sunny morning when the train pulled into San Luis Obispo, and a new conductor came on board. He was an elderly man and something of a philosopher. As he went down the car in his uniform checking our tickets, he soliloquized about the *summum bonum* of life. Before long the trip ended at Union Station in Los Angeles, and as I walked through the waiting room, I realized that I had seen it in many TV shows and movies.

I stayed at the Biltmore Hotel near Pershing Square and got a room with a single bed for fifteen dollars and seventy-eight cents. When I went downstairs, I peeked into the ballroom, where a Jack Lemon movie was being filmed. During the afternoon I took a Grey Lines tour of Hollywood and Beverly Hills and recall seeing the homes of Lucille Ball and Jimmy Durante, along with the columned mansion that served as Tara in *Gone with the Wind*. We stopped at the Hollywood Bowl, and I got out and wandered around. We also stopped at the farmer's market downtown, but I decided to remain on the bus. I struck up a conversation with our driver and learned that he was originally from Albany, Georgia, my hometown. He had moved to Los Angles twenty-five years previously.

That evening I walked from the hotel to the Ahmanson Theatre for the opening night of Shakespeare's *Richard II* with Richard Chamberlain in the lead role. I had read the play while I was a graduate student at Emory University, so I knew the plot. As a result, I greatly enjoyed the performance, especially since I remembered Chamberlain in his role as Dr. Kildare on TV. This was one of two opening nights I have attended. The other was the premier of the 1967 release of *Gone with the Wind* at Lowes Theater in downtown Atlanta, with Olivia de Havilland as the featured speaker outside the theater before the film began. I stood in the lobby of the Ahmanson Theatre to see the celebrities as they pulled up in their limousines and then stepped out onto the red carpet. Steve Allen and actors from his show were the ones I immediately recognized. But one of the most interesting aspects of the evening was overhearing two women sitting behind me in the balcony as they talked about Richard Chamberlain. Wrapped in their fur stoles, they chatted about his days as a student at Beverly Hills High School. I returned to the Biltmore pleased with the evening, and the next morning took an airport limousine to Los Angeles International Airport.

On the flight to Atlanta, I occasionally looked out the window and marveled at the arid landscape of Arizona and New Mexico. At one point the window framed a swirled pattern of orange and rust-colored sand on the ground below. I was reminded of certain abstract paintings I had seen at the Metropolitan Museum of Modern Art in New York. At the time I had accepted the paintings as art objects within themselves, rather than as representations of reality. But in looking out the window of the Boeing 747, I realized that even abstract patterns depicted in art are also present somewhere in nature if only we have eyes to see them. Abstract art depicts observed reality at some level.

CHAPTER 23

Fort Meade, Maryland

I went home on leave for a week and then took a Trailways bus to Washington and another bus from there to my duty station with the Navy detachment at Fort George Meade, Maryland. It was mid–March when I arrived. I was assigned to secretarial duties in the computer division of NSA, which was only a short walk from my barracks. There I encountered a few of the guys who had trained with me at DLIEC but had not been assigned to Vietnam. I also made new friends among both the civilians who worked in my division and the Navy men assigned to NSA.

Fort Meade had a special significance for me. During World War II my father was stationed there in the Army before being shipped out to Europe. He and my mother rented a house in nearby Laurel, Maryland, and I realized that I was probably conceived there. As a result, being in Laurel was in a sense like coming home, although I had never before visited the town. After my father left for the war, my mother took a train back to Colquitt, Georgia, to stay with her mother. My father told me that he learned of my birth when he received a letter from my mother while he was quartered in a stone barn as part of Patton's Third Army, which was engaged in the Battle of the Bulge.

On certain afternoons during my time at NSA, it was my responsibility to check the office before I left for the day. I went to every desk and tried the drawers and tugged on the doors of all the cabinets to be sure they were locked and secure. If I overlooked anything that was not locked, I would be in trouble with the Marine security guards who later checked the office. These guards were somewhat intimidating. They stood with their rifles at order arms at intervals along the hallways. If someone's ID badge was turned backwards, they abruptly reminded that person to flip it over so that the picture and number were visible. After securing the office, I then took the burn bag from my area down to the incinerator in the basement. All classified trash was kept separate from other trash and had to be burned at the end of each day.

The civilians who worked in the computer division were kind to me.

Many of them had worked for NSA for several years and had high civil service ratings. One of the men across the way from my desk was Fred, originally from Boston. He and I enjoyed comparing accents, and he joked about "paking the ca in Havad Yad," and I made jokes about "Y'all." Knowing my interest in the history and literature of New England, especially since my master's thesis had been about Robert Frost's poetry, he regaled me with stories about the culture of the region and also brought me some copies of *Yankee Magazine*, which I still have. Richard Screven also had a desk nearby. He was always impeccably dressed in coat and tie and frequently made me laugh with his humorous sayings and ironic remarks. Ray Mix and Navy Chief Grimes were others in the office who befriended me.

Georgetown

I sometimes visited the Savile Book Shop on P Street in Georgetown when I took the bus to Washington on the weekends. There was a separate room for books in French. A middle-aged woman who knew French literature well supervised this department. She had a desk in the center of the room, where she recorded the purchases, taking note of which books to reorder. Customers paid her and enjoyed chatting with her. I admired the Gallimard deluxe editions bound in leather but could not afford them, so I had to settle for less expensive volumes. On different occasions I purchased *Lettres Choisies de Mme. de Sevigne* and *Poesies choisies de Pierre de Ronsard*, both writers I had admired since studying French literature under Professor Jane Barrow at Georgia Southern College. The woman, accepting my payment, remarked that those were good editions for the price. As I remember, the Savile, located in an old brick townhouse, had a small café up front where one could order fondue and a variety of coffees. It was a pleasant place to spend an evening, but I have read on the Internet that it closed several years ago. *Quel dommage*!

Washington

According to my journal, on April 30, I was in Washington, touring the area near the intersection of Eleventh and Massachusetts. One of the sights I encountered was a bronze statue of Edmund Burke, the great Irish statesman and philosopher, best known for his book *Reflections on the Revolution in France*. The right hand of the statue was raised with the figure tilted slightly forward, giving it, to my imagination, the ludicrous appearance of trying to hail a taxi. I noticed that the statue was placed there in

1922, so for fifty-year-old Burke had in vain been trying to catch a ride, since I imagined that Washington's political atmosphere was perhaps a little too liberal for his conservative views. To add insult to injury, across the street was a memorial to Samuel Gompers and the American labor movement, forcing Burke to gaze upon the bronze figures commemorating ideas that he might have opposed. The scene was not too bleak, however, for nearby, facing his little green space, were the massive stones and airy steeples of the Church of the Ascension and Saint Agnes, a reminder of traditions that he would perhaps have approved of. I attended services at this church one Sunday that spring but forgot to set my clock ahead and arrived near the end of the service. I sat at a pew in the rear and enjoyed the concluding part of the liturgy with the priests in their vestments, although as a Baptist I was somewhat confused about when to stand, sit, or kneel.

An Enlightening Encounter

Late that April afternoon I went back to the Greyhound bus station to return to Laurel and Fort Meade. I sat down on the retaining wall of a flowerbed in front of the station, pulled out a paperback I had purchased, and began reading. Also sitting nearby on the wall was a middle-aged African American man in an old Army jacket, who was talking to a young white man, apparently in the military, since he had a crew-cut and wore combat boots with his blue jeans. Occasionally, as I read, I overheard snatches of the conversation, which seemed to be mostly about race relations. From his speech and the loudness of his voice, the black man seemed to be drunk. After a while there was some type of disagreement, and the African American man rose and staggered along the sidewalk in my direction. I tried to appear deeply engrossed in my book, so he passed by and attempted to sit down beside another young white man and engage him in conversation, but this man immediately picked up his briefcase, moved further along the wall, and then slammed the briefcase down, clearly showing that he did not want to be bothered. The black man then staggered back in my direction and sat down beside me.

It was clear that the man was drunk and also maybe under the influence of drugs. His speech was thick and slurred, more like a mumble than clear enunciation. He began talking and admitted that he was not making much sense and could not gather his thoughts to express himself the way he wanted to. While he talked, I remained silent most of the time, making only an occasional comment to show I was listening. I did not want to insult the man by abruptly moving or rebuking him, yet I realized that any attempt at rational discussion with him was impossible since his remarks were irrational and he spoke in an embittered way, filled with latent hostility. I listened and told him that I preferred merely to look and listen so that I could learn. He told me he did not have anything to teach me. As he talked, though, I realized that he was giving me an insight into the way some African Americans felt about the racial injustices of the nation.

He stated that he hated the country and wished he could blow the heads off the D.C. policemen. He said he wanted to see the country destroyed, and pointing to one of the Greyhound buses pulling into the station, remarked that blowing up that bus would accomplish something. When I ventured that doing that would accomplish nothing but merely create more problems, he became loud and shouted, "You think that won't accomplish something? It'll stop that bus! You think that blowing up that building," pointing to the station, "won't accomplish something?" I saw that it would do no good to continue a discussion, so I reverted to silence with only occasional brief remarks. His tirade revealed that he was completely disgusted with American society and in particular with the white race. I suggested that he might start over in his life, and he became angry, saying he had started over twenty years ago when he returned from Korea and it accomplished nothing. Then he asked me if I thought he was a fool, and I replied that I did not, observing that, if I did, I would not still be sitting there listening to him. It was at this point that I mentioned I wanted to listen and learn. The man calmed down and continued to talk, mentioning one of Stokely Carmichael's points that there are more dark-colored people in the world than white people. He said all of these people could rise up and defeat the whites. He declared that he was a Black Muslim and claimed that two-thirds of all blacks in America are Muslims.

I looked up at the sky and saw that a rain cloud highlighted with sunlight was approaching from the west beyond the steeple of the New York Avenue Presbyterian Church, the church that Lincoln had attended and where Peter Marshall had served as pastor. During my walk earlier in the day, I noticed that the cornerstone for the present sanctuary had been laid in 1951 by President Truman.

I offered to give the man some money for a sandwich because, when he sat down beside me, he said that he was hungry. He admitted that he was drunk and needed to get himself in shape and asked if I would give him money for a beer and a sandwich. I tried to persuade him that eating a sandwich first would be better. Near the end of the conversation I gave him some money while he continued to talk, saying that he knew who he was and what he was, that he had no desire to be anybody else and that he was pleased with being himself. At this point the bus driver came and began taking tickets for those about to board, and I was relieved since I had been listening to the man for over thirty minutes. As I stood in line to get on the bus, the man said, "Peace, brother!" I gave him the peace sign and replied, "Peace!"

During his talk, the man told me that he was from Westminster, Maryland. It was obvious while he talked that he was deeply embittered and frustrated. When he remarked that he wanted to kill the D.C. policemen, he said that he did not mind dying. As I sat on the bus leaving Washington, I realized that within this man and perhaps thousands of others like him there was a great potential for violence. We were fighting a war in another country halfway around the world while at home racial discontent was fulminating, ready to explode into war. I trembled to think what the future might hold for the United States. The view of this man was that of the "have not's" against the "have's," and that perspective leads to the frustrated conclusion that "if I cannot have what you have, then you are not going to have it either!" It is the image of Samson, blinded and in chains in the midst of the wealthy and victorious Philistines but still seething with power, capable of collapsing the building on himself and all alike. In looking back, I wondered why this veteran of the Korean War had received no help, why no one had paid sufficient attention to his need and his hurt and reached out to thank him in a tangible way for serving the nation. If someone had done this, maybe things would have been different for him. In thinking about this man today, I am reminded of Vietnam veterans who returned home and had trouble re-entering society.

Boston and Concord

One weekend in May I took a trip to Boston. I caught a train from Union Station in D.C. to Pennsylvania Station in New York and then walked to the Port's Authority Terminal to catch a Greyhound bus for Boston. It was late that night before the bus departed, and I sat for a long time listening to the roar of arriving and departing buses and smelling the fumes. Finally, I was able to board my bus and sat next to a tall, thin black man with a huge Afro. He was eating a barbecued leg of some animal, and, I swear, it looked like a dog's leg. As we departed from New York, he kept gnawing the meat off the bone and wiping his fingers on his trousers. I took out a peppermint for myself, and having finished his repast, he leaned towards me and asked if he might also have a peppermint. I gladly obliged.

As the bus traveled in the pre-dawn darkness of Connecticut, I looked out the window, hoping to catch sight of a white birch. I had always wanted to see these trees after reading Robert Frost's poem "Birches." Finally, I glimpsed a straight line of white against the blackness of the forest, and afterwards I occasionally saw other white trunks of birches.

In Boston I walked from the bus station across the Common to a small café to eat breakfast. The young woman behind the counter asked me what I would have, and I ordered pancakes. She looked at me without understanding, so I said, "I'll have some hot cakes, please." She still did not understand, so thinking that surely the people in Boston watched western movies, I ordered flapjacks. But the woman still did not know what I meant. In desperation, having used up all my words for pancakes, I looked at the items on the menu posted on the wall and said, "I'll have griddle cakes." Then she comprehended, although I was not sure what I had ordered, but when she brought the plate to my table, it was pancakes.

That morning I walked to the State House and was surprised to see a table set up in front of it by supporters of George Wallace as a candidate for the presidency. Wallace campaigners in Boston, the home of abolitionists! The idea seemed absurd, but there they were, wearing straw boater hats and passing out Wallace bumper stickers, buttons, and pamphlets. I was equally surprised earlier that spring when I was walking on the southwest side of the White House grounds. A tour bus from Michigan parked and people wearing Wallace for President straw boaters disembarked. I had no idea that people from Michigan would be in favor of the notorious supporter of segregation from Alabama. I was from Georgia, and I definitely did not support him.

The sidewalk in front of the State House was crowded, and I wended my way through the tourists, the Wallace supporters, the war protestors, and the Hare Krishnas in their saffron robes, chanting and clanging their finger cymbals, to continue my tour of Boston. I visited the Museum of Fine Arts and the Old North Church, from which the lanterns were hung to let Paul Revere know that the British were marching towards Lexington and Concord. Earlier that morning I was surprised to learn that there was also an Old South Church near Copley Square. I went to the top of the fifty-story Prudential Building and took photos of downtown Boston. In the distance I could see Fenway Park. I spent some time on the Boston Common and strolled past Louisburg Square in the Beacon Hill area, thinking of Henry James and *The Bostonians*. I visited Faneuil Hall and the nearby farmers' market.

Saturday night I stayed at the YMCA, and the next morning went out to Harvard Square, where I had coffee, and then walked around Harvard University. I went to Harvard Yard and saw the seated statue of John Harvard. The simplicity and relative bareness of the Yard surprised me. I thought that the Quadrangle at Emory University was more impressive. Next, I strolled past the Widener Library. Since it was Sunday morning, nothing was open, and I regretted that I could not go inside the library. In the vicinity of the library, I spoke to a campus policeman and asked if

Concord had become part of the Boston metropolitan area, overrun with used car lots and fast-food franchises, or was still a separate village. He assured me that it was still a village and worth seeing, so I determined to take the bus to Concord that afternoon.

But first I walked in the neighborhood near Harvard and saw the outside of Longfellow's home and, on the Cambridge Common, a Civil War memorial that included a bronze statue of Lincoln. Protestors of the Vietnam War had smeared graffiti in red paint on the base of the memorial. "Revolution Now" was one of the slogans that marred the stonework of the monument. The graffiti also included the names *Nixon* and *Spiro* with swastikas for the "x" in *Nixon* and the "s" in *Spiro*. The previous day I had seen another memorial near the State House in Boston with graffiti in huge red letters that stated, "Viet Cong Take Saigon." Even on this trip I was reminded of how divided the country was over the war, and in looking back at that time from the present (2021), I and others of my generation realize that the nation has had serious divisions before and survived them. That reflection offers hope.

That afternoon I took the bus to Concord and was surprised that the bus did not go into the village itself. Instead, it stopped at a prison outside of the village. Quite a few people got off the bus, crossed the highway, and began walking up a low hill towards a modern brick building. I guessed that this might be a visitors' center for the historic area, but upon entering the building, I was again surprised to learn that this was a correctional facility for juvenile offenders. The crowd consisted of family members who had come out from Boston to visit their incarcerated sons. I retraced my way down the hill and noticed a sign for Concord on a side road. Then I walked the mile or so into Concord, and it was just as the police officer had said it would be, a village that had preserved its charm.

I must have walked eight or ten miles that afternoon to see the sites I wanted to visit. First, I went out north of the town to the Old Manse, where Emerson and Hawthorne had lived. I thought about Hawthorne's collection of stories *Mosses from an Old Manse*. I visited Concord Bridge and the area near it where local men had skirmished with the British troops on that day when the shot heard round the world was fired at Lexington. Then I walked across the bridge to see the Minuteman statue by Daniel Chester French. I visited Sleepy Hollow Cemetery, where I saw the graves of Emerson, Hawthorne, Louisa May Alcott, and Thoreau. I was touched by the simplicity of Thoreau's headstone. Admirers of his writings had placed pinecones and a bundle of wildflowers on the grave. Then I walked to Emerson's home, where I took a tour that included only myself and a mother and father with their young son. At one point in the tour we were in Emerson's bedroom, where his black clerical robe was hanging, and the middle-aged woman who was our guide mentioned that he had been a preacher. The boy misunderstood and in astonishment asked, "Creature?" The lady calmly replied, "No, preacher." On the lower floor I admired Emerson's library and also saw near the backdoor leather "buckets," which, according to our guide, were hung there in case of a fire. Before departing from the house, I bought a copy of a book titled *Emerson in Concord: A Memoir Written for the "Social Circle" in Concord, Massachusetts*, by his son Edward Waldo Emerson.

From Emerson's house I walked about a mile to Walden Pond and went to the spot where Thoreau had erected his small cabin and lived for two years. I plucked a leaf from a white birch tree near the spot and placed it in the book I had just purchased at Emerson's house. I had read Thoreau's *Walden* during the summer after the eleventh grade. In Mr. Billy Bragg's English class that year, we had read excerpts from the book, but I wanted to read the rest of it. My mother insisted that I needed to weed the front flower bed that June, so I propped a radio in the living room window and pulled out Bermuda grass to the sound of country music broadcast by WJAZ. That was hot, sweaty work, so every now and then I took a break and sat in the rocking chair on the front porch to read on *Walden*. This book, along with Wordsworth's poetry, changed the way I looked at nature. Across the road from our house, I no longer saw just scrub oaks and broom-straw that concealed rattlesnakes. Everything—dandelions, blackberry vines, hawthorn trees, live oaks draped with Spanish moss, even the rattlesnakes—became a part of the marvelous whole of nature. The drainage pond in the swamp near my house became my local version of Walden Pond, and I enjoyed just standing beside it and meditating, but I also kept a sharp look-out for water moccasins and alligators that might be hidden among the lily pads and algae. Although I looked at nature from a new perspective and agreed with Emerson that its aspects were symbolic of the spirit, I did not enter the la la land of Transcendentalism.

New York

I went to New York for the weekend in August and visited the Frick Collection. I was drawn to the painting *The Polish Rider* by Rembrandt. This is a striking painting uncharacteristic of his style that I had learned to recognized in the National Gallery's collection of his works. In looking at the painting, I was reminded of the dramatic subjects and style of the nineteenth-century French painter Eugene Delacroix. The rider is depicted with his bow, arrows in a quiver, and a hatchet. He wears a fur cap, and the horse has a fiery eye. The light on the horse's bit and bridle reminded me of Rembrandt's characteristic treatment of light reflected off jewelry and metallic objects. Also, on exhibit were his black and white sketches. I noticed that even in these works Rembrandt has a remarkable ability to suggest light. The blank spaces in the drawings emerge as light since they are so well-defined and contained by the dark lines. As in his paintings, he highlights certain spots, such as the center of a tree trunk or the side of a house above seated figures.

The next morning, I traveled downtown and walked past the World Trade Center Towers, which were still being completed. In my journal I wrote that they are "impressive because of their mammoth size, but they are no more interesting architecturally than two up-ended cracker boxes. They seem to throw Manhattan off balance, as though they were going to tip it over into the Hudson River." Today, in 2021, there are other tall, thin skyscrapers that also seem to throw the New York skyline off balance. As I strolled past the towers that morning, I had no inkling of what would happen twenty-nine years later. In looking back, I am glad I had the opportunity to see them.

On October 21 and 22, I was again in New York. In my walk around lower Manhattan the first morning, I noticed that on the approach to the Brooklyn Bridge there were black boxes on either side filled with sand to be used during icy weather. In my journal I described what it was like to be on the bridge: "There is a very loud humming of cars beneath me as they constantly speed over the iron grating on the bridge. I can feel the planks of the pedestrian walkway vibrating beneath my feet."

At the Pierpont Morgan Library, I viewed an exhibit of the illustrated medieval book *The Egmont Breviary* and admired its bright, rich colors. Also, on exhibit that morning was a letter from Thomas Jefferson to his daughter, Martha. The letter was written on white birch and mailed from New York in 1791. Many years later, while a graduate student at the University of South Carolina, I would return to the library with one of my professors, Dr. James B. Meriwether, along with other students, to attend a meeting of the Bibliographical Society of America. At this gathering I had the honor of meeting Fredson Bowers, perhaps the greatest scholar of bibliography and textual criticism at that time.

The fragrance of roasted chestnuts was everywhere along the streets of Manhattan. This was a pleasant smell that came from small carts pushed by vendors who sold the nuts and large pretzels. That evening I wrote in my journal that "the moon is shining through a slight haze of clouds and is very beautiful, like a pearl seen through a frosted glass. I am sitting at Rockefeller Plaza now, and a chilly wind is blowing. A few moments ago, I admired the haze-covered moon against the illumined spires of St. Patrick's Cathedral."

That evening I went to a performance of *The Lincoln Mask,* a play by

V.J. Longhi, with Eva Marie Saint playing the part of Mary Todd Lincoln. I remembered her from the movie *Raintree County*, starring Elizabeth Taylor and Montgomery Clift. I enjoyed her performance because I admired her refined beauty and grace. She had a distinctive voice, and it was a pleasure to hear her speak. The play itself was interesting but rather heavy. The mood it created was too ominous with the future in all of its tragic consequences apparently foreseen by the characters as though they were aware of themselves as actors in a drama whose conclusion is foreknown. I preferred dramas that portray characters who are more life-like in their uncertainty about the future. The idea of fate moving along a foreordained path did, nevertheless, impart to the work the idea of a classical tragedy in which the characters are inexorably bound in the web of things. There were times during the Vietnam war when I had that sensation myself.

The following day I noted in my journal that New York is one among a few American cities where one can still see horse manure on the streets. I noticed horse dung on Seventh Avenue a block below Times Square and recalled that New York still maintained mounted policemen.

In trying to go to Columbia University that morning, I took the wrong subway line and ended up in Harlem. When I came out of the subway exit onto the street, I knew I was in the wrong place. Two African American men standing near the exit held out their hands panhandling for money and said, "Hey, man!" I walked past them and looked around. As far as I could see the street was strewn with trash, the buildings were run down, and there were broken windows in them. A middle-aged woman came along the street, leading a dog on a leash and carrying the Sunday *New York Times*. She asked, "Are you lost?" I almost wanted to laugh because it was glaringly obvious that I was lost. I explained that I was trying to get to Columbia University. The woman was very kind and told me that, if I stood on the corner across the street, a bus would come along shortly and take me over the hill to Columbia. She gave me the bus number. Soon after I reached the corner, a young black man with a pencil-thin moustache and a hat cocked at a jaunty angle on his head approached me. After a moment or two of conversation, I realized that he was a pimp. He was courteous in all that he said and assured me that the girls at his house were clean and young, around seventeen or eighteen. All that he asked of his customers was that they not be drunk. He said, "We been trying to get some of you white cats to come back to Harlem." I realized I had to walk a thin line in talking with him since I was afraid that he might pull out a gun or knife. I did not want to offend him, but neither did I want to accept his offer. As a result, I talked politely with him, thinking that this was a unique opportunity to get some insight about a kind of man I might not otherwise encounter. I was grateful when the bus finally arrived.

At Columbia I strolled around the campus and regretted that the Butler Library was closed. I walked up the steps to the Low Memorial Library to view the seated statue of *Alma Mater*. Then I walked to the Cathedral of Saint John the Divine, which was nearby, and admired the huge bronze doors with panels depicting scenes from the Bible. A young man from Sierra Leone asked me to take his photograph in front of the doors. I explained that I had slide film in my camera, but that was fine with him. He gave me his address and asked that I send him the slide with his photo, and that is what I did when I returned to Fort Meade and had that roll of film developed.

That evening I went to Carnegie Hall to hear British vocalist Dorothy Squires sing and greatly enjoyed her performance. The hall was not full, so I was able to get a box seat near the stage instead of the balcony seat for which I had paid. Although the audience was small, it was enthusiastic and lavished Squires with flowers at the end of the show. She was obviously touched by this mark of their admiration for her and by a message from Mayor John Lindsay sending her his best wishes on behalf of the city in her comeback to the stage. Among the songs that she sang were "For Once in My Life," "My Way," "This Time We Almost Made It," and "Say It with Flowers." This was exactly the kind of evening in New York that I wanted, and I became an admirer of Dorothy Squires.

On one of the weekend trips to New York in 1972, I attended an off-Broadway performance of a new play by Tennessee Williams titled *Small Craft Warnings*. Williams himself was in the play, which depicts the interactions of a small mixed group of people confined to a seacoast bar during stormy weather. Dressed in a white suit, Williams had the role of the alcoholic doctor. To some extent, the play reminded me of Sartre's *No Exit*. Almost as interesting as the play were the comments before the performance by the young couple sitting behind me. As people entered the theater and took their seats, they made sarcastic remarks about them, noticing the ratty furs, the gaudy jewelry, the mismatching colors, the overdone hair styles, and the snobbish facial expressions. I was reminded of similar comments in the seventeenth-century dramas I had read in Dr. Paul Hunter's course on Restoration comedy at Emory University.

Reconnecting with my Da Nang Roommate

On another weekend that fall, I reconnected with Rusty Harrison, who had been one of my roommates in Da Nang. He invited me to spend the weekend with him, his wife, and young son at their condominium in Columbia, Maryland. Rusty was also assigned to the Navy detachment at

Fort Meade. That Friday night we enjoyed talking and reminiscing about our time together in Da Nang, including those occasions when we listened to classical music on his cassette recorder, intermittently drowned out by the roar of an F-4 taking off. Then on Saturday we took a road trip to Harpers Ferry, West Virginia. We visited the brick armory and arsenal that John Brown and his men seized in their 1859 raid that was intended to spark a slave rebellion against their owners. I thought it ironic that the first man to be killed during the raid was a free African American man, a railroad employee, who stepped off a train that was stopped by Brown's men as it approached the bridge over the Potomac River. My most vivid memory, though, is our visit to Jefferson Rock, a spot on a trail above the town that offers a view of the confluence of the Shenandoah and Potomac Rivers. According to the historical marker at the site, Jefferson visited this spot in 1783 and described the scene as "worth a voyage across the Atlantic." The view was beautiful, but I was not sure that it was majestic enough to warrant a voyage across the Atlantic. I considered, though, that, since Virginia was his home, Jefferson admired the scene because he loved this place as part of the region where he had been born and grown up, and to visit a beloved place near one's home was indeed worth a trip across an ocean. That was the way I felt about my part of Georgia, a landscape that people from other regions of the country would consider plain and uninteresting since there are no majestic mountains, beautiful valleys, mighty rivers, or exotic coastlines. But while I was on the other side of the world in Vietnam, I would gladly have crossed the Pacific Ocean and the North American continent to be at home and enjoy its pine forests, peanut fields, country stores, and small towns, in other words, just to be at home in my country of the heart. I took a snapshot of Rusty, his wife, and their son standing in front of Jefferson Rock, and it is a photo that I cherish, especially since Rusty passed away in 2017. Just as we were preparing to leave the site, an indigo bunting lit for a moment on a nearby branch, adding its resplendent blue feathers to the beauty of the scene, and then flew down into the valley.

Thanksgiving, 1972: The Chesapeake Bay

The people in the computer division at NSA were always kind to me. I could not go home for Thanksgiving in 1972, so Ray Mix invited me to spend the holiday with him and his wife, Dorris, at their home on Chesapeake Bay. They prepared the traditional Thanksgiving dinner with all of the trimmings. I remember Mrs. Mix making the dressing in a different way than I was I accustomed to in the Deep South. Instead of using cornbread, she used light bread. The dressing, though, was delicious. Some of their friends from Philadelphia were also present for Thanksgiving dinner, and after the meal they all enjoyed playing cards while I watched or read in a volume of Douglas Southall Freeman's *Lee's Lieutenants* that was placed on a side table in the living room. I walked around the yard, which had a beautiful view of the bay and noticed that there were oyster beds next to the shore. Later that afternoon or the next Mr. Mix took me out on the bay in his boat. Although it was very cold, I enjoyed being on the water. On Saturday afternoon he drove me down to Point Lookout, which was only a short distance from their home. I had told him that my great-grandfather Joseph Johnston Shippey had been a prisoner there at the end of the Civil War. According to records I had located, he was taken prisoner after the Battle of Petersburg and then incarcerated at the prisoner of war camp at Point Lookout, located where the Potomac River merges with Chesapeake Bay. The only trace of the camp that still survived was an earth embankment on the Potomac River side of the point. We stopped for something to drink at Buzz's Country Store in Scotland, Maryland, and this business had copies of an old print that gave an artist's aerial view of the Point Lookout prison. The print copies were complimentary, so I took one that I still have today as part of my family history materials. On Sunday evening the Mix's returned me to Fort Meade.

Readjusting to Life Back in the World

When I went home on leave while stationed at Fort Meade, my parents and family welcomed me and were supportive, but no one was interested in hearing about the war. On one of these trips, Daddy and I rode out to the edge of Albany to see a watermelon patch planted by a distant cousin on my mother's side. My father always enjoyed riding around to see how crops were doing, and I liked to go with him since this gave us bonding time. On this occasion, though, we bonded in a different way. Daddy drove to the back of the field where the melons were planted, and we got out of the truck. Suddenly, there was a loud explosion, and I immediately hit the dirt. Daddy began laughing because, as a World War II veteran who had often come under fire, he understood my reaction. He helped me get up and then explained that my cousin had placed in the middle of the field a device with a chemical drip that occasionally made a sound like a shotgun blast. The device was intended to prevent birds from pecking his watermelons. This was just one event involved in my readjustment to life after Da Nang.

Sometimes, while eating, I think that I startled my family by giving the salt shaker a sudden, loud rap on the edge of the table before using it. This was customary for us in the mess hall at Da Nang because the humidity made it difficult for the salt to come out, even though rice was placed in the shaker to facilitate this. My difficulty in swallowing certain kinds of granular foods continued for several years because of the tension and stress I had endured while in Da Nang.

CHAPTER 24

Fort Meade Continued

Gettysburg and Monticello

While stationed at Fort Meade, I went somewhere almost every weekend. In addition to going to Washington, New York, and Boston, I traveled to Baltimore, Gettysburg, and Charlottesville, Virginia. At Gettysburg I wandered across the field where General Pickett had led the charge that fateful July day in 1863 against the Union forces on Cemetery Ridge. I also stood on the ridge and looked back over the field where so many Confederate soldiers had died. In later years, in remembering this scene, I recalled what Faulkner in his novel *Intruder in the Dust* had one of the characters say about the charge:

> For every Southern boy fourteen years old, not once but whenever he wants it, there is the instant when it's still not yet two o'clock on that July afternoon in 1863, the brigades are in position behind the rail fence, the guns are laid and ready in the woods and the furled flags are already loosened to break out and Pickett himself with his long oiled ringlets and his hat in one hand probably and his sword in the other looking up the hill waiting for Longstreet to give the word and it's all in the balance, it hasn't happened yet, it hasn't even begun yet, it not only hasn't begun yet but there is still time for it not to begin against that position and those circumstances....

As a Southerner who was a child in the 1950s when many people still insisted on referring to the Civil War as the War Between the States, I understood what Faulkner wrote but had no desire that the outcome of that battle or the war should have been different, only that it, and the Vietnam War, too, might have been less traumatic, that so many people might not have died. In not winning the Vietnam War, the nation had a taste of what the South experienced in losing the Civil War, including both the regret and the guilt, as well as the tragic view of how the world works, a perspective, as C. Vann Woodward points out in *The Burden of Southern History*, that most other nations know only too well. After walking along Cemetery Ridge, I visited the cyclorama of the battle and was surprised that, although impressive in its dramatic details, it was smaller than the cyclorama of the Battle of Atlanta.

My trip to Charlottesville occurred on a beautiful October day. I took a taxi from the bus station to Monticello, and the driver kept referring to "Mr. Jefferson" as if he had only recently died. When we passed over a level place on the way up the mountain, he remarked, "This is one of the bridle paths where Mr. Jefferson used to ride his horse each day when he was at Monticello." The driver let me out at the back of the house, where golden leaves were dropping from the trees lining the walk to the entrance. Once in the house, I and the other visitors were conducted on a tour by a middle-aged blue-haired lady with her glasses, attached by a cord, resting on her bosom. I was impressed by Jefferson's bed, which was positioned between his dressing room on one side and his library on the other. In walking around the grounds, I enjoyed the view of the misty Blue Ridge Mountains in the distance and then strolled down to Jefferson's tomb, where the inscription stated that he was the author of the Declaration of Independence and "The Statute of Virginia for Religious Freedom," as well as the father of the University of Virginia. There was no mention that he had been President of the United States. In later years, I noticed that the tombstone refers to three types of freedom, political, religious, and intellectual, and regretted that it had not also referred to a fourth, namely, the freeing of his slaves. I realized that he is a controversial figure, praiseworthy in some ways but not so admirable in others. Natasha Trethewey skillfully presents Jefferson's duality in her poem "Enlightenment," which records her own visit to Monticello with her white father. She describes how a portrait of Jefferson is two-toned with the forehead illumined and the rest of the face "darkened as if the artist meant to contrast / his bright knowledge, its dark subtext." Jefferson, in his role as slaveholder and the one who wrote that "all men are created equal," is in some ways an apt representative of America, which in its history has been both an oppressor and a beacon for freedom. Jefferson reminded me that we are all flawed in some way, regardless of how good we may be in other ways. That reflection led to the thought of our involvement in Vietnam. Perhaps our initial intentions in intervening might have been understandable, but in conducting the war, we had also done much harm. I thought of all the men who served in Vietnam and had been killed or wounded or become ill as a result of exposure to Agent Orange and of those who returned but were not fully at home again because of PTSD. But I especially thought of the Vietnamese people, who today still deal on a daily basis with the scourge of Agent Orange, along with injuries and losses from the heavy bombing.

In pondering Jefferson, I am also reminded of my own flaws, some of which are revealed in this memoir, and I recall what the Apostle Paul wrote in Romans 3:23: "For all have sinned and fall short of the glory of God...." As a follower of Christ, I know the truth of this verse. We can point a finger at Jefferson, and deservedly so, as well as at others who have conspicuously done wrong, but we must also point a finger at ourselves because in God's sight we are all flawed creatures in need of redemption.

Before leaving Charlottesville, I walked around the quadrangle at the University of Virginia and remembered that Edgar Allan Poe had attended the university for a while. At one end of the quadrangle was the Rotunda, and at the other was an open view of the mountains, misty blue in the distance. In later years, while working on my doctoral dissertation, I would return to the University of Virginia to visit the Clifton Waller Barrett Library of American Literature in the Alderman Library. I would also have a daughter-in-law who received her Ph.D. from the university.

Walking in the Woods

I enjoyed walking in the woods at Fort Meade. Excerpts from my journal record walks that I took in June 1972:

> There is a pleasant wooded area near my barracks, and there are inviting pathways all through it. Some of them are crisscrossed by branches, and I have to constantly stoop as I walk. But I do not always keep to the paths. I like to walk through the tangles of briars and vines also, listening to the dead branches cracking beneath my feet. I like a wood with some wildness to it.
>
> A green-bordered lane in the woods, a myriad leaves tremoring on each side, shadows dappling the way, small bits of straw and dry leaves blowing across the ground, the whole day in movement with the wind, as if the entire countryside were sailing someplace, sweeping me along with it to some far exotic land or to some nostalgic scene back in time.

Another entry:

> I went out walking again late this evening; indeed, it was almost dark. The air was cool and bracing, like autumn, and I walked rapidly along the dirt lanes through the woods, thrilling with a kind of animal wildness at the darkness of the woods on either side. The sky was still light and I exited the woods into a straw-covered field dotted with patches of small, dark pines. A black cat with a white chest and wearing a silver collar appeared on the lane before me. It crouched low to the ground in a bundle as I walked towards it. I called 'kitty, kitty,' trying to be friendly, but it bounded into the woods. I penetrated a little ways into the trees further on and squatted down on a carpet of moss to experience the mystery of darkness coming in the woods. All was quiet, except for the sounds of cars passing at a little distance on the Washington-Baltimore Parkway. After a while I rose and returned by way of Schrafft's restaurant, where I stopped for coffee and a piece of cheese cake. A dinner theatre adjoined the restaurant,

and there was a pleasant hubbub of people dining, a warm contrast to the darkness I had just experienced in the woods.

In walking in the woods at Fort Meade, I was continually amazed that this spot, with its natural beauty and tranquility was within sight of the NSA buildings, a nexus with connections to all parts of the world.

An Interesting Phone Call

One night in the barracks about 12:30 I received word that I had a phone call at the desk downstairs. I picked up the phone and, after saying "Hello," heard a booming voice that said, "Herrrrbert, how are you!" The trilling of the "r's" let me know that this was Fahad, my Arab roommate at Georgia Southern College during the fall term of my senior year. I immediately faced a dilemma. I was delighted to hear from Fahad after a long time being out of contact and wanted to know where he was and what he was doing, but I also was in some trepidation because I suspected that, since I was on the same military post as NSA, the phone could be bugged and wondered how it might sound for an enlisted man to be receiving a call from an Arab man in the middle of the night. Personnel who became part of the Naval Security Group were told that they were not to have contact with foreign nationals. During my time overseas, Fahad had occasionally called my home in Albany and talked with my parents, and I realized that my mother had probably given him my phone number at Fort Meade.

Hearing Fahad's voice carried me back to those days at Georgia Southern. He had come to America from East Jerusalem, Jordan, to study. His sponsors were a political science professor and his wife at the University of Georgia. The house mother of my dormitory assigned him to room with me because other students had refused to be roommates with him. Fahad was broad-shouldered and muscular, but his forehead had scars from injuries he had received in the fighting around Jerusalem when he was a child. A letter from his sponsoring professor informed me that he had spent time in a refugee camp. From what Fahad later shared, I understood that his family were Catholic, but he had converted to Islam. He had spent some time in England and talked with a British accent, often prefacing his remarks with the word "Blimey!" He came to be well-liked by the students for his friendliness, politeness, and good sense of humor. Fahad patiently put up with all the stereotypes about Arabs. Sometimes a student passing him on the sidewalk would say, "Hey Fahad, where did you leave your camel?" And he would reply, "Oh sir, I left him at the zoo."

During his first week at the college, Fahad went to the gym where the gymnastic team trained and tried to do some exercises on the rings, but he fell and broke both of his wrists. A doctor came out from town to see him at the health clinic, and the nurses put casts on his wrists; however, Fahad did not like the casts and removed them. Back to the clinic he went, and the nurses put new casts on his wrists. The doctor told Fahad, "If you break these off, I will put casts on up to your shoulders!" The doctor also told him that he should not get the casts wet, so Fahad and I drove around Statesboro, looking for plastic bags long enough to cover his arms up to his elbows. We finally settled on freezer bags for chickens. That evening I helped him put the bags over his arms and secured them with rubber bands. Then Fahad walked into the shower, holding his arms out on both sides. On this occasion, as on others, while he was showering, Fahad chanted the cry of the muezzin calling the faithful to worship. Since the bathroom was tiled, and the windows were open, his voice resonated over that part of the campus. Quite likely, the call of the muezzin had never been heard before on the Georgia Southern campus.

During the first two or three weeks I roomed with Fahad, I tried to be super polite, but he realized that this was a false front and wanted to get to know the real me. One night as we were going to bed, I set my alarm clock and lay down. Fahad reached over from his bed and clicked the alarm off. I lay there for a moment and then pulled the alarm stem out again. Fahad reached over and turned it off again. Then he extended his foot and pushed my bed out of alignment with the wall. I got up and straightened it. He waited a moment and then pushed the bed again with his foot. I got up and straightened it. Next, he went to his closet and brought back his dirty clothes and plopped them onto the foot of my bed. I lay there silently fuming. He returned to the closet, got his basketball and running shoes and dropped them onto my bed. At this point, I stood up in the bed, pointed my hand at him, and said in a loud voice, "Stop acting childish and go to bed!" Fahad smiled because he realized he had finally broken the ice that prevented us from having a real relationship.

Thereafter, we had our ups and downs, but at least we could be honest with each other. One afternoon we had a disagreement about something—I do not remember what—and Fahad took a roll of toilet paper and unrolled it across the room. He taped one end to the wall in his closet and the other end to the wall between our beds. He said, "Now we will have divided city, just like Jerusalem. That is *your* side of the room, and this is *my* side. You do not cross to my side, or I will thrrrrow you from the window!" I had no doubt that he could carry out the threat because he was much stronger than I was, but I knew this was all bluster. I replied, "Fahad, you have forgotten one thing." He looked at the ceiling, as if he did not care, and said, "What is this?" I said, "The door is on *my* side of the room. How do you propose to go out and come back in?" Crossing his arms, he assumed a magisterial air and said, "We will not worry about this trifling problem."

We got over that disagreement after a while, and Fahad wanted me to teach him dirty words in English. I told him that I was not going to do that, so he proceeded to teach me dirty words in Arabic. Then when we were on the way to the cafeteria, he would stop to introduce himself to some students. They asked his name, and he used one of the dirty Arabic words. The students would try hard to pronounce the presumed name correctly, and Fahad would burst out laughing. He would say, "No, no. Like this," and pronounce the word again and laugh once more as the students struggled to say it correctly. One night he went downstairs in the dorm to visit with an Iranian student, who taught him some dirty words. Fahad came rushing back upstairs, burst into the room, and unloaded all of the words on me at once. These were some of the foulest words I had ever heard, and he went on for a minute or two saying them. I felt as if I had been plastered to the wall and held there by this flow of vulgarity. So Fahad got his wish, learning not only proper English and colloquialisms but also dirty words. He could curse in English if he wished.

The women of the campus liked Fahad because he was polite to them, using elaborate Middle Eastern courtesy in talking with them. They also liked his sense of humor. Sometimes when I walked into the cafeteria for supper, I could hear his booming laughter at the far end of the hall, where he sat with a group of students, enjoying the conversation. He became friends with the nurses who had prepared his casts and sometimes dropped by the clinic to visit with them. After the casts were sawed off, he sometimes put them back on and slept with them. I suppose this gave him some kind of security.

We had a friend from Savannah who had converted from Catholicism to Judaism. Fahad seemed to enjoy talking with him, but every time that he saw him at a distance in the hallway of the dormitory, he yelled out "Jew" in his booming voice. Our friend was patient and did not become offended. In this respect Fahad reminded me of a Muslim friend that I later had at the University of South Carolina. We got along well and enjoyed talking about books and various intellectual topics. But on the subject of Jews and Israel, he had nothing good to say. As a result, we avoided this topic most of the time.

Over the term Fahad and I continued to have our disagreements from time to time, but we also became friends. Sometimes on the weekends Fahad went out with other male students and drank too much. When he returned, he lay down on his bed and waved his hands back and forth, saying, "Oh Herbert, I am a bad person! I am a Muslim, and I should not drink." Then I would dampen a washcloth, put it on his forehead, pull the trash can near the bed in case he vomited, and sit up with my sick Arab roommate. I watched him carefully to make sure he did not throw up while lying on his back.

When the fall term ended, Fahad went home with me for a few days in Albany. Rooming with Fahad that fall had been quite an adventure, and the adventure continued during the break. My mother and father were pleased to have him visiting us but did not quite know what to make of him since he was unlike anyone they had ever met before. During Fahad's visit, my father arranged for us to go on a deer hunt at one of the area plantations. The truck dropped Fahad and me off at a point in the woods where the dogs were expected to pass after scenting deer. We stood beneath a live oak tree overlooking a field of broom-straw for a long time without hearing the dogs or seeing any deer. Eventually, Fahad just wanted to shoot the rifle. I tried to dissuade him, pointing out that the shot would scare off any deer in the area, but finally, he could stand it no longer and fired the rifle. Doing this seemed to please him, and not long afterwards the truck came back to pick us up.

After a few days, I drove Fahad to Athens to spend Christmas with his sponsors, but en route he wanted to stop in Macon to see his girlfriend from Georgia Southern. That afternoon while we were visiting with her, she arranged for us to go up in a small plane from the Herbert Smart Airport. Her father, who had passed away, had worked at this airport, and she knew a mechanic who was also a pilot. We arrived at the airport and climbed into the four-seater plane. Fahad and the mechanic were in the front seats, and the girlfriend and I sat in the back. We flew over downtown Macon. I remember seeing the Ocmulgee River just north of downtown and a train passing through the yards in back of the railroad station. The pilot then executed some turns, climbs, and dives that made me rather nervous since this was my first time to fly. During the dives I felt as if the top of my head were going to blow off. At one point the pilot gave the controls to Fahad, who was ecstatic. He turned around to me and said, "Look, Herrrrrbert, I am *flying*!" He said this with both hands in the air. I shouted back, "Fahad, get your hands on the controls!" The pilot resumed control, and after a few more turns over downtown Macon, we landed. We visited a while longer with the girlfriend and then continued to Athens. After that first flight, little did I dream that in the future I would experience several more climbs and sudden dives.

Fahad returned to Georgia Southern for a few days at the beginning of the winter quarter, but he had not done well academically during the fall, mainly because he did not yet know how to write well in English. During those days the college did not have an ESL course, and so far as I recall, there was no writing center to help him. Rather than continue at the college, Fahad decided to go to Washington to the Jordanian embassy to see if they could assist him. I carried him to the Trailways bus station, and that was the last time I saw him. I felt sad parting from him. For the next few years, he wrote letters and sent Christmas cards and occasionally a gift. I remember some of these gifts. One was a nice gray and red neck scarf, which my mother eventually claimed, and another was a Bible that someone had probably given to Fahad. He also gave me bookmarks decorated with tiny pressed flowers from Jerusalem, and I placed them in my Bible.

So that night in the barracks at Fort Meade when I picked up the phone and realized it was Fahad, I was both happy to hear him and a bit nervous, not knowing who might be listening. I said, "Fahad, where in the world are you?" And he replied, "I am in London, working at the Jordanian Embassy." This announcement made me even more nervous, but I said, "It must be around 5:30 in the morning in London." Fahad laughed and said, "I have a girl on each arm. Are you still stuck in your fanatical Baptist ways?" At this point it was my turn to laugh. He was obviously still the same outrageously funny, extravagantly courteous, sometimes exasperating, yet kind Fahad. He said that he planned to be in Washington soon and wanted to know if we could get together. I told him to let me know when he would be in town, and we could arrange to see each other.

I did not have any repercussions from that phone conversation, but that was the last time I talked with Fahad. Days and weeks passed, but he never got in contact with me again. Now I look back on my friendship with him and can say he was one of the most interesting persons I have ever known. I have tried to locate him on the Internet, but his name is fairly common. As a result, I have not been able to find him. Recently, though, in going through old letters, I came across a note that he left for me when he departed. He wrote, "I don't know how I am going to thanks you, always you were with me so nice and kind. The only wish I ask God … keep Herbert for ever.… God bless you, Herbert." I hope that one day I will hear from him.

Shooting in Laurel, Maryland, May 15, 1972

During my duty at Fort Meade, Governor George Wallace of Alabama was shot while campaigning in nearby Laurel for the Maryland primary. The shooting occurred at a shopping center that I often passed whenever I took a Greyhound bus into Washington. Wallace was transported to a hospital in Silver Springs, where it was reported that he was in critical condition. As a result of that assassination attempt, he was forced to drop out of his campaign for the presidency, and he remained in a wheelchair the rest of his life.

Here is what I wrote about the shooting in my journal that evening:

I have not been a Wallace supporter; I do not share his views; but I am certainly a supporter of his right to state those views and to run for office. I deplore insane acts of violence which have cut down too many of America's public figures in recent years.

It would be interesting to make a study of assassins or would-be assassins. In nearly all of these incidents they have been maniacal young white men who have been alienated from society and have failed in life. One can point to Lee Harvey Oswald, James Earl Ray, Sirhan Sirhan [an exception], and now this would-be assassin of Governor Wallace [Arthur Bremer].

How do you protect a public man from a mad dog like this? I do not know. But I am afraid that America is going to be forced to sacrifice some of its cherished democratic freedoms to stringent law enforcement simply to prevent the country from coming completely apart at the seams.

I learned that Bremer had initially planned to assassinate President Nixon but could not get close enough to him, so he settled instead for Wallace, even though he apparently did not hate him and even agreed to some extent with his views. I was shocked and saddened by the assassinations of President Kennedy and Senator Robert Kennedy, and I marched in the funeral procession of Dr. Martin Luther King, Jr., in April 1968 while I was a graduate student at Emory University. Although I disliked Wallace's racist views, this assassination attempt also saddened me, and I worried about the future of the nation that I was serving.

In thinking further about assassins during the next month, I wrote the following in my journal: "If you cannot be liked, it is better to be hated than to be a mere mediocrity noticed by no one. I think something of this same spirit inspires would-be assassins. They cannot become notable by hard work or inherent genius, so they desire to become famous by causing the death of some well-known man. This is achieving notoriety by the parasitical method. If you cannot build Rome, you can achieve fame as the one who tears it down."

Baltimore

On some weekends I went into Baltimore on an Army bus, which stopped at the USO downtown. One of my favorite places was the Enoch Pratt Free Library, where I obtained a library card. As a result, I could check out books that were not available at the post library. Some of those that I borrowed included Thomas Browne's *Religio Medici*, Julia Ward Howe's

Reminiscences, 1819–1899, Emerson's *English Traits*, John Henry Newman's *The Idea of a University*, *Swann's Way* by Marcel Proust, *The Flowering of New England 1815–1865* by Van Wyck Brooks, Walter Pater's *The Renaissance*, and the *Foundation* trilogy by Isaac Asimov. I also checked out and read Milton's *Paradise Lost* since in high school and college I had read only excerpts from it. One afternoon at the post library I picked up a book on the South by Robert Coles and learned about an up-and-coming Southern writer named Cormac McCarthy. I also visited the library at Johns Hopkins University and thumbed through some of their volumes by Sidney Lanier, a Georgia poet of the nineteenth century who eventually went to live in Baltimore. All in all, I read more books in the Navy than I had read in college.

Sometimes I frowned at the idea of going into Baltimore because it was dirty and run-down in some areas, but as I returned each time from a trip to the city, I realized that I had had a good time. Here is the way I described central Baltimore in the journal that I kept during that time:

> Parts of the city have an almost bombed-out appearance, like pictures of German cities at the end of World War II. There are brick row-houses with huge holes in the walls and no glass in the windows and vacant lots covered with brick rubble and streets littered with all kinds of papers and trash. Small children sit in open doorways where green paint peels from the doorposts. Nearly all the people in these areas are black. Three small steps extend onto the sidewalk from each of these row-houses, and people sit on these steps or stroll along the cracked sidewalks past broken-down cars parked along the curb, calling out to each other in loud voices from across the street…. One part of the downtown area is dominated by dingy office buildings with stone lion heads growling down upon the pedestrians. The buildings here speak of high finance with their massive stones and fluted columns and lower windows covered with pot-bellied iron grills. Here and there a more gracious gothic skyscraper rears its tower into the air surmounted with a green copper roof encasing a huge clock face. The upper stories of some of these buildings are done in elegant French renaissance style, reminding me of the Philadelphia city hall.

In all of my strolling, though, I never visited Fort McHenry or Edgar Allan Poe's grave, two omissions that I later regretted.

Thoughts About War and Art

On one of my weekend trips to Baltimore while I was stationed at Fort Meade, I visited the Walters Art Museum and was pleased to see the breadth of its collection. It did not have the range and depth of the National Gallery in Washington or the Metropolitan Museum of Art in New York, but the collection was, nevertheless, impressive. That May afternoon I was drawn to a large oil canvas by the late nineteenth-century French painter Alphonse de Neuville. I stood entranced by its grim depiction of a battle scene from the Franco-Prussian War of 1870–1871. The painting, *The Attack at Dawn*, depicts a winter-morning skirmish between French and Prussian infantry in a village. A street covered with dirty snow divides the canvas in half. On one side the attackers pour onto the main thoroughfare from a side street, firing their rifles at French troops who have been startled from their sleep at a small inn. The defending soldiers run down the steps with surprise written on their faces. A bugler puffs out his cheeks to sound the alarm; an inquisitive young face peers from a basement door to see what is happening; and leaning against the door is a soldier, mortally wounded, struck by a bullet in the neck. He clutches a hand to his throat, and blood trickles onto the snow. Another soldier lies face-down dead in the snow. Down the street the attackers fire their muskets from behind a wagon beneath the sign of a grocer's shop. It is a dismal winter morning. The street at one end is still wrapped in fog, and a single upper-story window glows dimly in the distance. The sky is pinkish-gray, and the scene is depicted in somber hues appropriate to death. Rifle muzzles flash brilliant orange in the dim light, and a lone street-lamp sheds an eerie glow over this scene of startled sleep and sudden death. This painting by de Neuville, as well as others by him I have viewed online, reveal that he was skilled at portraying the grim realities of war. He had himself been a soldier and knew first-hand what was involved in battles and their aftermath.

Seeing this painting led me to reflect on the power of art and literature to convey the impressions of war. Sailors tell sea stories about their adventures aboard ship, in port, and in war. Soldiers, like my father in returning from World War II, also tell stories, although for some what they experienced was so painful and horrific that they remain silent. Sharing stories through photographs, art, fiction, poetry, or memoirs can perhaps help men and women who have been in combat to cope with their emotional reactions and turmoil when they return home. Doing this provides a needed catharsis and at the same time communicates to some extent what they experienced. The problem is that sometimes it is difficult to find someone who is willing to listen or read. As for myself, all I can say is that I felt compelled to record my experiences, but for decades I had to remain silent.

While writing this memoir, I learned that between 1967 and 1970 the Army appointed soldiers skilled in art to accompany units in Vietnam and to depict what they witnessed honestly and realistically. The result was compelling and hauntingly beautiful works of art depicting the war. These artists, like de Neuville, were there and knew first-hand what the patrols and the fighting were like. All of this reminds me that only those who were there can truly tell the story of the Vietnam War; but sometimes fiction, like Tim O'Brien's *The Things They Carried*, may give an account that somehow seems truer than what actually happened. Aristotle in his *Poetics* made this kind of argument about tragic drama, affirming that, if done well, it presents the universal laws of probability rather than the facts of particular historical events and, as a result, seems truer. Putting all of these stories, photos, and works of art together creates a mosaic of the Vietnam experience for future generations. This memoir, although it does not recount the horrors of patrols and fighting in the rice paddies and jungles of Vietnam, nevertheless, constitutes my small contribution to the grand mosaic of the Vietnam War and the time period during which it occurred, my tessera, if you will, telling what it was like to be in the Navy and, more especially, to be part of Det Bravo in Da Nang between January 1971 and February 1972. This was an experience that has endured in my mind and heart and that will always be a part of me because it has profoundly shaped who I am and how I view life.

Fort Meade Friends

      I was not a total egghead while at Fort Meade. Marston was a lanky, somewhat nerdy guy in the Navy who wrote and illustrated his own bizarre comic books and then printed them on a mimeograph machine. He gave me one or two copies of his work that I still have among my boxes of papers. But my chief memory of Marston is centered on the night that he suggested we visit the infamous Block in Baltimore. We rode the Army bus to the USO downtown, ate supper at a restaurant, and then walked to a small establishment in the Block that had a go-go girl who danced on top of the bar. She did not do a strip tease, but she did make some provocative moves. After her routine she sat at our table and talked. We bought her drinks and noticed that she quickly dispatched them without any apparent ill effects. Marston and I realized that was her main purpose, to get the customers to buy plenty of drinks, hers being non-alcoholic. I was not into spending time with go-go girls, but Marston seemed to enjoy the evening. After a while, though, we had to leave in order to catch the bus back to the post. It was bitterly cold, even though we both wore our pea coats, and I had on ear muffs, an article of clothing I never needed in South Georgia. We walked through the streets with our breaths frosting and Marston taking long strides, talking, laughing, and slapping his gloved hands together. It was good to see him enjoying himself. I was not sure he had many friends.

      Another of my friends at Fort Mead was Richard Allen, an African American sailor from New York City. He was also a CTI, and his language was either Urdu or Farsi; I forget which. Some evenings I went down to the detachment cafeteria after it had closed to sit and write in my journal at one of the tables. Richard stopped by from time to time, and we talked about books and writing. He was working on a novel but had also written a one-act play, as well as some poems. When I returned home after being separated from the Navy, he wrote me two letters. He said that he had finally finished the novel and was working on his Ph.D. in comparative literature at SUNY in Binghamton. He mentioned that he had had an opportunity to work with some outstanding faculty, including the African American playwright Loften Mitchell and the Canadian novelist Robert Kroetsch. His play had been produced and presented at the university. He was glad to have his work before the public but said that working with some of the student actors and directors could be annoying.

Laron Matthies, whom I called "Larry," was another friend. The detachment roster shows that he served several months in Da Nang during 1971. I did not get to know him there, but he was part of a group at Fort Meade with whom I associated. I recall one cold morning when I was walking with Larry and some others from the Navy barracks to work at NSA. It is likely that Randy Bennett, another friend, was with us as we walked. Across the huge parking lot, we could see the NSA buildings, from which a plume of steam rose straight up into the clear blue sky. I complained about how bitterly cold it was for a South Georgia boy, and Larry laughed, remarking that back in Minnesota, where he was from, it would be a spring day. I noticed, though, that he, like the rest of us, was wearing his pea coat.

Reconnecting with a Friend from Home

Skip (Edward Gnehm, Jr.), my best friend while I was growing up in Albany, was living with his wife and their baby daughter in Alexandria, Virginia, in 1972 and working in the State Department. We arranged to meet one Sunday and go to the worship service together at Calvary Baptist Church, where he attended. We met at the Jefferson Memorial. I approached from the tidal basin side, and he arrived in his car in the parking lot on the other side. We glimpsed each other through the open center of the memorial past the huge statue of Jefferson and then walked around to greet one another. I had not seen him for a few years, so it was good to be with him.

I met Skip when I was ten years old. Strolling around the yard one afternoon shortly after we had moved to our new house on Gordon Avenue in Albany, Georgia, I came around the corner, and there he was in the back yard. He had walked down the alley to meet the new kid in the neighborhood. I accompanied him to his house, and then we climbed into a pecan tree on the other side of the alley, where he had built a tree house. We talked until sunset. The next summer his mother invited me to spend a week with the family at Fernandina Beach, Florida. Skip, his mother, his two sisters, and I enjoyed walking on the beach, collecting seashells, and building drip castles that were washed away by the incoming tide. We also visited nearby Fort Clinch, a Civil War fortification. His father had to stay in Albany, where he worked for the Metropolitan Life Insurance Company. When we were in junior high and high school, we often did things together. We drew maps of cities in imaginary countries on the floor of his room in the garage behind his family's house. Sometimes other friends came over, and we played Uno, Flinch, or hearts and listened to music as we talked and the cards were dealt. I recall one rainy Sunday afternoon when Skip and I, while drawing, listened to Bach's *Mass in B Minor*. We also enjoyed music from Broadway musicals such as *Oklahoma, Pal Joey, Show Boat,* and *My Fair Lady*. We played with the toy World War I soldiers that his father had given him, and on Friday nights we watched *The Twilight Zone* together. Sometimes I spent the night in Skip's garage apartment, and we sat up late, telling scary stories to one another. I remember, in particular, his story about the hunchback of Camp Osborne, a Boy Scout camp near Albany, where Skip, as a scout, spent time during the summers. We walked through the fields of broom-straw in front of our subdivision and dug fox holes, naming them Hole #1 and Hole #2. We worked like day laborers digging these deep holes, but to us it was all fun. We took branches and straw and covered Hole #1 to create a shelter, which we lighted with a candle set in a niche in the wall. One afternoon while we were down in the hole, we heard two buzzing sounds zoom overhead, and immediately two objects struck the ground at the entrance of the hole. We realized that someone at a distance had fired a rifle into the air, and had we been standing at the entrance, we might have been struck by the two bullets that hit in the leaves. We rode bikes and walked through the swamp that bordered the railroad track near our homes and one March afternoon discovered white lilies blooming in a boggy place. We dubbed these wild lilies the true Easter lily. Sometimes when his mother picked us up after we had gone swimming or been to the movies, we stopped at the public library. Skip and his mother helped me to get a library card and check out some books. At my home we had only a few books: copies of the bible, a bedtime story book, and some agriculture volumes that my father had acquired while attending training courses for farmers at the experiment station in Tifton, Georgia. But Skip and his family were readers, and they subscribed to *National Geographic*. Skip also, received *Boys' Life* magazine, and I enjoyed reading it. His mother gave me two volumes of *Reader's Digest Condensed Books*, and I placed them on the shoe cabinet in my room and admired their elegance. Later, I subscribed to this series and received a volume in the mail for each season of the year. I still have those volumes, which served as a starter set for more in-depth reading. Because of my friendship with Skip, I became a lover of books. When he went on vacations with his family to other parts of the country during the summer, he sent me post cards and brought back maps of the states and cities he had visited. I still have the map of New York City that he gave me during the late 1950s, and although, it is old and torn in places, I value it because of our friendship.

Skip and I were boys and then adolescents together, but when we graduated from high school, our paths diverged. He enrolled at George Washington University in D.C. while I went to Georgia Southern College in Statesboro, Georgia. He later attended the Foreign Service Institute and became a member of the diplomatic corps with many exciting adventures at his different posts overseas. I prepared to be a college English teacher. Skip was assigned for a while to the American embassy in Saigon but had already left by the time I arrived in Da Nang.

Thus, when we attended church together that Sunday morning, we had many wonderful shared experiences, and it was good to reminisce with him when we returned to his apartment after the service and enjoyed lunch with his wife and their baby daughter. Skip asked me to write something in their remembrance book, and if I recall correctly, I wrote, "Good friendships, like a fine wine, only improve with age."

Preparing to Return Home

One night in November I went outside to take a short cut from one wing of the barracks to the other. As I crossed the open space, a flock of geese passed overhead at a low altitude. Illumined by the barracks lights, they were white against the night sky and honking to one another as if debating which direction to go. I heard them for a minute or two as they flew southeast over the woods towards the Chesapeake Bay. This was an amazing sight, for at that time I had seen very few geese in the wild. Before long, I too was going to return south.

I applied for entrance to the graduate program in English at the University of South Carolina for the fall of 1973 and was accepted. In preparing to apply, I went into Washington one Saturday to take the Graduate Record Exam (GRE) at George Washington University. I had taken the GRE several years earlier while at Georgia Southern, but so much time had elapsed that it was necessary for me to take it again.

As mentioned earlier, the people who were in the department at NSA where I worked were always kind and considerate. Shortly before I left active duty in the Navy, they invited me to a farewell luncheon at a restaurant in Laurel. There were several people at the long table in the private dining room, including the head of the department. I was surprised and humbled by their willingness to take time out of their busy schedules to honor an enlisted Navy man. The NSA has come under much criticism in recent years, but I look back with pleasure upon my time there because of the people I met.

Before I left the D.C. area, I hoped to see a snowfall similar to those I had experienced in the winter of 1969–1970 while quartered at Fort Myer, but we had only a brief flurry in October, which I watched from the window of my office area at NSA. Ironically, in February after I arrived home, Middle and Southern Georgia had one of the heaviest snowfalls on record, with Macon recording six inches and Albany receiving an inch.

CHAPTER 25

Home

While I was stationed at Fort Meade, I spent a lot of time traveling, walking, and sight-seeing on weekends and holidays. My duties at NSA were somewhat monotonous, and these trips gave me something interesting to do. I realize that my narrative of all these experiences is rather long and perhaps tedious, but I wanted to include them to show the means by which I readjusted to being back in the states after my duty in Vietnam. I am glad that I had all of these experiences before I finally went home. They were educational and perhaps helped me to deal with the anxiety and stress that I had known while flying out of Da Nang and undergoing several rocket attacks. They to some extent kept my mind off what I later rehearsed over and over, remembering the details of being involved in the war. I do not know to what extent other men who served with the Fleet Support Detachment in Da Nang experienced after-effects from the war. Some, I think, were affected by being exposed to Agent Orange, which was stored and loaded onto planes not too far from our compound on the west side of the airfield. In 2019 the Veterans Administration extended eligibility to file claims for exposure to Agent Orange to veterans who had served in the Blue Water Navy off the shore of Vietnam, so as a veteran who had feet on the ground in Vietnam, I was presumably exposed to some extent. For almost four decades after being in Vietnam, I had difficulty swallowing when eating and avoided certain types of foods on which I tended to choke. Many times, as when I was in Da Nang, I had to get up from the table and spit out a mass of food that I could not swallow. Whether this was the result of Agent Orange or prolonged stress, I do not know. Finally, after many years I was able to eat and swallow in a more normal way. Today, I rehearse my memories of Vietnam only occasionally when I choose to do so.

Some readers of this memoir may say that those of us involved in air reconnaissance to protect the planes and ships of the Seventh Fleet during the war were implicit in the sufferings of the Vietnamese people. They may argue that, even though we did not shoot guns or drop bombs, we, nevertheless, bear part of the blame for the harm done during the war since we helped protect the Navy, Air Force, and Marine aircraft that dropped the bombs and fired the missiles. Critics may assert that, instead of joining the Navy, we should have become conscientious objectors and been active in the protests against the war. There is no escaping the fact that we were involved, even though our motives were not to cause harm but to protect American lives. Great nations and empires in their actions produce both harm and good. This is simply a fact, whether one thinks of Assyria, the Han Empire, the empire of Alexander the Great, the Roman Empire, the Ottoman Empire, the British Empire, the Soviet Union, or present-day America. Powerful nations and empires by their very nature both destroy and build up, and I suppose that this is also true for all humans as individuals. We have within us the power for both evil and good. I like to think, however, that America, a lumbering giant that both wreaks havoc and dispenses good, overall, has worthy aims and intentions, although many today focus on only the harm that the nation has caused. Seeing both the dark and the light sides of America's history provides balance and may, one hopes, eventually lead to wiser actions in the future. Only time will tell. History shows, though, that optimism must be tempered with realistic pessimism. In the meantime, I can offer no excuses for my part in the war other than to say I did what I saw as my duty and hope that, when my life is over, I will have accomplished more good than bad and made some recompense. I look to the One who sees all yet extends grace. Knowing this, I must also extend grace, even to those who criticize Vietnam veterans for having been involved in the war.

On Friday, January 26, 1973, I completed active duty in the Navy. The office for the Naval Security Group at Fort George Meade gave me my separation papers, and Captain Karl B. Kohler, the commanding officer, presented me with the Air Medal (5th Strike/Flight award). I have two Polaroid photos of this ceremony taken by a staff member in the office. In one Captain Kohler is reading from the award certificate as I stand at attention beside him in my winter dress uniform, and in the other photo he is presenting me with the certificate and shaking my hand. No one else was present for the award.

After the ceremony I picked up my sea bag in the barracks and called a taxi to take me to Laurel, where I caught a bus to the Greyhound station in Washington. Then I walked to Union Station to catch an Amtrak train for Atlanta. It was dark by the time we were underway. We crossed the Potomac and passed by the office buildings of Crystal City, Virginia, where approximately three years earlier I had taken Vietnamese lessons with DLIEC. When the train stopped in the middle of the night at a station in North Carolina, I noticed how neat the houses near the track were with their clean white paint and windows embraced by shutters. I slept fitfully

January 26, 1973, the day I separated from active duty in the Navy. Captain
Karl B. Kohler, commanding officer of the Naval Security Group at Fort George
Meade, presented me with the Air Medal (5th Strike/Flight award). Other than
the officer who took the photograph, no one else was present for the ceremony.
Over the years some of the writing on the back of the photograph bled through
(photograph by the author).

in my seat, and when morning came, I went to the dining car for breakfast.
The Atlanta Constitution had been brought on board at one of the stops, and
I read the paper while drinking my coffee and eating toast and scrambled
eggs. I noticed that we were in South Carolina. The woods were dense with
tangled underbrush, unlike the almost park-like woods of Virginia, and the
track was bordered with shanties surrounded by dog fennel and an assortment of junk, including old cars mounted on cinder blocks, rusted scrap
metal, and broken commodes discarded in the tall weeds. I was back in
the Deep South. In Atlanta I took a taxi from the Amtrak terminal to Five
Points downtown and late that afternoon boarded a Trailways bus bound
for Albany. We had a twenty-minute rest stop in Butler. By then it was dark.

I went to the bathroom and noticed that the paint on the walls looked as if it had been mixed with spider webs. That, I assumed, was to discourage graffiti from being written on the walls. When we re-boarded the bus, I sat behind the driver and watched the road unwind before us in the headlights as we continued south along U.S. 19. When the bus pulled into the station in Albany, I went to the pay phone and let my father know I had arrived. That is how I returned home from the war and active duty in the Navy—no fuss, no fanfare, no crowd holding welcome banners and waving American flags, no glorious sunset—just my father waiting for me in the truck and my mother at home turning on the back-porch light for me. That was enough.

Epilogue

It is a stereotype now, after all the movies and TV programs about war, that men who have been in combat together form a bond unlike any other they may ever have. In Da Nang we Spooks did not have to trudge through rice paddies or along mountain trails wary of snipers or trip wires, we were not in firefights, we were not dropped by helicopters into the midst of country overrun by North Vietnamese regulars, we were not pinned down by fire or subjected to nonstop shelling, but we did have our dangerous moments. There were times when we did not know if we would die in the next few minutes or even seconds from a MiG-21 attack or a SAM launched from the jungle below us. The planes we flew in had electrical problems, or engines failed. We had to vent fuel, and even the slightest spark could have blown us out of the sky. Sometimes we put on parachutes and lined up ready to bail out, not knowing if this was a drill or the real thing. We knew about the EC-121 that had crashed at Da Nang, killing nearly everyone on board. Rocket attacks sometimes hit the base; Air Force guys across the field died in these attacks. We felt the barracks shake when a rocket struck nearby. During attacks we sat in the bunker, slapping mosquitoes and listening to explosions in the distance while guys with M16's stood guard at the two entrances. Anywhere was potentially a place for a C4 plastic explosive or grenade suddenly hurled. We were acutely aware of the morgue at the north end of the airfield. At night some of us avoided dark paths between buildings for fear of trip wires. We knew that some of the local people who worked on the base by day probably lobbed the rockets in by night. Typhoons struck the base and stripped the roofs off barracks. The aircraft were sent away, but the men remained. We could be more easily replaced than a jet worth several million. At night returning from the head to the barracks, toothbrush in hand, we glanced at the stars and wondered, "Will they hit tonight; will there be a rocket attack?" No, we did not do the most dangerous things perhaps, but we knew danger every time we flew. We had our different political and religious views, we came from different parts of the country, we had different cultural backgrounds. Sometimes we had annoying habits or foul mouths. We became irritated with each other. Some sneaked women into the barracks from Dogpatch, the village next to the base, or they went to the "massage" parlors. Some got drunk and puked all over the floor of the upstairs mess. With all our faults and diversities, however, we had been through danger together. We had flown in the planes and endured the rocket attacks. We had been chewed out by officers from time to time, and we had known homesickness for our families, wives, girlfriends, and buddies back in the States. We had been so wound up with stress that we could hardly eat, or we acted just plain crazy at times, seeking relief from the demons of war that oppressed us. Sometimes late at night we sang, "We gotta get out of this place if it's the last thing we ever do." We satirically referred to ourselves as "war heroes." When we returned home, there were no parades down Main Street or welcoming committees at airports, only the ones who loved us to give us a hug. We were ignored, and eyes glazed over if we tried to talk about what we had been through. Sometimes we received outright criticism for having gone to the war. The media vilified us. Most us went quietly back to school or our jobs and continued with our lives. Some were unable to make the adjustment and truly to come home because of severe PTSD. But through all of this, there was still the bond. We knew what we had experienced that could not really be shared with others. We were willing to listen to each other, and we could empathize with a detter who received bad news from home. Now that we are old and have not often seen each other, and though some of our number have died after returning home, succumbing to illness or being injured in a car wreck after going uninjured through Nam, there is still a connection. Some of us have ideological or personal disagreements; nevertheless, deeper than all of this the bond remains. We were there; we know.

Index

Numbers in **bold italics** indicate pages with illustrations

223